To dearest June,

Who bravely and
expertly presented
this material for me
at M. Met. Uni

from Andy

24 / 5 / 2016

The Origins of Collective Decision Making

Studies in Critical Social Sciences

VOLUME 84

The titles published in this series are listed at *brill.com/scss*

The Origins of Collective Decision Making

By

Andy Blunden

BRILL

LEIDEN | BOSTON

Cover illustration: Leveller Women in the English Revolution 1647 – © Hidden project
www.redsaundersphoto.eu

The Library of Congress Cataloging-in-Publication Data is available online at http://catalog.loc.gov
LC record available at http://lccn.loc.gov/2016011384

Want or need Open Access? Brill Open offers you the choice to make your research freely accessible online
in exchange for a publication charge. Review your various options on brill.com/brill-open.

Typeface for the Latin, Greek, and Cyrillic scripts: "Brill". See and download: brill.com/brill-typeface.

ISSN 1573-4234
ISBN 978-90-04-31496-2 (hardback)
ISBN 978-90-04-31963-9 (e-book)

This book is printed on acid-free paper and produced in a sustainable manner.

Printed by Printforce, the Netherlands

Contents

PART 3
The Post World War Settlement

Preface

The very essence of political life is participation in making collective decisions. Individuals are utterly powerless on their own, but through making and sharing the responsibility for carrying out decisions collectively individuals become agents in the wider world. Consequently, nothing better characterises the political life of any community than how it makes collective decisions.

It is remarkable then that the Left, which agrees on a very wide range of social issues from economic inequality and freedom from discrimination to protection of the commons, is sharply divided on the question of collective decision making. Especially since the emergence of the alterglobalisation movement, traditional decision-making procedures and structures of the social democratic and labor movements have been criticized for being intrinsically hierarchical and exclusionary.

Marianne Maeckelbergh (2009) goes so far as to characterise the division over methods of collective decision making as an opposition between Horizontals versus Verticals. According to Maeckelbergh the new social movements of the 1960s and 1970s crossfertilised with the peace and identity-based movements of the 1980s, combining the ideals of participatory democracy and diversity with practices of consensus decision making that favour multiple outcomes. The alterglobalisation movement of the 1990s and 2000s developed these traditions into the new concept of 'horizontalism'. Maeckelbergh understands horizontalism as "the active creation of non (less)-hierarchical relations" (Maeckelbergh 2013, p. 31). According to Maeckelbergh, "Voting cannot lead to equality because it always results in unequal outcomes – outcomes which favour one group over another" (2009). Moreover, 'vertical' representative democracy based on majority decision making creates uniformity, which erases the plurality of voices. Homogeneity has to make way for diversity, which is to be achieved by an active politics of inclusion. Maeckelbergh emphasises that inclusion and diversity should not be restricted to equal participation of individuals and minorities at the input-side of the decision making process: "If equality partly lies in the outcomes of decisions, and if it requires that people should feel that they can play an active role in reaching these decisions, then often those decisions cannot be singular. Equal outcomes are often diverse outcomes" (Maeckelbergh 2011, p. 322). Yet Consensus meets with scepticism from the labour activist who would respond that inequality cannot be eradicated so long as the wealthy minority have a veto over everything. Moreover, for the labour movement diverse outcomes are practically unfeasible, as they undermine solidarity in strike action and make the maintenance of union resources impossible. Here the diversity of goals can become a threat to the collective.

Although Maeckelbergh sees horizontalism as having a prehistory in anarchist traditions of the nineteenth and early twentieth century, its proper history appears to commence with the rise of the New Left in the 1960s. Hence today the progress of history itself seems to vindicate the 'new' model of the Horizontals over the 'old' one of the Verticals. However, both majority and consensus decision making have historical roots that are older than the New Left of the 1960s. Curtailing the history of collective decision making in this way obscures the emancipatory historical role of the labour movement.

In the pages to follow I trace the real historical relations of 'participatory belonging' (Ricœur, 1984) back and forth over more than 1,000 years to discover how the various paradigms of collective decision making have originated and been transmitted to us today. I believe that my investigations serve to make the ethical antagonisms between 'horizontals' and 'verticals' intelligible, hopefully to the extent that adherents on each side can see virtues in the others' stance and be prepared to work to transcend this antagonism and devise new, revolutionary paradigms of collective decision making.

I make no effort to anticipate that task however, and terminate my historical investigation at just the point when the landscape which spawned the Occupy movement was coming into being. I have abstained from current debates on this question.

Throughout, the focus of my enquiry is the *principle* governing collective decision making; while the structures of delegation, mandation, cooperation and representation are described, partly because they shed light on the motivations and anxieties of the participants and partly because further enquiry will call these structures into question. I must emphasise from the outset, however, that the procedure for making collective decisions is an *ethical* problem, and until the ethical dilemmas which arise amongst a group of people trying to decide upon what they do together can be resolved, there is no chance of resolving the pragmatic problems which arise when participants try to extend their decision making processes beyond those together in the here and now.

Hopefully history can provide the sense of distance from which the reader can empathise with the efforts of oppressed people to create just and effective forms of organisation based on ethical means of making collective decisions.

Acknowledgements

Covering 1,000 years of history was only possible thanks to the willing help of numerous people, either experts or participants in the relevant events who freely gave of their time to guide me through unfamiliar territory. In particular I must thank Mitch Abidor (Historian, translator), Malcolm Chase (Professor of Social History, University of Leeds), Ben Dandelion (Centre for Postgraduate Quaker Studies, University of Birmingham), Brecht de Smet, Bernard Muir (Anglo-Saxon Culture, University of Melbourne), Ann Upton (Friends Historical Association), Robert Gribben (Methodist historian), Jo Freeman (radical feminist activist), Casey Hayden (former SNCC, WSP and SDS activist), Mary Elizabeth King (former SNCC activist, non-violence activist), Keith Laybourn (President of the Society for the Study of Labour History), and Barbara Mott, Betsy Raasch-Gilman, Carol Hollinger, David Fasenfest, Helena Worthen, Janette Martin, Jeremy Dixon, Kotaro Takagi (Japan), Lars Klüver (Denmark), Lyn McKenzie, Lynn Beaton, Maureen Murphy, Maureen Postma, Riki Lane, Robert Williams, Ron Lubensky and Ted Crawford.

Introduction

A word about how this book is structured. I have set out to write a history, but the entities whose history I have written are the products of my investigation, not objects or events given at the outset. Consequently, the broad structure of the book is that of my investigation, going back from the present into the past to find origins, and then working forwards again, and on a number of occasions, stepping back again to follow up leads which would later prove to be byways. And I do this twice, once for each of the types of collective decision making which were known to me at the outset.

To begin with I provide an outline of the question which this book is intended to answer and anticipate in outline the results of the investigation so that the reader may be better able to follow the logic of my investigation.

The historical investigation is then given in three parts. In Part 1, I start from the present and trace the origins of Majority decision making back until its origins in medieval times becomes clear, and then I go directly to Anglo-Saxon England and work my way forward from there, following the evolution of majority decision making up until the eve of World War Two.

In Part 2, I start once more from the present time and trace back to the origins of consensus decision making in the aftermath of the English Revolution of the 1640s, and follow its evolution forwards up to the 1970s. The Quakers, and the Civil Rights and Peace Movements in the USA are the main focus of this narrative. In the course of this I make a number of steps back, notably to look at decision making in the Africa from which slaves were brought to America and the Anarchists of nineteenth century Spain.

In Part 3, I present a brief explanation of the political terrain in the decades following the Second World War and how this changed over a period of 50 years, to understand how collective decision making came to be problematized.

In conclusion, I sum up the results of this investigation as far as the advent of the new millennium, setting the scene for how the problem of collective decision making confronts social change activism today.

Collective Decision Making

How do communities make collectively binding decisions about their activity? How have such decision making procedures figured in bringing about historical change?

Collective decision making, that is, the determination by a group of individuals of their collective will, is a subject-forming process. It transforms social groups and the individuals who participate in them into social subjects and further develops their subjectivity – that is, their self-consciousness, their way of understanding the world and their capacity to act in the world. Undoubtedly, shared conditions of life and the need to collaborate always underlie the formation of subjectivity, but nonetheless, subject formation in human societies is always mediated by the making of collectively binding decisions. The same conditions do not always lead to the same responses – there is not a causal relationship between social conditions and collective response. How a community responds to a given situation is always mediated by the collective decisions they make. The making of collective decisions is therefore constitutive of social and therefore human subjectivity. The individual whose life decisions have always been made by someone else is not yet truly human. Knowledge and identity as well as agency can be formed only through the making of collective decisions. Likewise, social groups which do not make their own collective decisions may be the objects but never the subjects of social policy and action. No wonder that for many of us, learning only begins after we leave school.

However far we look back in history, even into the world of our animal predecessors, we do not find a starting point of isolated individuals coming together to create groups, but rather already-existing groups who make decisions together and negotiate their interaction with other such groups. The individual is a product not a premise of social history and development.

Individuals are always engaged in a number of projects, and it is not so much their belonging to social groups which is decisive in the formation of subjectivity, but their participation in *projects*. Individuals have agency, an identity and a way of understanding the world only in and through their participation in projects and it is through projects that people construct and change the larger social formations which govern their lives. It is projects not social groups which must be our presupposition, even if at the beginning there is no meaningful distinction between a social group and a project. Accordingly, projects make decisions through some kind of collective decision making process and it is these processes, which are as ancient as the human species itself, which are the focus of this investigation.

© KONINKLIJKE BRILL NV, LEIDEN, 2016 | DOI 10.1163/9789004319639_002

We must therefore see the problem of the formation of political structures from two interrelated aspects: the internal will-formation of already existing projects and the moderation of external relations between such projects. These are essentially different processes. The extent to which the internal decision making processes of a project may become the means of moderating collaboration between different projects, and vice versa, can only be determined by an historical investigation. Likewise, the extent to which an internal decision making process can be maintained as a project expands in scale cannot be a matter of speculation, but must be the subject of investigation.

In fact, *there has never been an historical investigation of collective decision making*, far less an historical investigation of how the internal decision making processes of a project prefigure the decision making processes of a larger community. "Just So Stories" such as David Graeber's (2013) speculations, are no substitute for a real historical investigation. I will deal with the problem of a methodology for a "realist" historical investigation of collective decision making in the next section. First I have to establish exactly what it is that requires historical investigation.

Collective decision making is a profoundly ethical problem, governed by deep-seated convictions and intuitions which persist over centuries and escape all the efforts of social engineering and political persuasion to orchestrate. At the same time, all our intuitions about how collectively binding decisions ought to be made are confounded by the complexity entailed by living in communities of tens and hundreds of millions of people spread over large portions of the globe. We need a method.

The Germ Cell of Collective Decision Making

Marx began *Capital* with a consideration of the commodity exchange, which he took to be the 'germ cell' of bourgeois society. In the same spirit, I take *a group of people in the same room, deciding what to do together* as the 'germ cell' of collective decision making.

Beginning with a germ cell allows us to gain a firm grasp of the essential contradictions of collective decision making in an immediate and visceral way without calling in advance on any theory of sociology or political science. What is at play when you are in a room together with a group of people trying to come to a collective decision can be understood without reference to any social theory. It is the simple, irreducible cell or unit of analysis of collective decision making. All the complexities of social and political history arise either from contradictions which are already inherent in that cell, or from difficulties which arise in attempts to expand the process to a larger number of people. *If only* we could all gather together in a room together and talk this through, we think, there would be no need for all the complicated and alienating apparatus of political life!

This germ cell masks two distinct instances however. In one case, all the individuals in the room already take it for granted that in the matter at hand they all share the same interests, and it is only a matter how best to further an already formed collective will. In the other case, two or more groups are seeking a modus operandi for what are taken to be and to remain distinct parties with distinct interests.

It is only the first case which I take to be collective decision making, and which is to be the focus of the historical investigation to follow. Finding a modus vivendi with people who have a different agenda and a different view of the world is a different matter in every respect, from the problem of making decisions within an existing project amongst people already committed to that project. However, arguments between Left and Right wing groups in a trade union or partners in a family on the brink of break up, are examples where the distinction is far from clear. The difference between internal and external deliberation is relative, and both instances of decision making will be kept in view. I will briefly return to this below.

In order to make this historical investigation as clear as possible, I shall anticipate the essential features of its outcomes, namely the four paradigms of collective decision making, as well as the three paradigms by means of which mutually independent parties agree on a joint venture.

I will refer to the latter cases as modes of *collaboration* inasmuch as the notion of collaboration presumes the joining of otherwise independent wills in a specific venture. The paradigmatic forms of collaboration have been the subject of earlier studies, and outlined for example in *Collaborative Project: An Interdisciplinary Study* (2014). The paradigmatic modes of *collective decision making* are here posited for the first time, as the outcomes of the historical investigation outlined below.

In each case, the paradigmatic modes of collective decision making and collaboration are to be grasped simply in terms of a number of people in a room, deciding what they are going to do together.

Under these conditions, the mode of collective decision making is determined by *ethical* considerations, being free of all the complexities of interacting with people who are not present, or in communicating with large numbers of individuals. The problems entailed in consultation, preparation and deliberation prior to meeting together to make a decision, and in following through on the implementation of decisions may extend beyond the time and place of a given meeting, but on the whole do not raise any issues which are not contained in embryo in the 'germ cell' itself. What matters is how we together here and now ought to make a mutually binding collective decision.

In the case of modes of collaboration, the relevant ethical considerations may be determined from outside, and those in the room deemed to be delegates. Nonetheless, it has been possible to specify paradigmatic modes of collaboration.

All the problems and complexities of social and political life unfold themselves from these paradigmatic modes of subject formation and collaboration when the parties endeavour to *extend* their ethically grounded decision processes beyond the bounds of face-to-face interaction. In our times of electronic communication the notion of people in the room together is open to expansion to include electronically mediated interaction, but this may be left to the side for the moment, retaining face-to-face interactions between a number of people who can see and hear each other, as the germ cell of subject formation and collaboration.

To repeat, the paradigms to follow are *outcomes* of historical research, not its presupposition. To begin with, I set out only to find the historical roots of Consensus and Majority decision making, but the investigation brought to light distinctions which the reader may have the advantage of being sensitized to at the outset.

Four Paradigms of Collective Decision Making

The four paradigms of collective decision making are distinguished by the ethical principles they realise.

Majority: The participants take each other as mutually independent and morally equal individuals with an equal stake in what they do together. In the event that consensus cannot be found, a decision is taken by majority vote. Where difficulties arise in finding a consensus, such measures as going into committee, referring resolution to a subcommittee, or tabling motions are used to avoid a division.

Three ethical premises underlie majoritarianism: (1) every individual is equal, irrespective of differences in knowledge, experience, commitment or stake in the decision, (2) every individual is sovereign and is bound by the majority decision through their free participation in that decision, and (3) a minority has no right to dictate to or obstruct a majority. The participants are probably members of some voluntary organization or delegates to some governing body. Minority views are always *tolerated*, but actual respect for minority views is not essential to majoritarianism.

Consensus: a decision may only be made to which every individual participant may freely consent. In rejecting majoritarianism, Consensus treasures minority views, but is intolerant of stubborn persistence in difference. In coming to a decision, Consensus places no value on plurality other than unanimity; whether or not individuals are equal is not an issue for Consensus, for individuals are not commensurable with one another. There are two main currents within Consensus which are distinguished by the tendency to reach consensus by protracted debate or by the use of silence and attentive listening. In either case, it is essential for Consensus that time is no object. All forms of Consensus however use measures such as straw votes to guide discussion, and allowing dissenters to 'stand aside' to resolve a deadlock.

Counsel: one of the participants – the CEO, the King or the Abbot, perhaps – takes the advice of the other participants, but bears sole moral responsibility for the decision. Counsel requires that the voice of every participant is attended to but specifically rejects the notion of equality among participants. The ethics of Counsel is a virtue ethics which requires certain characteristics of the Chief in particular. Because Counsel places moral responsibility for the decision on one respected and well informed person, it is eminently capable of achieving rational decisions and should not be belittled for its lack of democratic sensibilities. And nor should it be discounted as a *collective* form of decision making: a king is only as wise as his counsel.

Sortition: (also known as cleromancy) the decision is made by lot or some other arbitrary means. Given the impossibility of finding a fair and rational decision, the decision is outsourced to God or luck. Sortition may be used to make appointments on rotation, for example.

All collective decisions are made under one or another of the above paradigms, each of which allow for considerable variation in implementation, and each of which has distinct historical roots. Notwithstanding these ethical distinctions, it is very often the case that decisions made under the banner of Counsel or Majority are in fact made by Consensus or vice versa. Indeed, it is the aim of *all* collective decision making to achieve consensus. Majoritarians generally only put a decision to the vote when they have failed to achieve consensus. On the other hand, if consensus is not reached prior to a decision being made by Counsel or Sortition, then sincere consensus is achieved post facto. Indeed, it would often be possible to witness a decision being made under one or the other of these paradigms and not know which paradigm was in play. It is not uncommon that meetings apparently conducted according to Majority or Consensus are in fact operating according to the ethics of Counsel.

Nonetheless, the historical, cultural, ethical and therefore social differences implied in the mode of decision making are extremely robust. Meetings which make nonbinding decisions or decide to make no collective decision are not covered here.

Three Paradigms of Collaboration

"Collaboration" refers to limited joint action by independent projects, which may be in conflict with one another over some matter of material interest to both parties or may be interested in joining forces in some endeavour. These decision processes are all essentially two-sided, and those in the room may be delegates. In this context, "collaboration" does not refer to collaboration between individual persons; collaboration between individuals is called a 'project' and collaboration between projects is what is meant here by "collaboration."

Negotiation: The parties engage in a bargaining process, each with the aim of furthering their own project. The ethical principle underlying Negotiation are the mutual independence of the two parties in negotiation, and the understanding that individuals on each side speak with one voice as delegates. There can be no majority decision and no decision can override the will of other parties. In general, when agreement is reached and the parties make a contract, there is nonetheless no collective will, only a modus vivendi to which both sides are committed. Typical examples are labour negotiations, commercial contracts and peace treaties. Negotiation is *not* Consensus, where a collective will is taken as given from the outset. All that Negotiation requires is *good faith*. Good faith means that the parties do not engage in deceit and are open, honest and fair in dealing with each other.

Solidarity: One party voluntarily places themself under the direction of another, despite the fact that the parties are independent agents. Solidarity differs from Negotiation because while the party offering solidarity retains its independence, pro tem, it sacrifices its own agency and places itself at the disposal of the other.

Command: The Commanding Officer or Director simply tells everyone else what to do, and neither invites nor accepts advice. Typical examples are military groups in the heat of combat or artistic endeavours such as an orchestra or a theatrical troupe, where the authentic vision of the artist is valued. When scaled up, Command is more properly to be called Colonization, since the will of the other is subsumed under that of the co. Counsel is not Command, as the requirement to attend to the view of all the others is a strong ethical requirement for Counsel, and is absent in the case of Command. Time is often a scarce resource.

Command and Negotiation may subsume one another in commercial relationships.

The chief concerns of our historical investigation are Majority, Consensus and to a lesser extent, Counsel. Sortition is of only marginal interest. The three modes of Collaboration are frequently confused with decision making procedures, and may constitute pathologies of collective decision making where there has been a failure to form or maintain a single will uniting all, but rather a relationship between distinct parties. So it is important to clearly distinguish between collective decision making and collaboration.

Although attention is focussed on Majority and Consensus, the importance of Counsel became clear in the course of research. It transpires that Counsel is the oldest form of collective decision making and to an outsider, Counsel may look like Consensus. There is no voting, everyone has a voice and at the conclusion of discussion there is a decision with which all are in furious agreement. Only the observer who is closely attuned to the status differences among participants and the linguistic nuances of contributions may observe what is really going on. Indeed, there may be no material difference between a meeting conducted according to the norms of Consensus and one conducted according to the norms of Counsel; the difference is ethical.

The above are ideal types; in reality, modes of collaboration may be mixed with modes of collective decision making.

The Realisation of Decision Making in Procedures

The form in which the historian can find the various modes of collective decision making is in the records of decision making meetings and in the limited but sufficient number of procedural manuals and constitutions setting out meeting procedures that have been preserved. These rulebooks are invaluable because they transparently manifest the anxieties, aspirations and ethical orientation of the organisation and how these sensibilities are embodied in their decisions.

In the case of Majority, the rulebooks reveal an on-going struggle to scale up the procedures which are used in the meeting room to deal with larger numbers of participants who are not present. Formal meeting procedures have been drafted and revised over centuries until reaching a fairly stable set of rules in the mid-19th century.

Procedures for Majority are well known, but Erskine May (1844) has a set of procedures relevant to the British Parliament, Citrine (1939) sets out the procedures used by the British labour movement, and Brig. Gen. Henry Robert (1915/1876) published the rules of order used in the United States. Star Hawk (n.d.) presents procedures for Consensus decision making. There are procedures for decision making by Counsel and these are mentioned below.

There are a vast array of procedures which have been used at one time or another. There is no definite normative model for any of the paradigms, but the procedures do clearly indicate three distinct paradigmatic norms, with very little blurring or hybridisation. *In practice*, the procedures are interpreted and used in ways which indicate the influence of other norms. Majority meetings in which the General Secretary always proposes motions and announces amendments while participants always vote unanimously in line with the General Secretary's opinion; Consensus meetings in which a stubborn minority explicitly indicates that it disagrees with the majority, but agrees to 'stand aside'; Counsel in which the Chief bows to the majority of his advisers but distances himself from the decision.

These ambiguous forms generally reflect projects which have degenerated, are in transition or experiencing internal ethical conflict. Their existence only emphasises the need for a clear understanding of the distinct paradigms of collective decision making and their ethical foundations.

The ethics of collective decision-making have deep cultural and historical roots. These ethical principles may even survive revolutions, and yet they *do change*. An understanding of the ethical roots of the various modes of collective decision making is therefore of the most profound importance for those of us who are dedicated to achieving a social revolution.

I have referred to Majority, Consensus and Counsel as 'paradigms'. Using Weber's terminology we could call them *ideal types*. When one comes across them, in life rather than in literature, they appear as meeting procedures with various features or attributes. It appears that one could engineer decision making procedures, selecting this or that feature from one or another exemplar to build a better decision making process.

Public deliberation professionals are adept at organising randomly selected citizens into deliberative forums which do make rational decisions, decisions evidently better than those of their duly elected legislatures. And yet it is rare that their deliberations are accepted as a legitimate part of the democratic process. It is not enough to make good decisions; decisions have to be warranted by the ethical validity of their procedures, and the random selection of participants and sometimes facilitation by outside professionals violate the ethical demands of all paradigms of collective decision making and consequently usually fails to win the commitment of anyone other than the participants themselves.

The superficial approach which sees meeting procedures in this way, that is, as simply a problem of combining various features into a cognitively effective procedure, misses the fact that meetings are part of organisations and/or traditions of organisation which are deeply embedded in history and culture, and carry their ethics with them. Majority, Consensus and Counsel constitute three distinct lines of historical development through which they have been embedded in our communities. They do intersect and collide from time to time, but they can only be rationally understood as lines of development, each realisation being only a snapshot in a centuries-long line of cultural development. Each represents a distinct *concept* of collective decision making, not a collection of contingent features.

In informal or transitory situations, it is possible that the participants will be uncertain about how to make a decision together. In such cases it is possible that there will be some ambiguity until one or another paradigm is settled upon.

The aim of the historical investigation is to trace the origins of these three paradigms of collective decision making and discover the social conditions which gave birth to them, and then follow their development forward to the present time, to discover two things: (1) how the ethical principles underlying Majority, Consensus and Counsel have manifested themselves in social and political development, and the social basis they have in today's world, and (2) the problems which have arisen when the relevant projects have tried to expand themselves to a wider field of action, and how they addressed these problems.

The problem of the prefiguring of future collective decision making in the collective decision making of progressive organisations is not new. Anxieties and aspirations reflecting such concerns can be found in the documents of organisations over centuries. A systematic historical investigation can inform us of the issues involved in trying to implement decision making procedures on a mass basis.

In my historical investigation, I have had repeated occasion to study groups of people who made historic innovations in decision making procedures and contemplated and experienced the problem of scaling up the procedures which worked fine in a small group of people working face-to-face to a national level. Their efforts to adapt their preferred decision making procedures to implant them in a wider domain provide invaluable lessons.

Here I must briefly prefigure the problem of mutual transformation between internal collective decision making – amongst individuals participating in a given project, and projects dealing with other projects. The notion of 'subject' encompasses both individuals insofar as they are sovereign agents *and* groups of individuals constituting themselves as projects. In the sense in which individuals are subjects, the various modes of collective decision making may be extended via individuals acting as delegates for independent projects. This notion however stands in contradiction with the deep seated notion of the moral equality of *persons*. A delegate representing 100 persons does not carry the same moral weight as a delegate representing 2 persons. The moral equality of all persons does not imply the moral equality of all projects. This may obviously be a barrier to acceptance of Majority decision making by delegates, but even Consensus may not be accepted where there is perceived to be an extreme disparity in delegates' representativeness. But such issues can only be resolved in the light of historical experience.

Up to this point I have said nothing of *non*binding decisions or agreement to disagree. These are both undoubtedly significant features in the landscape of collective decision making. Meetings which make decisions which are not binding on the participants are *not* making collective decisions; information sharing perhaps, exploration, but they fall outside the scope of our study and on the whole they have no significant impact on the history of collective decision making. Likewise, parties agreeing to simply have nothing to do with one another and each go their own way is always an option, but lies outside the scope of this study.

Realist Historical Investigation

The methodology I have adopted to investigate the origins of the various modes of collective decision making was initially developed admittedly in reaction to David Graeber's approach to the same problem. Graeber (2013) took as his starting point hearsay reports that Consensus had originated either with the Indigenous nations of North America, who had passed the practice on to settlers before being exterminated by those same settlers, or with pirates operating off the North Atlantic coast of America, before they were exterminated by the Royal Navy and American pirate hunters. Based on these unlikely propositions, neither of which have been verified by historical investigation, Graeber proposed that a body of people all of whom were *armed* could not impose majority decisions on a minority but rather would make decisions by consensus – thereby lending plausibility to a uniquely American prescription for democracy. Elsewhere (2008) he claims that Majority rule requires an apparatus of coercive force to impose its will on the minority.

So much for origins, but more importantly, no theory was offered as to how these collective decision making processes were *transmitted* down the centuries from colonial America to the small American anarchist movement of the late 1960s or Wall Street protesters of 2011. Majority for its part was evidently deemed by Graeber to have *no* history. Faced with such absurdities it was obviously inadequate to simply counterpose to his my own "Just So Stories" (c.f. Rudyard Kipling 1902).

First hand experience with collective decision making in the labour movement and in the alterglobalisation movement, had already suggested to me that each mode of collective decision making constituted a distinct paradigm with its own social base. But why were they so? Where did they come from? How ancient were they? What form of collective decision making had been used by Indigenous people? Had Majority "trickled down" from Parliament or had Parliament appropriated it from the people? Were Quakers really (as I had been told) the inventors of Consensus? And who had created the elaborate regulations governing Majority decision making? Why was there such antipathy between proponents of alternative paradigms? Were there any other alternatives? Was there any positive precedent for 'prefiguration'?

These questions could only be resolved through an historical investigation. In the light of historical evidence then it would be reasonable to weigh up the social and political problems posed by the current juncture.

I call my approach to this historical investigation *realist*. The starting point is frankly my own experience. As an activist I have had occasion to participate

© KONINKLIJKE BRILL NV, LEIDEN, 2016 | DOI 10.1163/9789004319639_003

in a variety of models of collective decision making and I anchor my investigations in my own experiences. I then consult the historical records and, using *real relations of collaboration* at every step, track back to the origins of these practices. Finally, I step by step retrace the path forward from the supposed original act of creation, again using real relations of collaboration, back up to the present time. Along the way I shall describe the simple 'germ cell' from which the different paradigms unfolded. I hope in this way to be able to reconstruct my experience in collective decision making practices as the intelligible outcome of past history, that is, to be able to grasp just why things are the way they are.

The problem is this: if a certain practice bears some resemblance to a practice which existed somewhere else at an earlier date, we cannot conclude that the later practice originated from the earlier, or has any connection with it whatsoever. Consequently, any features or experiences of the earlier instance shared with a later instance give us no basis to conclude that such features and experiences are relevant to the present instance. If we hypothesise that the earlier formation is the origin of the later version, it still remains to discover the *concrete link* across the span of time and space separating the relevant events which transmitted the practice.

The method of comprehending and explaining social and historical phenomena in terms of comparison and appearances is what Ricœur (p. 122) refers to as subsuming events under a "covering law." Such approaches are generally fatuous, as amply illustrated by Graeber's efforts to determine the conditions of applicability of Majority and Consensus.

Historical precedents may have some interest in themselves, as examples or counter-examples for supposed 'laws of history', but in fact claims that a given practice was found in Roman times or amongst the Inuit people, or whatever, tells us absolutely nothing about the practice as it is now, until a concrete *line of transmission* from there to here can be established, through which its later instantiation can be made *intelligible*.

The leading alternative to positivist 'laws of history' is what Ricœur (1984) calls 'emplotment', which entails arranging heterogeneous narrative components together into a plot, in such a way that one situation follows from another in an intelligible and convincing way. As we have already indicated, we take projects – real relations of collaboration between persons – to be the basic unit of social life, and projects fit the description for what Ricœur (1984, p. 194) calls 'entities of participatory belonging', which are to be the quasi-characters of an historical narrative. It is these quasi-characters which mediate between the actions of individuals and the concepts of historical determination that we are looking for.

The projects which constitute the entities of participatory belonging in our narrative include organisations of various kinds which have their own practice of collective decision making and which in turn belong to more extended projects that Gadamer (2005) would call *traditions*. Preferences for this or that mode of collective decision making are associated with traditions. Projects are bound together into such traditions by the continuous participatory belonging of individual persons, and by the continuous participatory belonging of organisations in great social projects.

For example, over the years boilermakers have belonged to a number of different trade unions, but many individual boilermakers have belonged to a number of such unions in succession, demonstrating the continuity between them. Further, each of these unions was a part of the Trade Union Congress, itself a great social project, and notwithstanding changes of affiliation, name, rules and membership, all are participants in the trade union *movement*, a continuous tradition, to which trade unions have belonged over a period of centuries.

If we are to derive from an historical study of this kind a conceptual explanation of why individuals adopt this or that procedure for collective decision making, according to Ricœur, it is the intelligibility of the plots in which these quasi-characters figure which will provide the ground for such an explanation. Such a plot would have to make intelligible for us any change or modification or conversely the retention of collective decision making procedures.

The point is that a practice is transmitted from one person to another and from one situation to another only by means of shared participatory belonging, that is, by people actually collaborating in the given practice. Practices are transmitted not by observation or hearsay but by collaboration. Further, it is not enough that an individual become acquainted with a given practice in some situation for them to be able to institute it in another situation. New practices have to accord with the expectations and traditions of those who are to participate in them. Consequently, the task I set myself was to track back and forth between my own personal experiences and original acts of procedural innovation through actual collaborative links, which in general extend beyond the activity of individual innovators to whole social strata who participate in a given tradition.

From time to time someone hears or reads about a formerly unknown practice and tries to emulate it in their activity. For example, when I proposed to burn my draft card in Australia in 1966, I had got the idea, as did others, from television news footage from the USA where others like myself were burning cards. The YCAC (Youth Campaign Against Conscription) immediately understood the sense of what I was proposing and readily found other conscripts to participate. The young conscripts in the US were already engaged in the same anti-war movement that we were involved in and there were innumerable practical links joining draft-resistors across the two countries whose governments were collaborating in the war in Vietnam. So the plausibility of a draft card burning event in Australia was based on the practice having already been introduced in the US and that young people in both countries had been participating in the same world-wide anti-war movement. Numerous practices rapidly moved from country to country within that movement, based on existing relations of collaboration in the same project or tradition.

It is often said – and indeed in the course of my search for origins, I was told on more than one occasion – that sometimes an idea is just 'in the air'. When a new idea is 'in the air', then it certainly can prove impossible to reconstruct the precise chain of transmission, but the practical connections are still there. Sometimes, when the time has come for a change in some specific form of social practice, and a new concept arises within that project, it will appear independently at multiple locations. However, this is only because the new concept arises out of contradictions emerging within the same *shared practice*. The idea is not just 'in the air', but is located in contradictions which have emerged within a specific tradition of practice. Meaningful communication always takes place within some form of collaboration, direct or indirect. In their study of how Gandhian nonviolence was transmitted from 1930s India to 1950s USA, Isaac et al (2012) show that collaboration ("difficult interactive labour") is necessary for a significant new social practice to be embedded in a new location, and in fact that "movement schools" are required for the intense, emotional labour that such transmission entails. Contra Tarrow (2005), Isaac claims that mere exposure is never enough: real dialogue, self-conscious leadership and collaboration is required.

New social practices begin from somewhere. The first draft card had been burnt in New York in May 1964. What circumstances made that act intelligible? No-one burnt a draft card during the Korean War or during the Second World War.

I set out to locate those few creative acts of innovation which created the Majority and Consensus traditions of collective decision making, and I have been successful in that aim. I have been satisfied in some cases to determine the main innovations and changes that have been introduced during the intervening years to the extent of locating them at a specific juncture without being able to determine exactly which individual(s) were responsible.

In general, I am looking for decision procedures used by groups of people at this or that historical juncture, in organisations belonging to coherent and continuous traditions of organisational practice, so that the continuity and change of practices can be followed over extended periods of time, depending on the longevity of the organisations themselves and the extent to which they constitute a tradition. At those critical moments in history when fundamental change takes place, there remain whole classes of people within some social formation who share the same lived experiences, and are confronted with the same contradictions. But at those very times when contradictions arise in social practices which foster change in collective decision making procedures, there may not be the organisations with the continuity through the crisis to allow us to track the practices. In these instances we require so far as possible the actual *individuals* who innovate and in some cases carry what they learnt in one place to another place.

While tracking the development of the procedures for collective decision making I have also taken note of the relevant social conditions which bore on the organisations in question and the crises and difficulties which the organisations faced as well as their achievements. The means of collective decision making is always the thread running through the narrative, and the snap shots of broader social conditions which form the background to the narrative are included for the purpose of making the central theme of the narrative intelligible.

Also, I do not confine myself just to Majority or Consensus decision making, but pay attention to the whole rulebook for organisations. It is through the change and development of all the rules that we can see the values, the anxieties, aspirations and beliefs of the individuals involved in the tradition which make the long term changes in decision making procedures intelligible.

The practices for selecting officers is often conflated with collective decision making, and indeed it seems common sense to do so. Voluntary, charitable and religious organisations have generally been subject to law and their capacity to draft their own rules has been limited by the state. I have found that in general, the legislators who have authorised the formation of organisations, as well as the founders, seem to have regarded the means by which organisations elect their officials, and often the times and places of their meetings, as essential pre-requisites for the functioning of the organisation, and these procedures have been legislated from the outset by governments or founders, rather than being chosen by the participants themselves. On the other hand, the 'standing orders' – decision making processes and rules of order – have usually been seen as matters for the organisation itself to decide, and consequently form the subject matter of my investigation, whereas the rules which are handed down from above are not. However, the rules of order are very often not documented at all and have to be inferred from records of meetings. Consequently, our information about elections is much more comprehensive than what we have been able to find out about other decision making procedures. Election of officers is far more ancient and widespread than formal decision making procedures in general. It is the decision making processes which are of interest, but we will also take note of the associated processes for the election of officers as well as the structures, divisions of labour, forms of representation and hierarchies which are embedded in organisations. On the other hand, it is at those rare moments when traditional rules of order are changed that we do get information about how and why changes were made.

Nonetheless, the investigation was dogged by the fact that no matter what decision a committee or group made, both the individuals who recorded the decision at the time, and historians who have subsequently gained access to the archives and perused the original records, invariably do not bother to tell us *how* a decision was made, only the content of the decision itself. The method of collective decision making tends to be taken for granted.

The Subjective Starting Point

As explained above, I have chosen to begin and close the historical investigation with my own experience. This autobiographical starting point imparts an explicitly subjective character to the history. On the other hand, as soon as I search back for the origins of the collective decision making procedures in which I have participated, the narrative rapidly loses its autobiographical character. Nonetheless, because of my own location in social history, the narrative is heavily skewed towards being an Anglophone history, dealing almost exclusively with the histories of Britain and the United States. The fact is that I am not in a position to produce a worldwide historical survey of collective decision making. This is what I can offer, and I can only hope that in time others can contribute to complete the picture. In any case, I doubt that a more comprehensive study would bring to light anything that is entirely beyond the horizon of the narrative to follow.

I suspect that wherever you began, it is very likely that you would find your way back either to the very same times and places, or cultural equivalents thereof. If the reader finds the autobiographical starting points distasteful, simply skip the first page or two of each narrative.

Going Back and Coming Forward

The methodology for tracing the origin of practices, going backwards from the present to the past, differs from the methodology for following the relevant organizations forward through their various crises and transformations. Essentially, movement in both directions is always necessary to definitively reconstruct a convincing and intelligible narrative. The narrative itself moves from the past to the present; the movement from the present to the past is needed to discover the starting point for the narrative, and is a narrative of the author's journey of discovery. The movement backwards is always provisional, being based to a large extent on appearances and only secondarily on establishing real connections. A proposed starting point is only verified when we can trace the movement forward to the present through concrete relations of participatory belonging, through collaborative links.

In looking backwards we have no choice but to be guided by an apparent similarity of practices and possibly names, to determine possible originators. When a suspected origin is posited, we can see if indeed the proposed source does indeed lead to the present through relations of real collaboration. It is in the tracing forwards that we can review the relevant social conditions determining change and not only verify the source, but understand the process of transmission itself.

I know that *no-one has previously researched the origins of Majority and Consensus* decision making, because the people I spoke to who were either eye-witnesses to the relevant events, or are recognised experts in the relevant periods of history had never before been asked the questions I asked them or heard of them being asked.

Using the realist approach described above, I have been able to trace Majority back to its source over 1,000 years ago and follow it forward through a number of critical periods of transition up to the present time. I have found the origins of Consensus 350 years ago, but with a significant moment of rebirth 55 years ago. The origins of Counsel predate written history and lie beyond my horizon.

PART 1

Majority

∴

My first experience with Majority decision making was in 1973 when I became a teacher at Tulse Hill School in London and began to participate in the lively union life both at the school group meetings, and at the monthly meetings of the Lambeth Teachers Association covering all the schools in that borough.

Despite my naïveté, I found the local group meetings relatively easy to follow and participate in and after being at the school for a year I was elected to Chair the group meetings. The staff at this school were highly political and those were days of intense political conflict in Britain. When strike votes were carried by very small margins, it caused me considerable grief, and I experienced a steep learning curve.

The monthly meetings at Lambeth Town Hall were something else. To be honest, even at the end of three years of attending those meetings it was still all that I could do to follow what was happening in the meeting and know when to put my hand up, far less have any real influence on the business of the meetings. The furious political battles between rival political factions in the union mobilized all the resources of formal meeting procedure.

Later I went to work at North East London Polytechnic as a technician and was soon elected Secretary of the local ASTMS group. Over a period of six and a half years there I gained a great deal of experience as a unionist, both in representing the technical staff and in chairing the Joint Union Committee bringing the technicians together with administrative, maintenance and academic staff. But my one effort to represent the branch at the ASTMS Annual Conference introduced me to union politics at an entirely different level again. Eventually, by the time I retired in 2002, with experience in three more unions in Australia, I would say I had mastered union activity and the procedures required for participation at all levels. When I had occasion to participate in committees which were part of the university's collegiate management structure, I found that the procedures were basically the same as what I was familiar with from my union activity.

In each of these experiences, the procedures were a little different, but they were all part of a genre of procedures ably outlined by Sir Walter Citrine in his book "The ABC of Chairmanship" (1939).

In 2003, as part of my work with the Marxists Internet Archive (which operates by Consensus, by the way), I had occasion, a few years ago, to transcribe the Minutes of the General Council of the International Workingmen's Association, meeting in London from 1864 to 1868. I was struck by the fact that this body evidently operated the same meeting procedures as I had personally experienced in London in and Melbourne over a century later. The name of the Chairman is recorded, then the minutes are read, and acceptance moved and seconded; reports from branches, correspondence, and resolutions are moved, discussed, amended and resolved by majority voting, with abstentions, apologies, etc., etc.

This is no wonder. Look at the participants in the General Council: Peter Fox – a journalist who had been active in the British Labour Movement for many years, Eccarius, Lessner, Maurice, Milner, Stainsby, all active in the Tailors Union, as well as other labour movement organisations such as the London German Workers' Educational Association, the Reform League and the Labour Representation Committee; Applegarth, Cremer, Lochner and Weston – carpenters, Bradnick, Hales and Mottershead – Weavers; Morgan, Odger and Serraillier – Shoemakers; Dell, Lucraft – Furniture makers, the watchmaker Jung and the Mason Howell – all active members of their respective trade unions. Applegarth and Odger had also been members of the London Trades Council uniting all the unions active in the London area. In other words, the General Council was thoroughly a part of the same labour movement in which I had participated, and which had been in continuous existence from 1864 (at least) up to the present day.

A closer study of the procedures used in the International and in the trade unions then and since would be required to follow the changes, and how procedures had been adapted to suit the changing conditions and ethos of the Labour Movement. Also, how much did procedures differ between the trade unions as such, and working class political organisations like the Reform League, the Communist League and the Labour Representation Committee to which members of the General Council also belonged?

But being focused on *origins* for the moment, once I had found that the labour movement used Formal Meeting Procedure back in 1864, it hardly needs explanation that much the same Formal Meeting Procedure was used over the intervening period. Whatever changes have been introduced over the years, this remains one continuous line of development, and any changes which have taken place have occurred as part of changes affecting the entire movement and have generally speaking been adopted collaboratively.

But how far back does it go? and From where did the trade unions acquire these procedures, or did they invent them de novo, and if so when?

The London Workingmen's Association

So then I went in search of the minute books or rules of earlier labour movement organisations, in particular I wanted to find something from the Chartists of the 1830s. What I came up with was a page from the minute book of the London Workingmen's Association of 18th October 1836 a facsimile of which the British Museum had posted on their web site, along with a transcription. The minutes begin:

Oct 18th 1836
Mr. Glashan in the Chair
The minutes of the previous meeting having been confirmed the Secretary read the letter of I.B. Bernard for discussion as agreed to on the previous meeting.
After considerable discussion the following Resolutions were agreed to, they were introduced by the Secretary and being amended by Mr. Watson were refered to a Committee consisting of Messrs. Mitchell Moore Hoare and the Secretary for revision.
Resolution 1st
That the members of this Association have no confidence [... etc.]

So here again, in 1836, we see basically the same procedure which was to be found in any union branch meeting in my own times. But in 1836 the holding of such a meeting made all those participating liable under the Conspiracy Laws of the time to terrible penalties, and yet the gentlemen still thought it best to carefully minute their considerations including the true names of the participants!

Note that when the British Museum transcribed the text for the benefit of students, they neglected everything before "Resolution 1st." What followed is a precursor of the famous Charter which dominated the political landscape for the following decade and transformed the country. Certainly a momentous decision which is worthy of learning about, but the fact that the men making this decision thought it appropriate to first confirm the minutes of the previous meeting and then proceed to Correspondence, resolving on the Charter as a Matter Arising from Correspondence, that "considerable discussion" and formal amendments were dealt with before the resolutions were given to a committee for drafting – this is also of some interest in its own right. The systematic deletion of these apparently insignificant details of procedure from the record is a problem that will dog our research.

The British Trade Unions in 1824[1]

So my next step was to go back into the earlier history of the British trade union movement. Searching for information about how unions transacted their meetings in the early days of the union movement is complicated by the fact that all workers' organisations were subject to various draconian regimes of repression.

As it happened, however, the British ruling class had found that repression had failed to dampen industrial action and employers were reluctant to prosecute workers. Repressive laws had only forced the formerly conservative and non-political trade unions to make common cause with the radical political groups who were already subject to the Treason and Sedition laws. So in 1824 the Combination Acts were repealed and a Select Committee appointed to investigate the activity of the trade unions. The Committee interviewed unionists and collected the rulebooks of 13 unions, and their report, along with the rulebooks, have been preserved. After an upsurge of trade union militancy, Conspiracy Laws were introduced in 1825 with much the same effect as the Combination Acts, until 1859, when the Molestation of Workmen Act allowed peaceful picketing. The 1871 Trades Union Act finally gave trade unions legal recognition. So the only evidence we have of the procedures used by the early 19th century trade unions is through this brief window given us in 1824.

The collection of unions investigated was very diverse. One was not a trade union at all, but simply a friendly society, while another offered none of the services of a friendly society and suggested their members join a friendly society in addition to the union.

Some were very local, some united local branches across a county and one aspired to cover all of England, another all of Scotland. The trades covered included shipwrights, seamen, weavers, cotton spinners, miners, coopers and papermakers. Every one had a different structure – with councils, general committees, districts, grand divisions, and district meetings, general meetings, delegates meetings, works meetings, and appointed different officers – presidents, secretaries, chairmen, clerks, wardens, treasurers, trustees, delegates, etc. Different benefits were provided – benefits for sickness, injury, shipwreck, funeral, funeral of dependent, unemployment, strike, and contemplated different kinds of collective action against employers or even

---

1 My source for this section is *The Report of the Select Committee on the Combination Laws* (1825) http://www.marxists.org/history/england/combination-laws/1825/combinations.pdf.

collaboration with employers. One offered a reward for invention of a technical innovation which benefited the whole trade, another offered an employment referral system. Meetings were held at different frequencies from weekly or as and when required to annual. Some strictly forbad continuation in an office after serving one term, others did not. Some preferred half-elections to ensure continuity, others did not.

So it is clear that in 1824 there was *no clear model* for what a trade association or union should look like and further, *no single organisation was planning and orchestrating the process*. The diversity, complexity and sophistication of the structures of delegation, election, division of labour and services intertwined with identical solutions to many of the same problems makes it clear that these structures were invented in an environment *already saturated* with models from which to draw. These workers were already familiar with a range of possible organisational structures when they came together to form a union amongst themselves.

Let us look at some common features of the rule books.

Decision by majority voting is ubiquitous, except only that most societies specify that 5/6 of the general membership are required to pass a proposal to dissolve the society and many include a requirement for a 2/3 vote at a general meeting to make a rule change. Even when the rule asks for "the sense of the meeting" or "the sense of the committee" it is implicit that this is decided by a show of hands. There is not a single instance of requiring unanimity for a decision to be made, or even an approximation to consensus. Although Majority is usually taken for granted it is nonetheless written into the rules explicitly and repeatedly. Nor is there any suggestion that, for all the calls for unity and brotherhood, there is any virtue attached to a unanimous or consensus decision nor is any disapprobation attached to voting or speaking in a minority. It is very clear that these workers were very comfortable with majority decision and minority dissent and neither valued nor expected consensus.

The first thing that strikes the modern reader, though, is that every one of them legislates a whole raft of fines and other sanctions for all kinds of misdemeanour related to the union meetings and the obligations of union membership in general. The Durham shipwrights had fines for a member failing to attend a meeting or arriving late, for late payment of their dues, for failing to perform the duties of their office, for "disrespectful language against His Majesty or his Government" and intoxication, cursing, blaspheming or indecent language, striking another member, calling another member a liar, reflecting on his character at a meeting, being censorious of the conduct of council without good cause. Most have fines for interrupting someone speaking at a meeting or failing to keep silent when called upon to do so by the chairman.

The coopers were not alone with a fine for "introducing political or religious subjects during the hours of the meeting." The Sheffield coal miners did not stop at fines: in the case of a member refusing to pay contributions or observe union rules, "such means shall be used to enforce the same as the committee of management, at their monthly meetings, shall think necessary."

Apart from these fines relating to the conduct of union activities there were also severe penalties for indiscretions at work. The Seamen had a fine for "a member seaman failing to obey the command of a superior officer." The Coopers had a fine for a member continuing to work for a master who had a "hireling," that is, an unqualified worker or a woman. (The various sanctions against women were waived for the wife or daughter of a master or in certain circumstances, the union member's wife or daughter). Others had fines for boasting, even boasting at the pub. The journeymen papermakers had a severe 2 guinea fine for insulting a committee man, except "at a public meeting convened for debates."

A member could be appointed to an office by election or by rotation or even by lot. The ubiquity of fines for refusal to take up an office makes it clear that office-holding was an onerous duty not a privilege. For people working 12 hour days, it would be no trifle to spend 2 hours taking the minutes, or handing out tickets at an evening union meeting. Many unions paid small honorariums for the more onerous duties.

Nonetheless, most rulebooks betray an anxiety about offices developing into positions of power and privilege, and have provisions for election of offices as frequently as monthly, though more commonly annually, and most forbid holding an office for consecutive terms. The Coopers even forbad their stewards to propose or second their successors. The Ayrshire colliers, on the other hand, were comfortable for the "secretary to continue in office for as long as the members may think it proper."

All the unions specified the day of the week and/or month, time, duration and location of their general meetings. Invariably the venue would be an inn, and the landlord was invariably regarded as a particularly trustworthy person and treated with some deference.

There is meticulous, almost manic concern for the security of their funds against theft or fraud. Almost all keep their funds in a triple-locked box. (The Sheffield coal miners required four locks). Usually two committee men or two officials such as secretary and president, plus the landlord, each had a key. The Thames shipwrights specify that each key had to be of a different construction. Timely payment of dues is enforced by fines, and the penalty for secretaries or clerks who fail to adhere to the rules for carrying out and documenting transactions are severe. And the unions were not tolerant of various conditions affecting their members' ability to pay. Even the unemployed were required to keep up to date with the dues in some cases, and penalties were imposed on those who returned to the trade after an absence, even for military service.

Rules governing membership are revealing. Almost all specify that seven years in the industry, and almost invariably a seven year apprenticeship is a pre-condition of membership. The Ayrshire Colliers placed barriers against those joining who were not sons of colliers. The Sheffield coal miners held that only those who have followed the trade of coal-getter from the age of 16 shall be allowed to work in mines.

And these kind of rules were effectively imposed on masters as well as union members and anyone threatening to take the jobs of union members: no employment of women (in most but not all of the trades), no employment of unskilled workers, i.e., anyone who had not completed a 7-year apprenticeship under a master who was himself qualified (and the Thames River shipwrights went to great lengths to prevent employers getting around this provision with a 'corporate veil'). If a member left a job due to dissatisfaction with pay or conditions, no member was to take his place and the union would find him another job. The papermakers would not accept as a member anyone who, as an apprentice, had been used to do the work of journeymen. Some unions explicitly put aside funds for strike pay, but most (at least in writing) were cagey about this, and looked to indirect sanctions, but evidently sanctions which had a force equal to that of the law where their union was solid.

Almost all the unions had a grievance procedure, both for internal disputes and disputes between members and their employers.

Some of the provisions are transparently related to the union's function as a friendly society. As they offered superannuation, sickness and unemployment insurance, they were obliged to discriminate against those who might become a drain on their purse. The Durham shipwrights had an age limit of 45 for new members, unless "of a healthy constitution, and free of any defect which may prevent him from earning a competent living for himself and his family." Other provisions were transparently related to their function, usually declared up front in the preamble to the rules, of improving the pay and conditions of members. Though the Thames shipwrights believed that prices (i.e., the payment for specific work) should remain fixed and unaffected by demand, clearly understanding this to be a principle that ought also to apply to food and rent, etc. But others held that their trade had always been underpaid and dedicated themselves to remedying that.

The schedule of fines for disturbing the smooth running of meetings tells us that while these men took their debates and decisions *very* seriously, they were also cognisant of the fact that not all of their members could be relied upon to conduct themselves appropriately, and used financial sanctions to suppress everything from striking someone to calling someone a liar or introducing religious or political topics into the debate.

But overall, notwithstanding elements of modern trade union consciousness, there is a very strong sense in these organisations of the *guilds* – also known as 'companies', 'societies' or 'corporations' – those associations of artisans and merchants which, as we shall see, date back to before the Norman Conquest. The guilds had been in decline since the rule of Henry VIII and were more or less defunct by 1824, but among their offspring were friendly societies. By 1824, most of the guilds existed in some form, but side by side with 'box-clubs' – a form of microfinance where members met in the local pub to make a regular donation and then discuss claims for relief of distress. This author has witnessed these in operation in the East End of London as recently as the late 1970s. Eighteenth/Nineteenth century England was saturated with these small local forms of voluntary association, and the rules of the 1824 unions are taken from the palette of organisational forms from box-clubs to artisan guilds.

In short, in 1824, we see a transitional form between mediaeval guilds and modern trade unions.

My hypothesis is that the Majority decision procedure which became embedded in the trade union movement from its beginning was inherited from the medieval guilds. The same decision procedures, it would appear, were also inherited by capitalist firms, mutual societies, universities and friendly societies, all of whose functions were once combined in the guild.

To test this hypothesis I must begin from the earliest recorded history of England to discover the origins of the guilds, and how they adopted a Majority decision procedure, and from there move forwards to the present day again.

Anglo-Saxon England[1]

Anglo-Saxon England was an aggressively slave-owning society. Slavery was normal even before the Roman occupation (55 BC–400 AD) and until about 600 AD slaves were routinely exported. Conversion to Christianity during the 7th century had no effect on the practice of slavery which continued even after the Norman Conquest. The Domesday Book tells us that in 1086 10% of England's population were slaves. Anglo-Saxon England was altogether a very unequal society.

Slaves had no protection from the law and no rights, enjoying only the same protection as any item of their owner's property. A freeman could kill his own slave without any legal sanction, but would be subject to penalties if he were to kill another man's slave. Likewise, he would be subject to a fine if his slave were to commit a crime against another freeman.

A freeman in Anglo-Saxon England did have rights though, and could not be dealt with arbitrarily. He was entitled to full participation in the courts where his oath was respected. However, most ordinary Anglo-Saxon freemen did not need to rely on the protection of the public authority, as they were entitled to bear arms and if aggrieved, could call upon their kin to exact legitimate compensation. A freeman was not subject to mutilation or the lash, though if guilty of a serious crime they could be sentenced to trial by ordeal, which often meant death. Women had rights, especially widows who inherited their husband's property, but were not generally agents in Anglo-Saxon law, though women of the royal family did participate in political life and on several occasions there were female regents.

Inequality was finely graded. The main protection offered by Anglo-Saxon law was the wergeld. This was the price put on the life of every Anglo-Saxon man. If a man were killed then the killer had to pay the appropriate wergeld, half as compensation to the victim's kin and half to the king as a penalty, a practice common among all the Germanic peoples.

The ordinary freeman of late seventh-century Wessex had a wergeld of 200s. (shillings). A nobleman had a wergeld of 1,000s. and there was an intermediate class worth 600s. The king typically had a wergeld of about 12,000s., half of which belonged to his kin and half to the kingdom. The king, like any

---

1 My principal sourced for this chapter are Loyn, H.R. (1984). *The Governance of Anglo-Saxon England, 500–1087,* and Liebermann, F. (1913). *The national assembly in the Anglo-Saxon period.*

nobleman, was further protected because his kin and his servants had the protection of a graduated scale of wergeld.

Anglo-Saxon law was principally enforced by an elaborate schedule of fines. Failure to observe a festival incurred a fine of 120s.; a priest or thegn who failed to be present for the swearing of oaths would be fined, a deserter would be fined 120s. Fighting in the home of an ealdorman incurred a fine of 120s., forcible entry to his home, 160s. In the case of private wrongs, half the fine would be paid in compensation to the aggrieved party and half to the king or his agent, generating an income stream for the state.

Nobility brought obligations, so fines were graduated to represent these obligations. An ordinary freeman who neglected his military duty was liable for a fine of 25s., while a nobleman would be fined 50s. and a nobleman who owned land 120s. for the same offence.

Further protection for the nobility was provided, and the aura surrounding social class reinforced, by the wergeld attached to the servants and slaves of the king and landed nobility. A thegn was a servant of the king, who was not necessarily of noble blood, but due to his closeness to the king, his wergeld would be 1,200s. A female slave could be used by their owner without penalty but the penalties were 50s. for anyone lying with a maiden belonging to the king, 25s. for a slave of the second and 12s. for a slave of the third class. If the slave belonged to an earl the scale of fines was 6s., 2½s. and 1½s. respectively.

For serious crimes against the king, a freeman could be sentenced to death or sold into slavery. One of the most serious penalties to which a freeman could be sentenced, however, was outlawry. A person who was placed outside of the protection of the law could be murdered with impunity and anyone harbouring them would be subject to penalties. Going to another kingdom was ruled out because as a foreigner you would still be regarded as an outlaw. So to be outlawed was to be flung alone into a state of nature.

This social system functioned well and developed for 500 years. The main causes of insecurity were invaders from outside and warring between contending kings. By the middle of the seventh century, there were seven kingdoms in England and the royal dynasties which provided the kings were not subsequently added to. From this time forward, no ruler would be accepted as king unless he could claim membership of one of these royal dynasties.

Kingship was the chief pillar of government in Anglo-Saxon England. By the time Alfred acceded to the throne in Wessex in 871 AD, Wessex was the only English kingdom not governed or ravaged by invaders. Alfred pushed back the Danes (and converted the Danish king to Christianity) so that well before the Norman conquest, an English king governed a single kingdom extending across the whole of England.

As life became more settled and agriculture more productive, Anglo-Saxon England moved from being a collection of tribal societies to a feudal society based on land right. The kingdom was divided into shires, hundreds, and later, boroughs. Lords ruled private estates and shires, exacting an income for themselves while collecting taxes for the king, and managing social and political life at the different territorial levels. Every family was under their lord and tied to the land through a chain of feudal tenancy. At the base of the pyramid were tithings, groups of ten freemen who met monthly, often over dinner, and were jointly responsible for security of their locality (a kind of Neighbourhood Watch) but also ensuring that every one of them did their civic duty, attended court, participated in festivals, etc. One of the ten would be delegated to fight as a soldier for the king and another nominated as the senior tithingman. King Cnut (1016–1035) made membership of a tithing a condition for enjoying the protection of wergeld and the right to swear an oath in court.

This was a well-organised, feudal order based on the land and governed by the king with the active assistance of a landed aristocracy.

When not leading his army in battle, the king took an active part in governing the land and its people, progressing around his kingdom with his household, holding court and collecting taxes in different shires. By the later centuries at least, the king was seen as *interpreting* the law as it existed in the form of folk-right rather than as a *lawmaker*, but nonetheless, English law grew through the will of the king, recorded in Charters, giving regular and stable shape to Anglo-Saxon England.

The first question which goes to our subject is this: in the course of governing his kingdom – how did the king make his decisions? Although the king was the ruler of the kingdom, the king was also subject to law in Anglo-Saxon England and the rights of individuals were not simply subject to his caprice.

The Witenagemot

When the king was to make a decision of any import he did so with the counsel of the *witenagemot* (*witen* = wise man; *gemot* = meeting), ensuring that his decision was effective, lawful and practical. The king could convene the witenagemot with sufficient notice wherever he was in his progress around the kingdom, and local figures would be included in the witenagemot as well as the king's household and members of the nobility from around the kingdom. The size and composition of the witenagemot varied and there was no fixed schedule of meetings.

Felix Liebermann (1913) believed that the witenagemot was the same institution that Tacitus described among the Germanic peoples in the first century AD, and which therefore pre-existed the English monarchy.

The form of decision making at work when the king decided with the counsel of the witenagemot was what I call Counsel – an archetypal form of collective decision making. It was the earliest form of collective decision making which can be documented in Anglo-Saxon England. It persists to this day in the board rooms of companies, public service departments and traditional families.

St. Benedict (480–547), the authority on the rules of monastic life, left us a concise definition of this mode of collective decision making:

> As often as anything important is to be done in the monastery, the abbot shall call the whole community together and himself explain what the business is; and after hearing the advice of the brothers, let him ponder it and follow what he judges the wiser course. The reason why we have said all should be called for counsel is that the Lord often reveals what is better to the younger. The brothers, for their part, are to express their opinions with all humility, and not presume to defend their own views obstinately. The decision is rather the abbot's to make, so that when he has determined what is more prudent, all may obey.
>
> THE RULE OF ST. BENEDICT, Chapter 3: Summoning the Brothers for Counsel

Counsel is indeed a *collective* decision making procedure even though it is manifested in the shape of the decision by *one* person (the king, CEO or whatever). It is a valid and successful form of decision making because once completed it is the best possible decision in the mind of at least one human individual. It is not the outcome of some process which escapes the rationality of the individual human mind, satisficing divergent views with some kind of compromise or arithmetical mean. But it differs radically from individual decision making because it is the outcome of a rule-governed process of discussion and the weighing of arguments by the entire group.

The effectiveness of Counsel depends on three inter-related factors: the quality of the king, the quality of the council and the relation between king and council, in particular, the *power* relation between the two sides.

The quality of the Old English monarchy benefited from a unique feature of the Anglo-Saxon folk constitution. In most monarchies, including post-conquest England, monarchy followed the law of primogeniture, that is, on the death of the king, the crown passes to the first born male child of the king. When not passing the throne to his eldest son, the king has the option of determining the line of succession, and tradition allowed for widows and daughters to rule in the absence of a suitable male heir. War and fratricide aside, the line of succession is more or less determined by the king himself in his own lifetime and the kingdom must take what it gets. In Anglo-Saxon England this was not the case. When the king died, whatever efforts he had made before his death to secure the succession to his own son, it was the witenagemot which determined the succession once the throne was vacant! The king had to be chosen from one of the royal families claiming descent from Cerdic, a West Saxon king from the early sixth century, but the new king could be up to eight degrees of separation from the former king, typically sharing only a great-great-grandfather with his predecessor. So the witenagemot had a large pool of royal blood to choose from.

Once elected and crowned, the king had absolute authority over all his subjects, witan included, but he did start off both with a debt to those who had chosen him and coming new to the role, a real need to secure the loyalty and support of the witenagemot. The witenagemot could never make a decision contrary to the king's wishes, but on rare occasions, the witenagemot met without the king to depose him. While this emphasises the fact that the witenagemot could not make a decision contrary to the will of the king, it raises the question of how it could elect a new king in the absence of a king. It appears that the archbishop represented and spoke for the witenagemot during the interregnum and sometimes acted as an intermediary between the witenagemot and royal candidates. On other occasions, a pretender to the throne would come to the witenagemot and negotiate. So the witenagemot always made a decision through its leading representative, normally the king, but in the absence of the king, the archbishop.

Even those who acquired the throne by conquest were careful to gain the assent of the witan. This equalisation and harmonisation of king and witenagemot generally ensured a balanced relationship between king and council, and consequently rational and lawful decisions. Although the king convened the witenagemot and was active in inviting people to attend, the king could not depose the bishops, ealdormen or hereditary thegns, who held their office for life.

The king and his council remained features of the English monarchy through the Norman conquest, but the election of a new king by his council rather than by primogeniture – the feature of Anglo-Saxon monarchy which defended the people from the arbitrary oppression of despotic kings – was terminated by the Norman Conquest.

A witenagemot included both secular and clerical figures, noblemen and thegns; it might also include women of royal blood and commoners revered for their wisdom, though less so in later centuries. Promulgation of new laws was always carried out by the witan, and the ecclesiastical members of the witenagemot were responsible for framing and writing the results of deliberations on matters of law and drafting up the charters.

Churchmen were active participants in social and political life, even warfare, and there was no consciousness of a separation of church and state. The clergy supplied literacy to the witenagemot. But on occasion there would be witenagemots with no ecclesiastical presence. Even visitors, such as a Welsh king, might participate. Commoners might attend on account of their local knowledge or wisdom, but only the most senior aristocrats had a permanent right to attend. The king was not necessarily present during the deliberations, though he would always be present at the moment when the law was declared. The only consistent feature of attendance at the witan was the presence of noblemen owing direct allegiance to the king. These would include senior thegns, as well as ealdormen (usually governors of shires) as well as other officers of the king. But membership of the witenagemot did not imply any kind of equality between its members, though it did enhance the status (i.e., the wergeld) of those who participated. There was no notion of *representation* in the witenagemot; that is, members of the witenagemot were not seen as representing any constituency; all were seen only as representing the interests of the whole kingdom. Nor was there any notion of consensus: in 1051, for example, the witan banished Godwin and his family, which could hardly have been a unanimous decision since Godwin was present.

Any governmental act of more than routine significance would take place in a witenagemot. Charters testifying to grants of land would be authenticated by a witenagemot, and the signatures put on the charters have left evidence of the highly variable composition of the witan, according to the matter being determined. These signatures also tell us that there was at all times a strict hierarchy among members of the witen, the signatures always being placed in descending order of status. The language of the charters sometimes used the first person singular, expressing the will of the king, sometimes the first person plural, expressing the collective will of king and witenagemot.

The witan normally met indoors, and there were over 100 locations around England where the king came to consult with the witenagemot, requiring the construction of large halls for the purpose. Some witenagemots were held in symbolic locations associated with ancient rituals, and some were held at centres like Winchester, Westminster, Gloucester and so on. Witenagemots were convened regularly at Easter, Whitsun and Christmas. Up to a hundred people could assemble for a witenagemot, many coming from far afield to participate. And of course, failure to attend when required rendered the offender liable to a stiff fine, up to the value of his wergeld or even outlawry. As Lieberman notes: "Judging from the universal aversion to the fulfilment of the political duties amongst the provincial witan in the shire and hundred courts, the seat in the witenagemot was rather considered as an unprofitable burden gladly to be shirked."

We have no evidence as to the rules of order observed by a witenagemot. But whether the witan reached a consensus or not is irrelevant because it was the king who actualised the deliberation as a decision, even if he had not been present during the deliberation.

There could be no question of a vote in the witenagemot, because there was and could be no notion of equality between the witan. Counting the votes of archbishops and ealdormen and comparing the number of them to those of ordinary thegns would be a meaningless exercise. Self-evidently, this applied with even greater force in the wider population. On the question of electing kings, Liebermann tells us:

> At the elections of kings, the witan were divided in 975, 1014, 1016, 1035, and 1066. If votes were at all given singly, an archbishop or earl was sure to speak with a more powerful voice than a mere thegn. Majority, therefore...could not possibly decide here.

Even the tithing was no exception to this. Each tithing had a senior man, the 'tithingman', who was responsible for the collection of the dues of all ten and also reported on their activity to the hundredman. The hundredman was appointed by the reeve, and he, together with the ten senior tithingmen, had the responsibility of controlling the money of the hundred. So it is clear that at the base of the pyramid just as much as at the peak, decisions were made by Counsel, and one appointed person had the moral responsibility for the actions of the group. *There could be no question of voting in this society, at any level.*

The functioning of the Church even at that time did include a combination of appointment from above (including the appointment of bishops by the king) and collegial election by majority voting with some form of secret ballot. But although the Church was active in social life, its internal political life would have been very remote from the population at large. The doctrine of papal infallibility in matters of faith and morals, a doctrine which extended to bishops within their own diocese, suggests that decision making inside the Church resembled at its best that in the witenagemot. Despite the fact that the Church was a literate community, and in communication with the rest of Europe, there is no reason to suppose that monks electing their abbot (subject to royal approval), entailed majority voting. As St. Benedict explained it:

> In the election of an Abbot let this always be observed as a rule, that he be placed in the position whom the whole community with one consent, in the fear of God, or even a small part with sounder judgment [i.e. a subcommittee], shall elect.
>
> THE RULE OF ST. BENEDICT, Chapter 48: Of the Election of the Abbot

The wider question of decision making in the early Church will be dealt with below.

The Shire Courts

The largest administrative unit the kingdom was the shire, and the shire court was convened by the reeve (later, shire-reeve = sheriff), no more than twice a year, normally at Easter and Michaelmas. There was no judge present, and an earl or bishop would preside and the suitors (male or female) did not have lawyers, but had to argue their case in terms of folk-right. Attendance was nominally required by all freemen in the shire, though in practice one man for each land-holding would have to attend. These courts were great social occasions, attended by all the local nobility and usually the king. The shire courts dealt with almost anything – taxes and payment of fines and debts, disputes over land or inheritance, as well as criminal matters. Guilt or innocence would be decided by compurgation – sworn oaths as to the innocence of the accused, or ordeal.

The Hundred Courts

The hundred was a key level of the administrative structure of Anglo-Saxon England. The reeve in charge of a hundred was responsible for convening a court every four weeks, at a regular open air location in the district, usually a location with religious or symbolic significant, on a regular day, and everyone who had business at the court was required to attend at pain of a fine should they fail to attend. The hundred court dealt with all manner of civil disputes, including the witnessing of all sales and the taking of oaths, as well as hearing criminal matters which could see people fined, sentenced to trial by ordeal or outlawed if found guilty. The hundred was crucial to the economic and social life of the community and its decisions were final, so no-one could afford to not be there. It was the hundred courts which had the most immediate and regular impact on the life of the people and the proceedings of the court were important social events.

The hundred courts have an ancient and obscure origin, but by the law made at Wantage by Ethelred II in 997, §13.2 required the criminal court to proceed as follows. A meeting would be held in which twelve of the leading thegns and the reeve would come forward and swear a public oath to make a true judgment and then they would seize the accused. Witnesses would give sworn evidence and then, according to Loyn:

> Proof of guilt or innocence continued to rest with the traditional methods of compurgation or ordeal but the thegns of the Wantage code were no mere emergency posse of lawmen summoned to perform an executive function only. They exercised judgment in the full sense and were expected to reach a *unanimous* verdict. If they failed to do so, a majority of eight out of the twelve was deemed sufficient, but the minority was expected then to pay the quite considerable sum of six half-marks. This is the first statement in English law to recognise the force of a majority verdict.
>
> LOYN, 1984, p. 145

The use of the number *twelve*, rather than the usual figure of ten more often inscribed in English law, suggests that the jury had Scandinavian origins.

So just 70 years before the Norman conquest we find the first, rudimentary instance of Majority. But what a restricted concept of majority decision! Not only is 'majority' to be at least 8 out of 12, but those who insist on retaining their dissenting vote must pay a penalty for their dissent! Very clearly, Ethelred had a mind that a unanimous decision was the norm, and this remains the case for juries to this day. Only quite exceptional conditions would oblige a thegn to cast a minority vote and pay the fine, but the point is that here there was apparently *some notion* of the members of this jury being peers, and consequently that the counting of votes was meaningful. In general, in the feudal society of Anglo-Saxon England the counting of votes was unthinkable because the notion of the equality of persons was unthinkable.

The Guilds

During the last century and a half of Anglo-Saxon England, there was a great flourishing of the towns. No borough was without its own mint and some towns had dozens of moneyers producing a voluminous quantity of coinage, servicing a vigorous commercial life. London (with a population of over 10,000 by 1066), Winchester, York and Lincoln were major commercial centres and middling towns such as Chester, Exeter, Oxford and many others also minted coins and flourished as commercial centres. Increasing use of the North Sea for peaceful trade rather than pillaging sustained urban growth and the old Danish centres in the north and north-east came to life. Likewise the Cinq Ports in the south gained strength as naval centres and the church moved its bases into the new urban centres – all functioning to stimulate urban commercial life. The variety and complexity of life in the cities and towns and the flow of wool, cloth iron and salt across the North Sea and the Channel stimulated population growth and the growth of a class of Anglo-Saxon merchants who travelled as far afield as Iceland and Rome. Attempts were made by the kings to confine trading to recognised boroughs, but the sheer pressure and volume of business doomed such efforts to failure. Trade was eventually legitimated outside the recognised centres, but the law still required that all trading had to be conducted with good witness via the hundred court. The movement of people into the towns also required new forms of land tenure to accommodate the increasing and fluid population, which put enormous stress on the feudal mechanisms of taxation and regulation. The legal regime became impossibly complicated by the overlap of jurisdiction between land-right and the newly emergent borough-right, with a network of lesser courts meeting weekly in multiple sites across London with the power to witness trade or outlaw people for criminal offences.

On their side, the merchants had to travel all over the country, not to mention their overseas voyages. Under the laws of the day they had little public protection and none of the protection of kin on which most Anglo-Saxon people relied for safety and sustenance. In the absence of adequate protection and regulation of their lives and business the merchants established *guilds*. They had precedents in the tithings, sometimes called 'peace-guilds' which were strongly promoted by king Æthelstan (924–939), and thegns' guilds, the first of which was established by King Edgar the Peaceable (942–975), who granted a group of thirteen thegns a plot of land near Aldersgate, conditional upon them performing a range of sporting feats, thought to be the first guild to receive a royal charter.

The merchants' guilds were mostly concerned with retrieving a member or his body from faraway places and bringing them home. Also, there were guilds which were solely concerned with promoting social and neighbourhood life in their guildhalls, and priests and deacons also had guilds. These guilds all sprang up to meet pressing needs which the feudal structure was now incapable of fulfilling and which could only be met by forms of *voluntary association*.

Thegns' guilds were mostly concerned with protecting their members in matters relating to feuds or vengeance for injury. Both merchants' guilds and thegns' guilds operated as what would very much later come to be called friendly societies, offering insurance in the event of illness or welfare for widows and children and funeral benefit in the event of death. A fragment of the statutes of the Bedwyn merchants' guild survives, enough to show what seems to be a set pattern: payment on death, payment and recompense at the burning of a house and reconciliation and peace-keeping among the brethren. Urki, who had been a prominent nobleman in the court of Cnut (1018–1035), in the 1040s gave a guildhall and its land at Abbotsbury for a guild and drew up its regulations. These concerned alms for the church, and social regulations aimed at keeping the group together including the regulation of the standard of brewing with a fine for unsatisfactory brewing, regulations for keeping the peace amongst members, provisions for support in sickness and decent burial after death and "if any one of us becomes ill within 60 miles we are then to find 15 men to fetch him – 30 if he be dead – and these are to bring him to the place which he desired in life." Such a commitment implied considerable resources of both people and money.

So what we see here is a new institution founded, not on feudal obligation, kinship and service to the king, but on the *voluntary association among equals* for mutual aid and comfort, and on that basis decisions could be made by Majority, the rudiments of such a concept having been created by Ethelred II in 997 AD. The need and opportunity for this new kind of institution arose from the weakening of the feudal structure due to the rising tempo of commercial life and particularly the growth of towns and the resulting complexity of legal, administrative and economic life which could not be contained within or supported by hierarchical feudal right.

No information about the forms of decision making has been preserved for this very early stage in the development of the guilds, but the guilds were to continue for a thousand years and enough has been left to us over this span of time for us to be able to piece together how they elected their officials, conducted their meetings and made decisions.

The Norman Imposition

By the time that William the Conqueror took the throne, England was already a well-ordered kingdom with deep-rooted administrative strength and firm traditions of law and governance at all levels and a sense of constitutionalism. William imposed over the top of this social structure the instrument of a foreign occupying power and acted as all occupying powers do, with utter ruthlessness and an extraordinary degree of self-belief, replacing the top layer of administrators with his own associates and kin.

The ruling Norman caste who were to run England spoke Norman French, not Old English, and for effective government they relied upon machinery inherited from Anglo-Saxon England. Both the power relations and communications between the king and his people were irrevocably changed. The king's council was now utterly subordinate to the king, having no more power than a puppet, and at the base of the hierarchy, the people quite simply did not speak the same language.

Felix Liebermann supports the claim that there is a continuous line of descent from the witenagemot to the British Parliament and says that no-one at the time saw William's ascent to the throne as constituting a rupture in the English system of government. William himself claimed (falsely) descent from the English royal line and always saw himself as acting within the constitutional norms of Anglo-Saxon England. However, Liebermann tells us that:

> Almost every single feature was radically changed; ...a trained staff of civil officers. They, and no longer the witan in mass, begin to attest royal documents in a much smaller number; they represent a permanent governmental board. The same 'peaceful revolution', shifting the most important state affairs from the witenagemot to a narrow court council, conquered at the same time in France. ...The barons of the Conqueror depended more directly on him, than earls and thegns had done on the Anglo-Saxon king. ...the barons owed all their land and *all* their social privilege to this present king...The Norman ducal court...spoke French. In the Conqueror's later years it consisted almost only of foreigners. The majority of its members sat because they held fiefs in chief. The rule of its three annual meetings came from France... Its criminal law and procedure were Norman. (1913, p. 75)

The Norman imposition lasted for 300 years, before Anglo-Saxon right was able to effectively re-assert itself against the new ruling caste. The rebellion of the barons against King John in 1215 was resolved when his son Henry III signed the Great Charter in 1225 passing significant parts of the *Magna Carta* into English law, and restored the rights of the nobility and limited the arbitrary power of the king. The Peasants Revolt of 1381 was crushed, but over the following century rural wages increased and serfdom ultimately vanished in England. It is only after this interregnum that the threads of development of collective decision making in England can be gathered together again.

The House of Commons, separate from the Lords, was created in 1341, elections to the House of Commons began in 1430, for those owning more than 40 shillings worth of property, but open conflict between Parliament and the king continued until it was resolved by force in 1649 and finally in 1688. Until that time there could be no rational, constitutional, collective decision making procedure for the British monarchy. The word 'majority' (in the relevant meaning) did not enter the English language until 1650.

The Question of Continuity

The claim that the UK Parliament is descended from the Anglo-Saxon witenagemot is only valid in the most formal sense and has no content. The Norman invasion constituted a *discontinuity* in the history of England, and the legacy of the witenagemot cannot fairly be traced through the councils which advised the Norman kings.

It is widely believed that formal meeting procedure with majority voting evolved in the Parliament and was disseminated to the wider population from Parliament. This claim is also without foundation. I have been unable to definitively determine what decision procedures were used by the two houses of parliament and the royal council in those early centuries. The only clue is that when the Commons elected the Speaker they were electing not a Chairman, but the *person who spoke for them*, and the Speaker was appointed only at the pleasure of the king, and cannot be otherwise replaced even in the event of temporary absence. He is known as the "mouth of the House," which implies that originally a collective decision was reached by *advising the Speaker*, rather than by what evolved into the formal meeting procedure.

The difference between the way the office of Speaker works in the House of Lords as opposed to the House of Commons is instructive. The Speaker of the Lords is the Lord High Chancellor, an officer more closely connected with the Crown than any other in the state and not necessarily a Peer. It is the Lord High Chancellor who speaks *on behalf of the monarch* when s/he addresses Parliament (May, 1844, p. 152).

Although the Speaker of the House of Lords is the president of a deliberative assembly, he is vested with no more authority than any other member; his office is limited to the putting of questions, and other formal actions. The speaker in the House of Lords does not have the power to act as 'mouth' unless specifically so directed, and when Peers speak, they address themselves to the House, not the Speaker (May, p. 197).

Thus, in the House of Lords, debate does not take the form of advising the Speaker, but is decided by a majority of voices among peers, i.e., equals.

However, there were no written standing orders for Parliament until 1685 (on the eve of the Glorious Revolution) and transcripts of the debates of Parliament were not published (illegally) until 1771. Whatever decision-procedures evolved behind closed doors in Parliament and the royal court, they could have had no impact on the collective decision procedures which developed in close connection with the social life of the mass of the people since before the Norman Conquest.

On the other hand, the guilds had been functioning for about 400 years before the Parliament broke from its subordination to the Norman kings and the House of Commons was created. By 1430, most if not all of those who were to be elected to the House of Commons would have been participants in a guild, so it is most likely *that the guilds themselves were the origin of parliamentary procedure.*

Medieval Church Practice

While decision making practices in the Roman Church are unlikely to be the source of practices in the general community, they are of interest in themselves.

St. Ignatius of Loyola, founder of the Jesuit Order, argued that the objective goodness of the decisions made by bodies within the Roman Church is guaranteed only because such decisions are constrained by the laws and previous decisions of the Roman Church over many centuries. Thus, in making a collective decision it is not only those within the room who participate in making the decision, but also all those who have gone before.

Every decision making body is acting *within some tradition*. All Churches are characterised by the traditional knowledge that they inherit and the weight they give to that tradition when making decisions. Those founding new churches, participating in new social movements or aspiring to rationality and freedom from the power of tradition carry an extra burden in making decisions in that they lack this guidance by tradition.

In 534 AD, Justinian's code of Roman law included the maxim "*Quod omnes tangit ab amnibus approbetur,*" that everyone who was affected by a decision had a right to a voice in its approval, but it is hardly likely that the Church ever made a broad enough interpretation of this maxim to satisfy the requirements of discourse ethics today!

Formally, the Roman Church was elected by a collegiate structure and made collegial decisions on the basis of majority voting and secret ballot when required. Bishops were elected by a majority vote of the clergy. In response to the unedifying wheeling and dealing which accompanied lobbying for votes, the Third Lateran Council in 1170 decreed that in all the world's dioceses, the electors more noted for their virtue, zeal, and disinterestedness – the *sanior pars* – must all vote with the majority if the election is to be valid. This measure of consensus provided by the unanimity of the *sanior pars* was taken as a more convincing sign of Divine endorsement of the elected candidate. Likewise, a Pope is deemed infallible in matters of faith and morals only when in agreement with a plurality of his legates, not in defiance of their advice. According to Zabarella (c. 1335–1417), a bishop cannot act alone; he must have either the consent of the whole chapter or at least of its *major et sanior pars*.

Nicolas of Cusa likewise qualified the Divine authority of majority decision of a clerical body when he "insists that the minority formally endorse the decision of the majority after the vote so as to produce the required unanimity especially in the definition of doctrine." This notion that God's will can be found in *the unanimity of the most respected members* of a decision making body has been traced through hundreds of years in the governance of the dioceses of Great Britain.

Nicolas of Cusa had written that "on account of the unanimity on which the authority of the acts of a council depends, we know that the Holy Spirit, who is the spirit of union and harmony has inspired the council's decision." Conversely, "where there is dissent, there is no council."

The hybridity manifested in the history of the Church shows the premium placed on unanimity, whilst recognising the need for resort to majority, and various measures used to manufacture the appearance of unanimity where it did not in fact exist, as well as the persistent assertion of the non-equivalence of different voices, which made the counting of votes problematic. And as St. Benedict tells us, at the base level of the Church, it is Counsel which prevails as the means of determining God's will, not Majority.

The Guilds[1]

In tracing the development of decision making through the guilds from their earliest times up until the early 19th century we have to deal with the problem that when a guild was given its charter, the standing orders were not generally spelt out. The charter would specify the scope of the rights and responsibilities of the guild, that is, the trade it regulated, the officers, the manner and timing of their election, their rights in the borough, their meeting place, rituals and livery (i.e., the ceremonial dress marking a person as an officer of the guild); but the charter would be silent on the rules of debate. It has only been as a result of disputes and crises that decision making procedures have come to be documented – and fortunately it is just these crises which are of particular interest to us. In most cases we have been able to infer the means of decision making from the minutes maintained by the guilds and referenced by historians.

The period we are chiefly concerned with is from the 14th century up to the 17th century. As has been already noted, there was no word for 'majority' until the English Revolution, after which the guilds were in decline. But the concept was there from as far back as we can see; generally speaking the phrase 'the more part' is used in lieu of 'the majority'.

The word 'vote' did carry its modern meaning by 1478, but its use was restricted to voting for (not in) parliament or a vote of funds or a vote of thanks. The words used in lieu of 'vote' for matters internal to the guild are 'chuse' or 'chewse' and 'prick'. When the word 'ballot' is used it has the sense of a secret ballot. This practice was found in the early church where it involved whispering in the ear of the scrutineer; the word is derived from the Venetian Republic of the 8th century where it involved putting a coloured ball in a ballot box. In the guilds it involved handing in a marked piece of paper somewhat like a modern ballot paper. The most common method of voting throughout was raising the hand however; sometimes a bill containing a list of the candidates would be posted at the front of the hall and the electors would come forward one at a time, beginning with the most junior up to the most senior last, and put a tick against the candidate of their choice. Elections were mostly but not always collegial, that is, a limited group of electors elected from amongst themselves,

---

1 My principal source for the factual matter of this chapter is Herbert, W. (1836). *The History of the Twelve Great Livery Companies of London*, and for a better understanding of their evolution, Chase, M. (2012). *Early Trade Unionism. Fraternity, Skill and the Politics of Labour.*

and often, the out-going officers elected the incoming officers. Elected officials were also often subject to approval by the mayor or the king.

At the beginning of the period, when the mechanisms of social and political power inherited from Anglo-Saxon England began to emerge from under the Norman yoke, guilds were both arms of government and voluntary, mutual self-help organisations, which had exclusive and absolute control of all the affairs of their trade. Throughout the period they were what we would see today as *employers'* organisations inasmuch as full participation in the political life and decision making of the guild was generally reserved for masters, that is, those who had completed a seven-year apprenticeship under a master of their trade, become a journeyman allowed to work in the trade as a wage worker and gone on to own a shop of their own employing journeymen and apprentices. This three-layer class system outlived the guilds themselves, and continued into the nineteenth century, and to an extent continues to this day. Apprentices had no say in the affairs of the guild at all, and journeymen only a limited say in some cases, but these relations would not have been seen as antagonistic or exploitative class relations as they would come to be seen much later. For much of the medieval and early modern periods many journeymen had a realistic opportunity to become a master on their own account and enter into full membership of their guild, which, in the meantime, represented both them and their masters. Generally speaking everyone working in the trade was a member of the guild, paid a subscription, was subject to its laws and received sick relief, poor relief, retirement pension, funeral expenses, etc. The guilds also generally employed a priest to look after members' spiritual needs and engaged in religious, charitable and patriotic activities in their locality.

At the beginning of the period, guilds had total control over their trade. Wm. Herbert notes the amelioration of the guilds' regulations from after the Restoration in 1660, corresponding to the decline of their power, but says that even then, by the standards of his day (1836), they would be regarded as 'despotic'.

The guilds both regulated the quality of work provided for their consumers and the prices (which were on the whole very stable) and kept out competition and regulated apprenticeship, ensuring adequate supervision of apprentices, their wages and above all, the 7-year term of apprenticeship. However, gradually over time, especially after the Reformation, with movement of goods and people between towns and increasingly rapid change in technology, they lost control of their trade. By the end of the 18th century the guilds went through their rituals whilst the world went past them having little regard to guild regulations. 'Betty's Law', the Statute of Artificers enacted by Elizabeth I in 1563, was an important measure which gave extended life to the guilds; it formalised the seven years' duration of apprenticeships, extended the guild regulations and gave them the force of national legislation. 'Betty's Law' would be spoken of with affection by artisans well into the 19th century. It could not stem the rising tide of commerce undermining the exclusivity of the guilds however. And it should be remembered that dear as Betty's Law was to the skilled workers who were unionised by the mid-19th century, it was probably not beloved of unskilled workers whose access to well-paid skilled work it blocked. Also, as guilds maintained their 'friendly society' functions while gradually losing control of their trade and consequently their capacity to discipline their own members and defend their members from outside competition, their internal democratic life was gradually eroded.

This erosion happened along two dimensions. The election of officials came more and more to be subject to royal or mayoral appointment rather than internal election, and the election process itself became more and more a ritual for the life-long appointment of an entrenched clique. Since entry to the trade was largely passed on from father to son, the guilds themselves tended towards family dynasties. The guild elected up to six Aldermen to the borough council where they in turn elected the mayor, but this democratic right was of declining value, as the king and the mayor increasingly interfered in the election of aldermen. The guild constitution was hollowed out, as their ancient laws were gradually emptied of their content. Nonetheless, the original ideals of the guild, in which the guild was an expression of the trade, protecting the interests of everyone in the trade while at the same time looking after the interest of the public and loyally serving the Crown, remained throughout in the consciousness of the artisan and merchant classes of Britain.

Guilds generally pre-existed their charter, and although the charter set down the rules of the guild, the guilds' powers were not limited to the election of their officials. They also had the power to make new regulations, subject to royal approval, and regulated day-to-day matters in their trade. These matters resembled the operation of a court, and indeed the regular meetings of the guild were referred to as a court. In addition to the courts, there would generally be an annual meeting open to the 'commonalty', that is to say, the wider general membership of the guild, which would take the form of a banquet and include election of officials for the coming year.

Just like in Anglo-Saxon times, the guilds enforced their regulations by fines (including fines for refusal to take up an elected office or failing to carry out its duties), confiscation of the tools of their trade, expulsion (which meant being unable ever to practice one's trade), removal from office or gaol in the event of failure to pay a fine.

The following excerpt from the ordnances of the Merchant Tailors' Guild gives a flavour of guild discipline:

Refusal "to hear and keep the office and room of master, after being indifferentlie named and elected by the muter [i.e. master] and wardens," with the advice and consent of the assistants, late masters, "agreeably to the ould aunicent rules and laudable customs aforetyme used"; and the person so elected wilfully refusing complience, was subjected to a fine of 100*l*. for the use of the fraternity, "without anie redemption, and never afterwards to be admitted into the said room [i.e. office], reasonable cause excepted." Lesser penalties were inflicted for refusing to serve the office of warden.

HERBERT, V. 2, p. 420

An example of the implementation of this rule is given in the Minutes:

In 1613, one Robinson is fined for not serving as renter-warden. This cause was brought before the lord mayor by summons "when his lordship in a mild speech informed the defendant, that if mildness of persuasion would not do, justice must follow." He then required him to enter into a recognizance in 100*l*, and on refusal committed him to Newgate till he complied. On the following 3d of November the Merchant Tailor's court again appointed Robinson to the same office, who still refused to either pay or serve; but ultimately being persuaded by his friends, he consented to pay a fine of 60*l*. by two instalments within the year, which the court agreed to accept.

HERBERT, V. 2, p. 424

Let us first look at the processes by which the guilds elected their officers, and then at the processes by which they made other decisions.

Election of Officials

The officials of the Guild Court were typically, the Master, four Wardens (sometimes Bailiffs or Ministers), about twenty Assistants, and an Auditor or Clerk; the remainder of the members were called "the commonalty." The Master was the head of the guild and its representative. The Master would often be a nobleman acting as a titular head. The Wardens had the duty to resolve disputes and complaints, and if unable to get agreement from the parties, using guild sanctions, then with the consent of the Master they could "go to the lawe" as a last resort. The Assistants helped the Wardens in their work, voted in all elections and resolutions of the court and would be candidates for Warden in the future.

As a result of a dispute in the Clothworkers Company we have an unusual amount of information about this trade, which included shearmen and fullers.

In 1432, the Shearmen's Company was granted a charter by Henry VI naming the master and determining that the two out-going wardens choose their two successors, who were, in presence of the twelve assistants, admitted wardens. So that the government was then vested in a master, two wardens, and twelve assistants.

In 1441 new ordinances were made by that part of the fraternity only that had formerly been master or warden, "with the advice of the whole company," suggesting that the new ordnances were put to a vote of the entire commonalty, though one suspects that this approval may have been a formality.

In 1498 Henry VII granted the Shearmen a charter with new ordinances drawn up and agreed, "by the major part of the twelve assistants and ten of the best of the clothing (i.e. livery men, past masters and wardens)," whose names are given. (Herbert, p. 652)

On 28th April 1481 Edward IV granted a charter for the Fullers Company of:

> three wardens and commonalty of the men of the mystery or art of Fullers, of the city of London and its suburbs, as well of the brethren and sisters of freemen as of others...
>
> That the same commonalty; that is to say, the freemen of the art or mystery aforesaid, may elect, every year, from amongst themselves, three wardens, to support the burthen of the business of the same mystery, and oversee, rule, and govern the same mystery, and the workers in the same, both in London and its suburbs, in order to correct and amend defaults therein.
>
> That the said wardens and commonalty may make reasonable ordinances and constitutions for the good government of the same mystery, as often as they please or find necessary, and may amend and alter the same, with the advice of the mayor and aldermen of London. ...(p. 649)

On 24th January 1507, Henry VII granted a charter for:

> the men of the mystery of Shearmen within the city of London...That they and their successors may be able, yearly, from year to year, at their pleasure, to elect one master and two wardens, from themselves, to govern, keep, and rule the said fraternity for ever. (p. 650)

On 18th January 1528, Henry VIII granted a charter uniting the two trades:

> that the said mysteries of Shearmen and Fullers may thenceforward
> become one entire art or mystery, and that they may in future, for ever, be
> in deed and name, one body, one art, one mystery, one fraternity, and one
> perpetual commonalty, by the name of CLOTHWORKERS only, and no
> other. ...
>
> to elect and make amongst themselves, and from themselves, one mas-
> ter and four wardens, to govern, keep, and rule the same fraternity; and
> the said master and wardens to amove, if it shall be found necessary, and
> to elect others in their places, from amongst the said conjoined fraternity.

The master of the new company was to be chosen by and from a meeting of
all those who had served as masters of either trade in the past. If the person so
chosen as Master, refused the office, he would forfeit 6*l*. 13*s*. 4*d*. None of these
ordnances make clear just *how* the election is carried out, but in this case we
read how the Clothworkers proceeded to the election of four wardens "after
the old use and custome": The three oldest of the four current wardens each
draw up a bill on which they each nominate three persons who have been wardens in the past. These are given to the Master, and then each member of the
court comes forward and chooses one name from each list. The one with most
votes on each list is elected a warden. The fourth warden, who has just completed his first year, then draws up a list of four nominations from those who
have not served as warden before, and everyone comes forward and chooses
one name from that list. The nominee with the most votes is then the new
"youngest warden." By this means a gradual flow of 'new blood' into the government of the Company was effected.

In 1563, the Fishmongers Guild had 12 wardens each serving a two-year term,
with 6 replaced each year, and 28 Assistants. Nomination and election of the
6 new wardens from the entire commonalty of approximately 1,000 was carried
out by a majority vote amongst the Wardens and Assistants. The Assistants on
the other hand were elected for life, unless removed due to misconduct by a
majority vote of the wardens. So the entire court of 40 was renewed by up to
6 new members every year.

From 1569, by a Charter of James I, election by the whole commonalty was
superseded by the practice of 'secret elections' as described in the following
example. In 1573, the election of master and wardens of the Merchant Tailors'
Company was conducted at the annual banquet. First, four persons are nominated for wardens by the out-going court. The court first chooses the fourth

warden, the third next, and then the first and second wardens, and finally the new master.

The election was conducted by the clerk, first beginning with the youngest warden, and up to the old master. "The clerk reading the names, and every one making his mark or tick against the one he wishes to be master. In case of an equal number of ticks, the master pricks again. The master is elected in a similar manner to the wardens; and if there be but two named for the election as master, and that the new master is chosen only by the tick of the old master and wardens, all others being put aside," there is added in a N.B. "This is called the secret election, and is generally announced to the Great Parlour," where the entire commonalty would be awaiting them at the annual banquet. The publication of the secret election was made with an elaborate ritual in the dining hall where a grand entertainment was given to the fraternity, who had to approve the new Master and Wardens by acclaim.

In 1641, on the eve of the English Revolution, Charles I took all power of election of officials of the guild to himself and used this power to milk the guilds of money; his son continued the practice of interfering in the guilds after the Restoration. Although the right of election was restored to the guilds by Charles II, he required that Masters and Wardens be members of the Church of England (thus excluding Dissenters and Catholics), and retained for the Crown the approval of all elected officials and the right to dismiss any of them. From this time forward, the guilds went into decline.

Nonetheless, in 1675, the Haberdashers Company made for election of assistants by "the major part" of the court. As time passed, it seems that the electorate from which officials of the guild were elected became narrower. Election by and from the commonalty seems to have been generally confined to the antiquity of the guilds.

In the case of electing officials, majority voting was the norm, but this norm was more and more limited, at first by limiting the domain from which candidates for office and their electors were drawn to a point approaching the self-perpetuation of a clique, and secondly, by interference from the Crown. By the time of the Restoration in 1660, the guilds had ceased to be accountable to their members, but they still defended the interests of their trade and provided vital welfare and insurance benefits.

Winstanley on the Guilds
Lest the reader suspect that as employers' organisations, the Guilds would never have been a model for organisation and decision making for the poor, Gerard Winstanley, leader of the Diggers in the English Civil War, can set the

record straight. In his *Law of Freedom* (1652), a utopian outline of the kind of government he wanted the New Model Army to implement, he says:

> And truly the Government of the Halls and Companies in *London* is a very rational and well-ordered government; and the *Overseers of Trades* may very well be called *Masters, Wardens,* and *Assistants* of such and such a Company, for such and such a particular trade. Only two things are to be practised to preserve peace:
> The first is, *That all these Overseers shall be chosen new ones every year.* And secondly, *The old Overseers shall not choose the new ones,* to prevent the creeping in of lordly oppression; but all the masters of families and freemen of that trade shall be the choosers, and the old overseers shall give but their single voice among them.
>
> WINSTANLEY, 1965, p. 549

So it is reasonable to suppose that the poor of England aspired to this model of self-organisation, according to the ancient custom, rather than the increasingly oppressive ways being imposed on them.

Decision Making Processes

Because there were no written standing orders in the Charters, we have to look to the minutes to see how decisions were made. The following excerpts are illustrative.

In 1512, according to the Minutes of the Merchant Tailors, "the common clerk of the company transacted certain affairs of the company, at the commandment and request of the master and wardens, with the advice of *the more part of* the most substanciall and discreet persons, assistants and counsellors of the said fraternity." And in 1518 an audit of the Company was again ordered by the "master and wardens, with the advice of *the more part* of the most substantial and discreet persons, assistants, and councillors of the said fraternity."

Here we see the subjection of majority rule to an explicit concern to limit the electorate to those members whose experience and standing guaranteed the value of their vote, just as was seen in the early Church. The limitation of the electorate to the Assistants, Wardens and Masters was supposed to regularise this provision.

In 1531 the Constitution of the Clothworkers Company provided for majority decisions by the court of 21 officers:

> As to the election of assistants: they ordain, That "at the same time be named and chosen sixteen persons, of the most wise and discreet

persons of the same mystery, to rule and govern with the said master and wardens; and that all judgment shall passed by the said master, wardens, and the 16 persons, or *the more part of them*, and none otherwise : and this order to be kept yearly, for ever."

This was the norm in the time of Edward IV (1470s). The Ordnances of Henry VI's time (1460s/70s) required: "All judgment and acts of government pass by *the major part* of all present."

In 1613, the Merchant Tailors' Company allowed that fines should be imposed "at the discretion of the master, wardens, and assistants, or *the more part of them*" – a gathering of about 50 people.

So these minutes make it clear that decisions were made by majority voting. There was one instance however where majority voting was written into the ordnances of the Company. There had been a dispute in the Fishmongers Guild and a group known as the Stockfishmongers broke away and formed their own guild. But in 1536, the dispute was resolved and the Stockfishmongers were persuaded to rejoin the larger Fishmongers Guild. But to protect their rights and their own elected officials, the court was expanded from 24 to 28, and the number of wardens from 4 to 6, and majority decision making was written into the Charter of the amalgamated guild.

> They further covenant, – that as long as the name of stockfishmongers shall last, *two* of the stock-fishmongers shall be admitted joint wardens with the four wardens of the fishmongers, – thus accounting for the present number of *six wardens* in the united company
>
> It grants that thenceforth for ever, there shall be six of the commonalty of the mystery, chosen in manner under mentioned, who shall be, and be called, the wardens of the Mystery of Fishmongers of the City of London; and likewise twenty-eight of the same commonalty, who shall be, and be called, assistants to the same wardens and commonalty, who from time to time shall be assistants and helping the same wardens and commonalty for the time being, in all causes and businesses concerning the same wardens and commonalty; that such wardens and assistants, *or the greater part of them*, being congregated together upon public summons, to that end to be made, shall have power to ordain and make, from time to time, in writing, reasonable laws, statutes, ordinances, decrees, and constitutions whatsoever, which to them, or *a majority of them*, shall seem, in their good discretions, to be good, wholesome, …[etc.], or *a majority of them*, as often as they may make such ordinances in the form prescribed, may appoint such penalties and punishments, by imprisonment of body, or by fines and amerciaments, or by both of them, for all offenders against

the same, as to a *majority* of the same wardens and assistants shall seem
fit and necessary...

WM. HERBERT, 1837. Italics added

The Skinners Company made similar provisions when they were obliged to
bring into their ranks a large number of skinners who had been working outside the control of the guild.

We have no information about the rules of debate, but even though the
processes of election of officials included substantial elements of deference
and over time were increasingly emptied of content, and despite the fact
that for most of their life the word 'majority' did not exist, nonetheless, the
norm was clearly majority vote with one-vote-one-value, among a limited group
of equals. All the courts had a quorum as well, so that majority decision making
could not be subverted by minorities meeting in the absence of the majority.

The Goldsmiths Company had been noted as early as 1180 and was given its
charter in 1327. In 1462, they had four wardens and ninety-four 'on the livery'. In
1529, there was a revolt amongst members of the Guild, objecting to the kind of
'secret election' described above. It is reported that "the livery, and all other of
the commonalty of Goldsmiths now assembled" declared that "they wold none
of the Eleccion or Chewsyng of Wardens, with moch other ungoodly language
and demeanour," and a petition was delivered to the Mayor. A Committee of
disgruntled members objected to the 'secret election' and insisted "conform-
able to the auncyent custume":

> That, whereas all ordinances and constitutions should be made by the
> wardens and commonalty, – They desire, that there be none made with-
> out the assent of the whole commonalty.

The wardens responded, claiming that they had been "duly and lawfully elected, from time to time, after the ancient rules and customs heretofore used in
the said mystery, time out of remembrance of any person, and not contrary to
the grants of the said king" and responded to the above point:

> That they make no ordinances, but by the consent of the most number of
> the livery: and such ordinances, when made, are approved and confirmed
> by the lord chancellor, lord treasurer, ...(v. 2, p. 145)

The rebellious Committee in turn responded that the Wardens had rigged the
election, held as required by the Charter, but secretly, with relatives and servants of the wardens acting as voters.

> The replicants contend that the said usurping wardens, &c., were not elected by the commonalty, pursuant to the king's letters patents, as would appear by such letters; if they should be read; nor were elected in the manner before used; which was, – 'That four of the names of the chusers should be pricked off by the commonalty, openly in the hall; ...'

So the *ideal* of one-vote-one-value, open, majority decision making lived, even while the reality of that ideal was being gradually corrupted. On one hand there was an ethos which asserted the moral equality of all members of the trade (an ethos which has been unthinkable in Anglo-Saxon England), but on the other hand, growing social differentiation and the development of antagonistic interests within the trade was promoting the perversion of the constitution of the guilds in favour of the perpetuation of self-serving cliques.

The English people generally treasured these ancient egalitarian customs, invariably believing that they had prevailed in Anglo-Saxon England and were corrupted only because of the Norman Conquest. More likely, it was during the early centuries *after* the Conquest that the ideal had prevailed, if ever.

Oxford and Cambridge University

A community of scholars was teaching in Oxford as early as 1096, and Cambridge University was begun by a group of scholars who left Oxford after a dispute with the townspeople in 1209. Both existed as communities of scholars prior to receiving a charter, and the other great universities of Europe originated about the same time and in the same way. In 1211, in the wake of the dispute with townspeople, the scholars were placed under a Chancellor appointed by the Bishop of Lincoln. Later in the century it became the practice for the Bishop of Lincoln to confirm in office the Chancellor elected by the Oxford masters themselves. In 1214, Oxford University was recognized as a 'lay corporation' and over the remainder of the century received various royal privileges. The governance of both universities was vested in the whole body of all those who held a Masters or Doctors degree from the University; in Oxford it is called the Convocation, in Cambridge it is called the Senate. Every member had the right to propose motions and vote in the Convocation, and decisions were made by majority. Although both Universities were formally incorporated by statute only in 1571, this constitution persisted until the seventeenth century, after which the rights of the Convocation where gradually eroded to the point where nowadays the Convocation only elects the Vice-Chancellor.

Clearly, the University began life as a guild, or, more precisely as one of a range of bodies called corporations, or in Latin, *universitas*, which also covered towns and political or religious groups as well as the occupationally based guilds. The topic which has been the focus of this chapter was guilds, because we began in search of the origin of the early trade unions. In fact, the guilds were typical of a diversity of interest groups, from town corporations and charitable trusts to universities and trading companies.

The East India Company

Capitalist firms also grew out of guilds. The only instance I have found of the standing orders of a guild or company being documented is the Standing Orders of the East India Company of 1621. The document contains 329 paragraphs, and refers to what we would call the Board of Directors as the 'Court'. Paragraph 8 requires:

> In debating the Affaires of the Company in a Court of Committees, where matter is brought to the question of the Govenour, Deputy and Committees onely (and no other persons whatsoever) shall have their voyces, and the resolution of the *greater number*, shall stand for an order.

Section 52–56 provides for the election of officers on the 24th June every year, by a quorum of 13 committeemen and the Governor or his deputy, "by order of the ballat or by erection of hands, as unto the greater number of them present shall seeme most convenient." But also that "There shall be a faire admittance of all men, but first and especially of the free brethren of this Company, who shall concurre at the time appointed, to the election and preferment of any office in the said company." Continuing the practice of a form of *consent* by the general membership of the company.

The East India Company was the prototype of the British capitalist corporation, and its standing orders bear the clear mark of the guild. It makes sense then that I found the decision procedures operating within the structures of the University of Melbourne broadly the same as those operating within the trade unions; the same observation could have been made in relation to a capitalist firm or Parliament – they all originated from the same formation in Mediaeval England!

Journeymen's Guilds and the Early Trade Unions

While throughout the middle ages journeymen had a reasonable expectation of becoming a master and becoming eligible for full participation in the guild, this expectation declined from the seventeenth century. There were some instances of the guilds opening themselves to journeymen. For example, at Beverly, changes to the ordinances of the weavers' guild in 1500 gave journeymen an equal share with masters in the election of the two aldermen, though they could not themselves serve in this office.

Efforts by journeymen to organise guilds for themselves appeared very early. The earliest and most extensive evidence for journeymen's combinations is to be found in London. As early as 1299 journeymen carpenters and smiths were accused of forming illegal associations described as 'parliaments'. An Act of 1361 prohibited alliances of masons and carpenters. Official recognition of a fraternity of journeymen in Coventry was given in 1384, but then quickly withdrawn. In 1407 journeymen tailors and other artisans formed a new fraternity that endured some seven years. An edict of 1430, forbad the Cordwainers' Guild wage workers to form a confederacy, but they seemed to have endured and were mentioned in 1506.

From the mid-fourteenth century, London found it increasingly difficult to contain associations of journeymen. Around 1400 a fraternity of London journeymen saddlers succeeded in doubling their wages in little over a decade, and journeymen bakers organising from the own 'revelling hall' struck for higher wages in 1441. Reduction in journeymen's hours in six London trades between 1321 and 1389, according to Chase (2012), were probably due to such association.

So long before trade union consciousness could have emerged, wage workers were improvising their own guilds, invariably imitating the guilds to membership of which they aspired. Motives for doing so were by no means narrowly economic. "The high degree of mobility, especially due to the labour shortages of the late fourteenth and fifteenth centuries, predisposed town dwellers to form credit and fraternal networks to replace the support systems of the more intimate rural world. Credit and mutual trust were necessary for survival, for workers generally neither owned the materials with which they worked nor received immediate payment for the goods they produced. To be of good standing in the community was therefore vital: it promoted trust, accessed credit and was likely to ameliorate the problems of ill health and old age." (Chase, p. 4)

Employers would also encourage the formation of associations of wage workers as a means of managing the supply of skilled labour, and many such organisations simply asserted their independence and claimed the authority of custom, for example the London Watermen and Newcastle-upon-Tyne Keelmen.

In 1685, The Coggeshall Combers transitioned from a guild to the Coggeshall Combers' Purse, a trade society, inscribing their founding statutes in the minute book of the former Guild. The rules called for an annual meeting, the place of which to be chosen by "the major part" while the Treasurer was chosen "by the consent of the whole." And four supervisors were to be chosen by "general consent" – these were to put up bonds for the Purse. Ordinary meetings were to be held monthly for consideration of claims not resolved by the Treasurer. Failure of any of the large number of officers to complete their term of duty incurred a hefty fine and exclusion from the purse. Failure to attend the annual meeting for election of officers incurred a heavy fine. The purse broke up in 1690 due to the excessive claims upon the purse by just one member. (Chase, p. 20)

The memory of the guilds, which had a legal right and responsibility to regulate activity in the workplace validated collective action by workers. Trade union history in the 18th and early 19th century was marked by the tension between authority's suspicion of workers' combinations in any form and a grudging recognition that such association was legitimate, traditional and in some respects even desirable.

So central was apprenticeship to the concerns of early trade unions that their emergence corresponded closely to the decline in effectiveness of the Statute of Artifices in enforcing it. In taking up the defence of the apprenticeship system, the trade unions were indeed the direct descendants of the guilds.

According to the evidence of a journeyman flesher recorded in 1785. it was "usual for servants of different corporations of Aberdeen in imitation of their Masters to hold meetings and elect Nominal Deacons and Boxmasters and from these nominal office-bearers they also form a nominal convener court and elect a convenor and master of Hospital." Although mimicking the officials and methods of the old guild in practice they operated like a rudimentary trade union in controlling entry to the trade. (Chase, p. 31)

The power to search premises and even destroy tools and materials had long been vested in the guilds. So the Luddites of the 1810s had clear roots in the guild regulation of production, a tradition that can be traced in the *officially sanctioned* destruction of knitting frames as far back as 1710. Technically, the London Framework Knitters Company still exercised this authority, upheld in an apprenticeship case contested through the courts only a few years before. (Chase, p. 75)

Box clubs, journeymen's associations within or in opposition to the guilds, masonic lodges and workplace cultures shade off into the activities of what would later be termed trade unionism.

Although there are no exact equivalents of the guilds today, what are formally descendants can be found in the Livery Companies of London, and in the vestigial survivals in a few other cities, such as the Sheffield Cutlers' Guild, now a modern trade association or the Shoreporters' Society of Aberdeen, originally the Pynours' Society but now a removal and haulage company run as a mutual partnership.

The claim of the trade unions to be the inheritors of the ancient customs and role of the guilds was spectacularly emphasised in Bradford on the eve of the great strike of 1825, when workers celebrated the feast of Bishop Blaize with a parade of "extraordinary splendour," displaying all manner of costumes, symbols, 222 decorated horses and their riders, with a flag and traditional bands totalling 447 musicians, styles directly referencing their ancient Woolstaplers, Worsted-spinners and Manufacturers, Woolsorters, Woolcombers, Charcoal burners, Comb-makers and Dyers guilds. (Thompson, 1963, p. 425)

According to Thompson, the early semi-legal trade unions:

> emblemised this tradition in their ornate tickets or membership cards: the shearmen with the coat-of-arms, topped with the crossed shears, between the figure of justice and the figure of liberty; the shoemakers with their motto, 'May the Manufactures of the Sons of Crispin be trod upon by All the World'; all the unions with their proclamations and manifestos, signed 'By Order of the Trade'.
>
> THOMPSON, p. 544

For our purposes the situation is clear enough: the ideals of the trade unions that led them to adopt Majority decision making were directly inherited from the guilds dating back to the last century of Anglo-Saxon England. While the masters were hollowing out the structures built on one-vote-one-value majority decision making, the journeymen remain dedicated to these ideals and were working to recover them, an ambition clearly expressed by Winstanley two hundred years earlier.

The guilds also gave the workers a range of models through which Majority could be implemented, as well as a rich historical knowledge of the forms of perversion which afflict such organisational structures. The discipline that went along with Majority decisions and left no scope for the individual conscience was a life-and-death matter for the unions: a strike or a ban was meaningless unless it was enforced without exception. Once a strike or ban had been decided upon it was obligatory upon all. This ethos of solidarity was fundamental to the very existence of the labour movement at its birth.

In his book on the secret societies, James (2001) shows that secret societies which cannot be distinguished in any way from Artisan Guilds sanctioned by Royal Charter other than by the lack of the Royal Charter, existed, according to his research from at least 1200AD and moreover are to be found in every corner of the globe in broadly similar forms. Excerpts from rulebooks and eye-witness reports he provides show all the same features we have described while concentrating on chartered guilds. He further shows that these secret societies continued to exist with all their rituals and costumes in working class communities up into the 20th century.

The Hanseatic League

Although to the side of our tracking of the origins of Majority in Britain, it is worth touching on the Hanseatic League because it was here that the guilds reached the pinnacle of their development. *Hanse* is the Old German word for guild and merchant guilds began to form as early as 1267 in various German cities. In each city, the Hanse elected a Hanse Assembly just as the London Companies formed the London Council. In 1241, Lübeck formed an alliance with Hamburg and it was this alliance of two independent cities which grew to become the Hanseatic League.

The aim of the League was to open surrounding territories to trade, and the cities each raised armies and armed their merchant ships to collectively form a powerful armed force which fought protracted wars with Holland and Denmark in the fifteenth century. Most importantly, the combined power of the League was able to bargain with the local nobility to gain the independence of cities from domination by the local nobility. As a result, the alliance grew to as many as 170 cities and extended its influence over a large region, protected from both feudal interference and pirates.

Of particular interest is the decision-making methods of this alliance of independent cities. Decisions of the League were made by delegates sent by each city to the *Hansetag*. Not every city sent a delegate, and cities sometime shared a representative. Following the Lower Saxon tradition of *Einung* (unity), consensus was defined as absence of protest: after a discussion, the proposals which gained 'sufficient' support were dictated aloud to the scribe and became binding decisions if there was no objection. However, delegates whose views did not have sufficient support were obliged to remain silent. If consensus could not be established on a certain issue, a subcommittee would be agreed who were then empowered to work out a solution which could muster sufficient support. In the absence of any notion of equality between the cities, voting would have been meaningless, however.

By the late 16th century the League was wracked by internal dissension and facing formidable pressure from Dutch and English traders, met for the last time in 1669.

The Methodist Church[1]

The activity of the guilds, from their beginning in Anglo-Saxon England to their gradual decline after the Restoration, left a legacy in nineteenth century England manifested in a myriad of box clubs, embryonic friendly societies, mutual aid groups, voluntary special interest, charitable and religious groups of all kinds, including trade unions like those whose rulebooks were published by the Select Committee on the Combination Laws in 1825. The imprint of the guilds is clearly visible in these union rule books, but the shape of the trade unions, political parties and voluntary organisations of our own times is less visible, beyond the norm of majority voting decision making.

Like the guilds, the 1824 trade unions are particularist, parochial, somewhat amateurish, and with a discipline enforced by fines. None of these features can be found in the trade unions, political parties and social movements of our own times, nor were they to be found in the International Workingmen's Association of 1864. It seems reasonable to ask then whether the guilds were the sole source of the organisational principles of the nineteenth century English working class. Were there other sources which the working class drew upon for principles of self-organisation based on Majority? Where did the workers' movement find the resources to overcome the particularism and parochialism of early craft unionism, and how did it learn to build politically conscious, universalist, nationwide, disciplined organisations among the poor, without fines or control over entry to the trades?

E.P. Thompson suggests that we should look to the Methodist Church as another important contributor in the making of the English working class:

> Methodism was profoundly marked by its origin; the poor man's Dissent of Bunyan …was a religion *of* the poor; orthodox Wesleyanism remained as it had commenced, a religion *for* the poor. …Wesley was a superlatively energetic and skilful organiser, administrator, and law-giver. He succeeded in combining in exactly the right proportions democracy and discipline, doctrine and emotionalism; his achievement lay…in the organisation of self-sustaining Methodist societies in trading and market

---

1 My principal sources for this chapter are E.P. Thompson, E.P. (1963). *The Making of the English Working Class*, Townsend, W.J. (1909). *A New History of Methodism, The Constitution and Polity of the Wesleyan Methodist Church*, with appendices which include *The form of discipline or code of laws issued by the conference of 1797* and John Wesley's *Deed of Declaration*, 1784, and Kilham, A. (1795). *The Progress of Liberty, etc.*

centres, and in mining, weaving, and labouring communities, the democratic participation of whose members in the life of the Church was
both enlisted and strictly superintended and disciplined. He facilitated
entry to these societies by sweeping away all barriers of sectarian doctrines. (1963, pp. 37–38)

Unlike the Old Dissent, Wesley did not set out to break people away from their
former allegiance, whether to the established Church of England or a dissenting
sect, but rather a discipline and a way of life over and above the sacraments and
services provided by the Church. He was an ordained Minister in the Church
of England, but following contact with Moravians while in America, began to
develop criticisms of the hierarchy and practices of the Church of England.

Since we will be asking where Wesley got his ideas about decision making
procedures from, and because it is widely accepted that the Moravians had a
significant impact on this thinking, it is worth mentioning that the Moravians,
who are recognised as the oldest Protestant sect, *drew lots* to make decisions
like selecting church sites, approving missionaries, electing bishops and so on,
on the basis that this would allow God to give them guidance. This practice,
known as *cleromancy*, was greatly curtailed after 1818 and finally discontinued
in the 1880s. Wesley never adopted this practice, but rather adopted Majority
consistently from top to bottom of his organisation, although the drawing of
lots was used for making certain appointments, as indeed it was used in ancient Greece and is widely used to this day in rotating offices.

Following a personal crisis, Wesley began to preach a stern doctrine of personal salvation through faith and soon found that most parish churches were
closed to him. Consequently, in 1739, at the age of 36, he began preaching in the
open air or in whatever hall or cottage would admit him. He organised his followers into a 'society' and with a small group of associates continued to gather
converts across England.

His following became too large for him and his friends to maintain contact
with, so he instituted an organisational structure which was maintained by a
staff of full-time itinerant preachers, lay preachers and other volunteers. The
lay preachers still had to earn their own living and remained a part of their
community, and through these lay participants, the Methodist Church maintained a firm connection with their congregations. The Methodists turned
particularly to the poor and working people, though they also succeeded in
recruiting members of the newly emerging industrial bourgeoisie. Each group
of worshippers was responsible for raising the money to build their own chapel, and self-sustaining Methodist congregations multiplied rapidly across
England. The local church groups also collected money which went to Wesley

to hire itinerant preachers who each took on responsibility, a few months at a time, for a Circuit where they fostered the development of local preachers and maintained the unity of the "Connexion" as a whole.

At this point we should summarise the structure Wesley created, largely, it seems, improvising in response to pressures as they arose, and relying on his immense charisma and organisational ability to implement uniform organisational measures on a wide scale.

Class

The base level of the structure is a Class: a group of up to 12 Methodists with a Class Leader which met weekly.

By 1742 Wesley had about 1100 Methodists in London, but he could not keep in touch with them all while continuing his other work. While in Bristol, Wesley met some members of the Society there. One, a Captain Foy, suggested that every member give a penny a week until a debt there was paid off. When one of them pleaded poverty, he offered that 11 of the poorest be grouped with him, he would collect the subscription, and make up the shortfall of any who could not pay. Soon afterwards, Wesley made the group of 12 for collection of money the basis of a weekly meeting for prayer, Bible study, and mutual encouragement. One is reminded here of the tithings which formed the base of the pyramid in Anglo-Saxon England.

The Class Ticket

One function of the Class Leader is the issuing of the Class Ticket, a quarterly membership card, to his class members, withholding it from those who are judged unworthy of being called Methodists, and renewing it or not when it expired after 3 months. The Class Leader had some pastoral responsibility for the Class as well as being responsible for collection of dues. In this way, the classes kept every single member in constant touch with the church while providing a training school for new preachers and leaders at ground level. Up until about 50 years ago many trade unions collected their union dues through shop stewards in much the same way, rather than having the employer deduct union dues from wages.

The class ticket issued by a Class Leader was the means by which admission of people to Methodism was regulated. Class Leaders were told:

> Give Tickets to none till they are recommended by a Leader with whom they have met two months on trial. Give them the Rules of the Society the first time they meet. (1797, p. 483)

The Society or Church

The local Society or Church dates from December 1738, and was often known by the name of the person in whose home they met. They were self-sustaining congregations and would generally take on the task of building a chapel.

Initially, Wesley forbad Societies to hold meetings during the normal church times when services would be happening in nearby Church of England churches. Likewise, they were forbidden from holding baptisms, burials or services for Easter, etc. However, as Methodism became the main denomination in parts of the country, this policy was loosened and ultimately abandoned, but a Society still required permission from the Conference to perform such sacraments. Societies also had Stewards, usually voluntary, to look after practical matters.

The Circuit

The Circuit is a grouping of Societies in a region or city, under a Superintendent Minister and other Minister and is the main functional unit of Methodism. Circuits are usually named after a town and typically include a dozen or so Churches and would hold quarterly general meetings. The first such quarterly meeting was in October 1748.

Ministers are first appointed to a Circuit and it is the Circuit which is responsible for paying their salary, and assigning them to specific Churches. Preaching appointments for both full-time Ministers and Local Preachers were organised by the Circuit and advertised on a Circuit Plan issued every 3 months by the Superintendent Minister. The earliest preachers under John Wesley were itinerant, and preached around a Circuit from a home base.

Local Preachers and Travelling Preachers

Wesley's main instruments were the Itinerant Preachers who paid for themselves from the income generated by establishing and maintaining societies. These preachers were full-timers but not ordained by the Church of England. They were appointed annually by Conference (though during his lifetime effectively by Wesley himself) and assigned to a Circuit for as little as a few months before being moved on to a new Circuit or wherever Conference would send them. These were the eighteenth century prototype of the union organiser or full-timer of a modern socialist party: professionals, whose conditions of life prevented them from forming enduring personal relationships and made them highly effective and dedicated instruments of the organisation, upon whose prosperity they were dependent. When they were 'worn out' they would be put on a pension but would still continue to contribute as 'supernumeraries'.

They were allowed to marry, but the conditions of their lives often made this difficult.

Local preachers were authorised to preach only within their own Circuit:

> Let no Local Preacher be permitted to preach in any other Circuit, without producing a recommendation from the Superintendent of that Circuit in which he lives; nor suffer any invitation to be admitted as a plea, but from men in office, with the consent of the Superintendent of that Circuit. (1797, p. 484)

The Local Preacher was also key to Methodism's success in capturing the working class communities. The Local Preacher was a layman, perhaps a farmer or an artisan, appointed by the Circuit to preach within his own Circuit. The practice of training and sanctioning lay members of the congregation to lead religious practices without being ordained and while continuing in their normal lives with work and family was revolutionary. This embeddedness of the Methodists in the lives of their congregation through the lay preachers is probably the reason that, despite Wesley's own high Tory political views, Methodists became associated with the advocacy of all the socially progressive issues of the day, such as abolition of slavery, prison reform, and the relief of economic distress. For this reason, it is easy to see how both Wesley's moral teachings and his organisational innovations had such an impact in the English working class.

District

By the time of Wesley's death in 1791, the Circuits in England were collected into 20 Districts which were organised around quarterly meetings. While the Circuits were the key functional unit, the Districts were introduced to mediate between the Circuits and the annual Conference. Thus the District would choose by ballot from amongst their Itinerant Preachers those who were to attend Conference. The District also selected from amongst its Local Preachers those it would recommend to Conference for appointment as Itinerant Preachers. They also had an important role in managing dispute resolution procedures. For instance, the 1797 code allowed:

> If there be a difference between two Preachers in a District, the respective parties shall choose two Preachers; and the Chairman of the District, with the four Preachers so chosen, shall be final arbiters, to determine the matter in dispute. In both cases the Chairman shall have a casting voice, in case of an equality. ...

The Chairman, in all cases which, in his judgment, cannot be settled in the ordinary District Meetings, shall have authority to summon three of the nearest [District] Superintendents to be incorporated with the District Committee, who shall have equal authority to vote, and settle everything till the Conference. (p. 504)

The Methodist Connexion

The Methodist Connexion is the whole of Methodism within a country under the authority of the annual Conference.

Conference

The first Methodist Conference took place at the Foundery in City Road, London, in June 1744. The Conference was a truly revolutionary innovation, which, leaving aside the Question and Answer format which is used in all the Methodist meeting agendas, gave us the model for trade union and political conferences ever since. E.P. Thompson remarked dryly:

> Those Wesleyan Annual Conferences, with their 'platform', their caucuses at work on the agendas, and their careful management, seem uncomfortably like another 'contribution' to the Labour movement of more recent times. (1963, pp. 43–44)

The annual Conference had a quorum of 40 and began with the election of President and Secretary. The Annual Conference is the supreme authority in Methodism and was to be held generally on the last Tuesday in July, at London, Bristol or Leeds. Decisions are made by majority vote, with the chairman having a casting vote. Minutes of Conference are published every year, signed by the Secretary and President, and every new Preacher "must have read and signed the General Minutes, as fully approving of them; nor must any one suppose, or pretend to think, that the conversations which have been on any of these Minutes were intended to qualify them, as in the least to affect the spirit and design of them" (1784, p. 476). The time and place of each Conference is determined at the end of the preceding conference. Wesley laid down for the first time a principle which would be the foundation for all labour organisations forever after:

> The act of the majority in number at the Conference assembled as aforesaid, should be had, taken and be, the Act of the whole Conference to all intents, purposes, and constructions whatever. (1784, p. 466)

Wesley introduced an element of flexibility, however, allowing that between conferences, subordinate bodies may by majority refuse a new Rule until the next Conference, which may then amend or confirm the Rule and impose it in opposition to a local majority. (This rule is no longer operative, but to this day every Methodist Minister keeps a copy of the Minutes of Conference close at hand.)

This governance by Majority in meetings at every level of the organisation allowed the Methodist Church to formally avoid structural hierarchy. Appointments were purely functional, and formally at least, authority always resting with Conference and the various meetings at subordinate levels, as determined by Majority.

Preachers were not to preach outside their own Circuit and were forbidden from publishing without the direction of Conference. Altogether, the discipline and laws of the Church were rigorously enforced. During his lifetime, Wesley dominated the life of the Church irrespective of its apparently democratic structure. Furthermore, this was a very circumscribed democracy which extended only to those itinerant preachers who were full-time employees of the Connexion, and excluded from participation in decision making in matters of theology or church policy the lay-preachers and volunteers who were so vital to the success of Methodism. Which meant, E.P. Thompson remarks:

> The 'grass roots' democracy, by which the societies were officered by tradesmen and working people, extended not at all to matters of doctrine or Church government. In nothing did Wesley break more sharply with the traditions of Dissent than in his opposition to local autonomy, and in the authoritarian rule of himself and of his nominated ministers. (1963, p. 38)

The working class communities, to which Methodism was bringing the gift of organisation, were also listening to the words of Tom Paine (who was by the way, raised as a Quaker) and developing radical democratic aspirations of their own, and after Wesley's death the pressures for democracy within the Connexion burst out.

> There were a score of demands being voiced in dissident societies: for an elected Conference, for greater local autonomy, for the final break with the Church, for lay participation in district and quarterly meetings. Wesley's death (in 1791), when the radical tide was rising, was like a 'signal gun'. (1963, p. 44)

The most insistent of these demands came from Alexander Kilham, who spoke up at Conference and throughout the Connexion and agitated by means of anonymous pamphlets, and was most likely, as accused, in touch with radical English 'Jacobins'.

> The dissenters of every denomination hold it as an axiom in religion, that every society of people have a right to choose their own ministers. And they consider it as injurious for any man to be fixed as a minister over any congregation, unless he be fairly elected by a majority of those that compose it.
>
> KILHAM, 1795, p. 28

In his 1795 pamphlet, *The Progress of Liberty*, Kilham proposed on the one hand greater rigour in the training and selection of the lay preachers, particularly by the lay members themselves, and a greater say by the lay membership all the way up to Conference, on both religious and organisational issues, side-by-side with the full-time itinerant preachers. Kilham was expelled at the Conference of 1797, and went on to found The New Connexion, based on the same theology as Wesley had preached but with the organisational measures he had outlined in *Progress*. Kilham died in 1798, but his New Connexion continued to grow, although always a junior player alongside Wesleyan Methodism. At the time of its union with the United Methodist Church in 1907, however, the Methodist New Connexion had some 250 ministers and 45,000 members. In the meantime, by 1888, Kilham's proposals had already been adopted by the Wesleyan Methodist Church, with lay members and Ministers having 50–50 representation at Conference, and:

> The strict preliminary theological examination of Local Preachers, and the formation of a Local Preachers' Meeting; the strengthening of the Lay element in Methodist administration in the District Meetings, in the Connexional Committees, and in the Representative Session of the Conference.
>
> TOWNSEND, 1909, pp. 493–494

The Church of England inherited from its Catholic origins the practice of collegial election of official by majority vote; although proceedings of Parliament were not published until 1771, Wesley himself would have been aware of the rules of debate, etc., operative in Parliament. Whether Wesley adopted majority voting from Parliament, or whether he adopted the practice as something already widespread in the communities I cannot say. The local 'branch' structure with its lay officials, the class ticket and collection of dues at weekly meetings can be traced to the guilds. But the binding of the societies into an integral, disciplined, *nationwide* organisation and embedded in local communities – the class, the districts with their quarterly meetings, annual conference with its delegates from districts, agenda, and binding power over the whole organization and the itinerant full-timers – all these are innovations which have been the basis for a *universalist*, that is to say, non-particularist, working class organisational culture ever since.

The Methodists entered the twentieth century divided into a number of separate churches, but by the end of the century, they were approaching complete reunification.

Wesley was extremely well-read – he had a book stand fitted to the saddle of his horse and would read books as he travelled tens of thousands of miles throughout England visiting his societies. He moved in ruling class circles, well aware of the methods used by the English in administering an empire and managing Parliament, but so far as I can see, John Wesley *improvised* the innovations he made under pressure of circumstances, and by force of his own character and leadership was able to implement them and create a nationwide grass-roots organisation.

There is one more question we have to ask: where did the workers' movement acquire the radical political consciousness and independence, something which is lacking in both the craft unions and the Methodist church. Where did the idea and the means of applying the ethos of Majority rule *universally* come from? For that we must turn to the radical 'Jacobin' clubs, such as the London Corresponding Society.

London Corresponding Society[1]

The London Corresponding Society (LCS) was a reform group active from 1792 to 1798. It can best be described as 'Jacobin', though British Jacobinism was a very different animal from its French namesake. Its aim was universal suffrage and annual elections to the House of Commons and it pursued these aims by public education and lobbying. It was egalitarian (though it never criticised the king nor advocated 'levelling') and was dedicated to promoting the political voice of the ordinary man (the ordinary woman did not figure in their concept of 'universal suffrage'), and everywhere directed its propaganda and recruitment activity towards the poor and the working people. It was not a working-class organisation however.

It was eventually shut down by the government using spies, provocateurs and police using the sedition and treason laws backed by horrific punishments. Its suppression was closely followed by the introduction of the Combination Laws in 1799, forcing both Jacobinism and trade unionism underground. At its peak in December 1795, the LCS had 3,000 members, and had established correspondence with over 80 like-minded reform groups around Britain and made face-to-face contact with many of them. Its leaders were charged with responsibility for the organising *all* the seditious activity in the kingdom. Indeed, the government had cause for concern, as working class communities across Britain eagerly followed the military successes of the French army and many were turning their minds towards armed revolt amidst increasing economic hardship and government repression. But the LCS had no such intentions; although granting themselves a leading role in the Reform movement, they were exclusively focussed on educational and political means of struggle.

The LCS was a part of an upsurge of radical democratic reform activity, and although it did not instigate a Jacobin revolt, it did play a very important role in leading the reform movement and because of its situation in London it was uniquely placed to do so. The legacy of the LCS resurfaced 40 years later when the Chartists united radical democratic reform with the labour movement. An examination of the operation of the LCS contributes to our theme because the LCS has left us a considerable amount of information about its internal operations, both via government spies and from the minutes of its meetings assiduously maintained despite the very real threat of repression. The LCS was very

---

1 My principal sources for this chapter are Thompson, E.P. (1963), *The Making of the English Working Class*, and Thale, M. (1983). *Selections from the Papers of the London Corresponding Society 1792–1799*, and LCS documents from the National Library of Australia.

© KONINKLIJKE BRILL NV, LEIDEN, 2016 | DOI 10.1163/9789004319639_008

much focused on affairs in Parliament and closely followed its debates, now public thanks to the agitation of John Wilkes and others in the 1760s and '70s. However, as we shall see, the LCS had to *invent* its decision making procedures, democratic structure and rules of order as it went along, and its documents allow us to follow the construction of these procedures as they were developed.

The Personalities of the LCS

The LCS was founded in 1792 by Thomas Hardy, originally a poor journeyman shoemaker, who had opened his own shop in 1791, thus becoming an employer. Hardy was the first Secretary of the LCS and a co-signatory of all its publications. Hardy retired from agitation after his trial for treason, returning to his life as a master shoemaker. Notwithstanding his fame as a democratic reformer, in 1795, his employees in the Journeymen Boot and Shoemakers conducted a strike against him in his capacity as their employer. He died in poverty in 1832.

John Thelwall was born poor, but his love of books and writing prevented him from completing his apprenticeship as a tailor. He was radicalised by the French Revolution and thereafter dedicated his life to agitating for democratic reform. The police described him as most the dangerous man in Britain. Thelwall willingly embraced the label of 'Jacobinism':

> I adopt the term Jacobinism without hesitation: 1. Because it is fixed upon us, as a stigma, by our enemies.... 2. Because, though I abhor the sanguinary ferocity of the late Jacobins in France, yet their principles...are the most consonant with my ideas of reason, and the nature of man.
>
> JAMES THELWALL, *The Rights of Nature*, 1796

Hardy, Thelwall and John Horne Tooke were tried for treason in 1794, but all three were acquitted and carried through the streets of London by a wildly enthusiastic crowd. At the time, the full penalty for high treason was to be "hanged by the neck, cut down while still alive, disembowelled (and his entrails burned before his face) and then beheaded and quartered" (Thompson, 1963, p. 17). This was the kind of risk members of the LCS were taking, but the jury of respectable London citizens had no stomach for such a sentence. Thelwall subsequently eked out a living as an itinerant lecturer.

Maurice Margarot already had a long history of agitation for reform and was in France at the time of the Revolution. He returned to London to become Chairman of the LCS and with Hardy was a co-signatory of its publications until 1794. He was sentenced to 14 years and transported to New South Wales in May 1794 together with three others. He returned to Britain in 1811 but died in poverty in 1815.

Alexander Galloway was machinist and a member of the Worshipful Company of Leathersellers, Assistant Secretary of LCS 1795–6 and President in 1797. Galloway continued to campaign for democratic reform, whilst rising to become one of London's largest employers and an opponent of trade unionism. In 1813–14, he led the agitation for the repeal of 'Betty's Law'.

Francis Place completed his apprenticeship as a leather-breeches maker in 1789 and led a strike in 1793 and was blacklisted by employers for several years afterwards, but used his time to read. He joined the LCS in 1794, and became its Assistant Secretary in 1796 and Chairman of the General Committee, but resigned after an internal dispute. In 1800, he set up his own tailor's business which proved to be very successful, and worked with Galloway for the repeal of Betty's Law. He continued his work as a propagandist, documenter and archivist of English radicalism from the LCS to the London Workingmen's Association, though as a moderate. He left the Chartists in 1838, on the basis that the Chartists were prepared to use violence, and became involved in the campaign for the repeal of the protectionist Corn Laws.

John Richter was a bank clerk when he joined the LCS in 1792 and was arrested for high treason along with Hardy. However, he was released after Hardy and the others were acquitted, and returned to his job as a clerk. He continued agitation for political reform, including agitation for the repeal of the Combination Acts, and died in poverty in 1830.

Colonel Edmund Despard, a former soldier and colonial administrator, was an ordinary participant in the LCS. He was hanged on a charge of high treason in February 1803, before a crowd of 20,000 supporters.

By 1799 nearly all the former leaders of the LCS were in gaol, transported, or had emigrated to America, and most survivors had retired from political life.

The LCS conducted its agitation in the coffee houses off Piccadilly as well as among the waterside workers of Wapping and the silk-weavers of Spitalfields. It was not that the LCS spanned class lines, but simply that the line between journeyman and master was still not clearly drawn, as was amply illustrated by the lives of the leaders of the LCS themselves. Over the decades to follow, these lines would be drawn, but the LCS can only be described as a 'popular radical' not working-class.

How the LCS Organised Itself

After reading material published by the Society for Constitutional Information, Thomas Hardy tells us (Thale, 1983) that he developed a view that "a radical reform in parliament was quite necessary," that every sane adult, however poor, had a right to vote, but that only a campaign launched on the widest possible scale would have any chance of bringing this about. He discussed the idea with three friends and proposed that the following Monday evening, they

meet at a certain pub whose landlord was "a friend to freedom" to found a
society for the reform of parliament.

> ...previous to this first meeting I had prepared and ruled a book for
> the purpose of every man putting down his name if he approved of the
> measure. I had prepared tickets also written upon them *London Corre-*
> *sponding Society No. 1., 2., 3...*

The idea of a 'corresponding society' Hardy had taken from an Irish Committee
of Correspondence, and after "a great deal of conversation," producing no better suggestion, his friends readily agreed to his proposed name for the society
and that a 'corresponding society' was the best means to gather "the sense of
the nation." Hardy had copied extracts from radical democratic writers which
he believed would speak to the tradesmen who gathered at the pub after work
with the plan that they would simply read to them. He then presented his ruled
book to his friends and suggested:

> making a small deposit, which I considered would give them an interest
> in promoting the success of the society. Having got eight to put their
> names down and to pay one penny each, the first meeting night then
> I gave each one a ticket with his name written upon the back of it. The
> next thing which they considered was to choose from among themselves
> some trusty servants to conduct the business of that friendly and well-
> meaning company. They appointed me Treasurer and Secretary. There
> they stumbled at the threshold. Two *very important offices filled by one*
> *person.*

The penny-a-week donation to get your ticket is reminiscent of the Methodist
class ticket. Hardy discovers that his friends are not as educated in these matters as he was, electing him to two different offices, something which had been
forbidden in the guild constitutions. And this is the point, the LCS was to be
educative not only in the propaganda sense, but also as practical training for
those who joined.

> And in our enquiries we soon discovered that gross ignorance and preju-
> dice of the bulk of the nation was the greatest obstacle to the obtaining
> redress. Therefore our aim was to have a well regulated orderly society
> formed for the purpose of dispelling that ignorance and prejudice as far
> as possible, and instil into their minds by means of the press a sense of

their rights as freemen, and of their duty to themselves, and their posterity, as good citizens.

By the following Monday they had grown to 12, and a Chairman appointed for the third meeting, when the following questions were proposed for discussion:

First   Is there any necessity for a reformation of the present State of the Representation in the British House of Commons?

Second   Would there be any Utility in a parliamentary reform? – or in other words – Are there any just grounds to believe that a reformation in parliament will be of any essential service to the Nation?

Third   Have we who are Tradesmen – Shopkeepers and mechanics any right to seek to obtain a parliamentary reform?

and after five nights debating them, they were all decided in the affirmative. Hardy wrote letters to another Society in Sheffield and when he read the reply he received to the members, now numbering about 50, "it animated them with additional ardour when they were informed that others in a distant part of the nation had *thought* – and had also *begun* to *act* in the same way with themselves" and a committee of six was forthwith appointed to "revise alter or amend the laws and regulations" which Hardy had prepared, and to draft an Address to the Nation.

The question then was who was to sign the Address? Publishing anonymous political literature was in itself seditious and the social cost of putting one's name to such an Address was also forbidding. Ultimately Margarot (who had authored the Address) joined Hardy in signing it.

Through sales of their Address and readings in coffee houses and pubs frequented by journeymen, their numbers grew rapidly. When Lord Daer joined LCS, someone proposed that he be Chairman for the next meeting, but Hardy objected that their cause should not "depend implicitly (as formerly) upon the mere ipse dixit of some nobleman or great man":

We were so scrupulous about the admission of any of those of the higher ranks that when any of them offered to pay more than we usually demanded on the admission of a new member we would not receive it but told them that we had money sufficient for all necessary purposes viz. for printing, postage of letters, and stationary.

Hardy reported that:

all members were admitted high and low rich and poor – After the three
following questions were proposed to them and answered in the affirmative their names and residences were entered into a book kept for that
purpose (but not *their titles*) each member had a ticket given to him with
a copy of the rules and orders and the Addresses of the Society

Question first. Are you convinced that the parliamentary Representation of this Country is at present inadequate and imperfect?

Question 2nd. Are you thoroughly persuaded that the welfare of these
kingdoms requires that every person of Adult years in possession of his
reason and not incapacitated by crimes should have a vote for a Member
of parliament?

Question 3rd. Will you endeavour by all justifiable means to promote
such reformation in parliament?

By this time we wore under the necessity of having printed tickets –
for the members multiplied so fast that the business of the society was
retarded by writing the tickets – printed tickets were talked of for several
weeks before they were ordered to be printed.

By the end of April 1792:

> it was found expedient to divide the society into separate bodies and
> class them so that it might be more convenient for the members and be
> as neighbourly meetings (which was the original design before any meet-
> ing at all took place) and each division to send one of their number as
> delegate to form a committee in some central place for conducting the
> business of the society and when that committee amounted to 60 mem-
> bers to be divided again into six parts each part or division to appoint one
> of their number to form another committee.

By the time of the printing of their second Address in May 1792,

> we began to be a little more particular about the admission of people
> into the room where the divisions of the society met on account of sev-
> eral improper persons intruding and intriguing to get into the room as
> members and afterwards endeavouring to disturb the harmony of the
> Society by their noisy and virulent declamations designing thereby to
> throw them into confusion and anarchy that they might become an easy
> prey to their evil designs – The method which we adopted in order to
> counteract as much as possible the nefarious designs of those men as
> this – In each of the divisions it was agreed to appoint a Chairman every

meeting night, by acclamation or a show of hands – on the next meeting night the Chairman was to descend to become door keeper in rotation. It was not deemed any degradation to the man who filled that high and elevated station of *president*, to stoop to take upon him the *lowest office* in society, *door-keeper*, when it was for the express purpose of promoting, and securing happiness, order, and tranquillity in the Society. [Hardy's terrible spelling has been corrected throughout.]

Spies and *agents provocateurs* only began reporting on LCS meetings from October 1792. In May 1792, the problem was simply that the LCS was dealing with people who had no more experience in political debate than could be had in the local pub.

In the first draft of the May 1792 regulations, divisions were to have 20 members, and divide in two when they reached 40; by the time it was printed, the division had been set at 30, dividing in two when it reached 46. In practice, divisions were always much larger, and Hardy's own division had well over 100 members.

The general structure of the LCS was as follows.

The division meetings began at 8.00 p.m. on any day other than Sunday (reserved for reading) or Thursday (reserved for meetings of the General Committee), and the first item on the agenda was the admission of new members, each to be recommended by two members who vouched for their "civism and morals." Each new member then had to affirm Hardy's three questions. On admission the new member paid dues for the ensuing quarter (or month), and then received the ticket which entitled him to attend any division, but to vote only in his own.

Next on the division agenda was the report of the delegate to the General Committee on the proceedings of the previous meeting of the General Committee. The division then debated and voted on questions which the General Committee had referred to the whole membership. Most questions originated in the divisions, were brought to the general committee by the delegate, and then referred to all divisions.

A division elected one of their members as delegate to the weekly meetings of the general committee. Later they also elected a subdelegate, who represented the division when the delegate was unable to attend the general committee, and later still a rule was made to allow the division secretary to proxy for the delegates. These representatives were elected by secret ballot, the names of those eligible being read at the end of one meeting and the ballots collected at the next. Though it was recommended that the same men not serve for successive quarters, the delegates did tend to be re-elected. The secretary kept lists of the members, wrote vouchers certifying the election of delegate and subdelegate, drew up motions to be presented to the general committee by the delegate, collected and recorded the dues, gave the delegate the money for the general committee and paid for the meeting room (which was not to exceed 1 s 6 d per week). From mid-1794, each division also elected tythingmen thus:

> The ten persons whose names stand first upon the book, shall nominate out of their number, and the Chairman shall collect the sense by a show of hands. If two persons nominated shall have an equal number, he that is the oldest member shall take the office : – So the second and third tens, ...

The duties of the tythingmen were to tell their assigned members if the place of meeting were changed, to call on members whose dues were in arrears and to notify their tything of any last-minute changes in plans for a general meeting. Remarkable to find this practice dating from Anglo-Saxon England still in use both by the Methodists and the Popular Radicals! But even at the level of the tything, election by majority show of hands was the norm.

After completing business, the division often listened to the reading of reform literature or relevant newspaper articles. Division meetings were to end at 10 p.m. A constitution proposed but not adopted in 1794 set the first hour of the meeting (8–9 p.m.) for reading.

The General Committee, originally called the Committee of Delegates, consisted of one representative from each division. Their function was to coordinate the activities of the divisions and to elect the officers of the Society. Every Thursday they met at 8 p.m. and although the constitutions stipulated that the meetings end at 11 p.m., they usually ran until 3 a.m. or 3:30 a.m.

The first item on the agenda were the reports from each delegate of the numbers of new members and of members present in his division. Then deputies were assigned to visit the unrepresented divisions. Then there were applications from large divisions to subdivide, and members were appointed to show the new division how to conduct their meetings. When a division failed to send a delegate to the General Committee, a member was often assigned to follow up and offer assistance. Next, letters to the Society were read, and replies (drafted by an appointed correspondent) were debated and approved, as were any publications issued in the name of the LCS, and any question which had been referred to the whole Society, and the delegates then reported the votes of their divisions. After that, motions from the divisions were read and finally, the secretary and treasurer announced the totals of new and present members and the amount of money received.

The agenda had not yet reached the standard form which we found in the London Workingmen's Association of 1836, but resembles the Methodist Conference, in its prioritising of the maintenance of the divisional structure.

The LCS created the Correspondence Committee for the purpose of drafting letters and addresses and it was initially called the Committee of Secrecy, because of the need to keep secret the identity of the author of any letter or address issued by the Society. However, notwithstanding the danger to the author of being identified, the very notion of secrecy immediately came under criticism, and so it was called the Correspondence Committee and then later the Executive Committee. It consisted of six members whose principal duty was to reply to letters and to write any notices, addresses or petitions sent out in the name of the LCS.

To prevent the Executive Committee from dominating the General Committee, its members were not allowed to vote or even speak at meetings of the General Committee. The work of the Executive Committee was very demanding and meetings of the Executive Committee were sometimes cancelled for lack of a quorum, and there were frequent unscheduled mid-quarter elections to replace a resigning member.

The Sunday night reading and debate meetings were not mentioned in any LCS constitution, but were invaluable in educating the members, obliging them to find reasons for their opinions and to listen to the opinions of others. The chairman, different each Sunday, read aloud a chapter of a book, and then during the ensuing week, the book was passed around for the men to read at home. The next Sunday the chairman read the chapter again, pausing three times for comments. No one was to speak more than once during the reading, and anyone who had not spoken during the first two pauses was expected to speak at the end. After that there was a general discussion during which no one could speak on a subject a second time until everyone who wished had spoken once. This practice, nowadays called 'speaking in rounds' seems to have been invented by the LCS in 1793.

At all LCS meetings certain rules of decorum were enforced. No one was admitted drunk, and habitual drunkenness could lead to expulsion from the Society. Members had to remove their hats. When a man spoke he had to stand and address the chairman. No one could speak a second time until everyone who wished had spoken once; and no one could speak more than twice to a question. The duties of the chairman included making sure that everyone was seated and not walking around the room, that no member was interrupted

when speaking (unless he wandered from the question), and that no-one ut-
tered "intemperate aspersions" or used seditious language.

These regulations were obviously products of experience. In the constitution
proposed in February 1794 noisy and contentious behaviour was reprobated so
often that unruliness was evidently common. According to this constitution,
"it is the duty of every member to study concord, and for that purpose to moderate his own passions, particularly his personal attachments and aversions."
When voting, a member should show one hand. "The practice of showing both
hands, or of calling 'all! all!' or other such exclamations are tumultuous, indecent, and utterly unwarrantable." Even approval should be expressed silently
(by holding up a hand), for "all noise is interruption." As for disapproval, "to
attribute the conduct or opinion of any member to factious combination, or
other improper motive, is disorderly, as are also all invectives and declamatory
remarks." The section headed "Order" ends with the warning, "A noisy disposi-
tion is seldom a sign of courage, and extreme zeal, is often a cloak of treachery."
Besides rules to restrain noisiness, this constitution proposed a regulation to
curb verbosity: No one was to speak more than ten minutes at one time. Lest
anyone forget this restriction, "over the seat of the President in each meeting of
this Society, shall be suspended a label with these words, 'Beware of Orators'."

The 1795 constitution provided:

> VII. The business of the Chairman shall be to order all persons not speak-
> ing to sit; to request each Delegate to give an account of the number of
> persons admitted into his Division the preceding week; – to demand all
> motions which may be sent from Divisions; (which shall not be taken
> notice of unless sent in writing, signed by the Chairman and Secretary
> of the Division) – to take the return of referred Questions: – to read all
> the motions twice over, and take the sense of the Committee upon them,
> in order, as they were delivered to him; – to see that no member is inter-
> rupted while speaking (provided he addresses the Chair, standing and
> uncovered); – to see that no speaker wanders from the question before
> the Chair; – to let every member fully deliver his opinion; – but not to of-
> fer his own till every other member has done, and then to take the sense
> of the Committee by a show of hands.

These regulations reflect the fact that they were needed. Anyone who was not
a householder or employer would never, over centuries, have had the privilege of engaging in reasoned political debate. While the leaders of the LCS
certainly followed Parliamentary debates closely and would have known how
Parliament worked, this was *not* public knowledge. Far less did the labouring

people of London have a *habit* of reasoned debate. Francis Place claimed that: "The moral effects of the Society were considerable. It induced men to read books, instead of wasting their time in public houses, it taught them to respect themselves..."

The first constitution was evidently drawn up by Hardy in advance. After a brief preamble on unequal representation in Parliament, it listed eight rules and resolutions, according to Mary Thale, most of them derived from the rules and practices of the Society for Constitutional Information (SCI). These eight rules instituted "The Corresponding Society of the unrepresented part of the people of Great Britain &c.," a Society to be (unlike the guilds or SCI) "unlimited in its numbers." Its members are to pay "at least one penny towards its expense" weekly. "As soon as twenty members are associated, a general meeting shall be called when all the several laws or regulations already agreed to shall be read over and confirmed altered or annulled and at the meeting there shall be elected a president, Treasurer, and Secretary." A new member must be proposed by one member and seconded by another. The names and addresses of members are to be recorded, as are "all proceedings of the Society and its committee," and no-one under 21 be a member nor anyone "who has not resided in this country for one year."

But these rules differ from those of the SCI in that membership was not limited to householders, i.e., those who had the vote (thus the one penny dues), as well as the age requirement and British residency.

A slightly altered version of this document was written about March 1792. But almost as soon as they were agreed upon these eight rules were inadequate, for they made no provisions for organizing divisions, electing delegates and conducting meetings. Early in May, a month after the divisions and general committee were established, a committee was elected to write a new constitution. The resulting ten rules – which remained the official constitution of the LCS until 1795 specify that a new member be proposed by two members and that he answer correctly three questions on parliamentary reform; that the divisions consist of between twenty and forty members who meet weekly on any evening except Thursday; that each member pay one penny per week; that the delegate give this money to the treasurer for postage, printing and stationery; that the delegates, elected quarterly, meet every Thursday (two-thirds of them constituting a quorum) to communicate the wishes of their divisions and to authorize answers to correspondence needing immediate attention; and that the delegates report these transactions to their divisions.

Four rules introduced in February 1793 were necessitated by a temporary slackening in attendance at the General Committee (five delegates to constitute a quorum, a list to be made of absent delegates and their divisions to be notified, the meeting to open at 8:00 p.m.). The need for a new constitution and the difficulties of producing it are indicated by the appointment in 1793 of three successive committees of constitution, in March, in July and again in October. The last of these committees published a constitution in February 1794, containing 218 numbered items. The provision for two new committees, a Select Committee and a Council, reflected the difficulty of dealing with the business of the Society. In 1792–3 most of the correspondence from other societies was answered by Hardy or Margarot, financial records were kept by Hardy, and addresses, petitions and other publications were drafted by an appointed individual or temporary subcommittee. The proposed Select Committee, a large body containing at least half the number of delegates and a maximum of the same number as there were delegates, were to be in charge of prospective publications of the Society. The proposed Council, consisting of a Treasurer, a Secretary and not less than four Assistant Secretaries, were to audit financial records, record laws and answer letters. The final section of this constitution specified how to deal with a charge that a member was a government spy, with seventeen steps to be followed in the accusation and trial of a member alleged to be "unworthy." This constitution was not accepted and gave rise to acrimonious discussions in both the General Committee and some divisions on the basis that it introduced hierarchy, thereby defeating the very purpose of the Society.

A new committee, again consisting of one member from each division, was appointed to revise this constitution. Completed in April 1794, their version contained only 77 numbered points and sub-points. In place of the two new levels of officialdom proposed in February (the Council and the Select Committee), this constitution would have a four-member Committee of Correspondence, charged only to answer letters, and three under-secretaries, who would see that the decisions of the general committee were carried out.

This constitution was discussed in the divisions at the end of April and the beginning of May. Consideration of it was dropped after the arrest of Hardy and other members, but at the end of June the General Committee voted to adopt it. Several divisions promptly protested and the General Committee then rescinded their vote, and the Society continued to function according to the 1792 constitution.

Following the revelation at Hardy's trial that delegates and even a member of the Committee of Correspondence were spies, stricter rules on admitting prospective members were needed. At the end of 1794 six such rules were proposed to the General Committee. John Bone objected to the wording of these rules and offered to draw up some rules by the next meeting. To the Committee's astonishment he brought a whole new constitution with 47 articles. That night they discussed sixteen of the articles, and the next week between midnight and 2 a.m. they finished the discussion, having locked the door to prevent delegates from leaving. The divisions were persuaded to accept this constitution without detailed discussion, but quarrels over the method of presenting the constitution to the Society led three divisions to secede and form two new societies.

This constitution, minus two articles, was adopted in March 1795, and is similar to that proposed in May 1794. Every quarter the General Committee elected a secretary (who also acted as Treasurer) and an Assistant Secretary. A six-man Executive Committee, with two members rotated each month, drafted all communications bearing the Society's name and carried out the orders of the General Committee. All letters sent to the Executive Committee and their replies were to be published quarterly and distributed without charge to the members.

By mid-1795 over one hundred delegates and sub-delegates were attending meetings of the General Committee, and proposals were introduced to manage its business more efficiently: divisions were enlarged from 30 to 60; the offices of Secretary and Treasurer were separated; the power of the Executive Committee was increased; and financial accounts were to be printed monthly.

The Seditious Meetings Act passed in December 1795 obliged the LCS to limit the size of unadvertised political meetings to 49 persons, and four district committees, limited to 30 members, were established to regulate the flow of delegates to the General Committee to ensure compliance with this law. In March 1796, a new constitution introduced a door-keeper to ensure that no more than forty-nine entered a meeting.

As is clear, a great deal of meeting time at all levels was taken up with discussing and changing the rules. By these means LCS continued to operate until 1799. Obsession with its own constitution and intense disputation over procedure is usually a sign of an organisation in terminal crisis, but in the case of the LCS, this kind of discussion was to a very great extent the *very content* of their project and their members found it exhilarating. Working out how to cultivate an egalitarian ethos by means of majority voting, in the face of state repression on one side and absence of political experience on the other, was a task which engaged the disenfranchised people of England.

Summary

The norm for collective decision making in the LCS was Majority, consistent with their fiercely egalitarian ethos. In this they were no different than their opposite numbers in France, where decisions in the Sections of the Assemblé Générale were made by "the greater part" (*la majeure partie de l'Assemblée,*) or by "the majority" (*à la majorité*) of the Assembly. (Procès-verbaux de l'Assemblé générale)

It is also clear that the ordinary members of the LCS were well aware of how an organisation based on majority voting can be corrupted by various forms of inequality – delegation, hierarchy and control of information, and they struggled in extremely difficult conditions, including the activity of spies and agents provocateurs, to see that majority decisions were based on full and open discussion among all those involved. Members enjoined their delegates to stand fast against repressive measures taken by the government and not to compromise their open and democratic procedures to avoid prosecution. They had no model available for them for such a task.

LCS explicitly sought to make its internal organisational forms a model for the kind of society it wanted to bring about. Its means were public education, not just by the dissemination of texts, but primarily through practical participation in LCS meetings. In this the LCS anticipated the concept of 'prefiguration'. The religious sects did not see their internal regimes as *means* to anything other than salvation, and for the guilds and secret societies, organisational forms were *solely* instrumental. This interval between the French Revolution and the imposition of the Combination Laws provided a short-lived opportunity for experimentation in the conformity of means and ends.

Few of the members of LCS would have had experience of democratic decision making in a guild, because the guilds had long since degenerated and in any case were open only to masters. Many would have participated in the emerging journeymen's guilds, and others learnt the basics of delegate structures from the Methodist Church. But the norm of decision making by majority voting by everyone, not just an elite, was well-known even if practically non-existent. They lacked the habit and skill of using this norm for collective action, and the LCS provided a "movement school" (Isaac, 2012) in which ordinary people learnt how to engage in formalised collective decision making. Furthermore, the LCS "signified the end to any notion of exclusiveness, of politics as the preserve of any hereditary elite or property group" and "implied a new notion of democracy" (Thompson, 1963, p. 21). In this sense, the ethos of the LCS was at odds with the exclusiveness we found still in the rulebooks of the trade unions of 1825. We must move to the 1830s to see how this *unlimited*, universal notion of democratic decision making could implant itself in the British working class through the activity of the Chartists.

The Chartists[1]

The period of the Chartist movement, from the founding of the *Northern Star* in November 1837 to the rejection by Parliament of the last great petition in April 1848 was one in which the principle of majority voting could be said to have reached its zenith, as a *universal* principle. We have already discovered that the principle was thoroughly embraced by radical democracy at the time of the London Correspondence Society in 1792, by which time it had already been developed to a high level of sophistication by the Methodist Church and was already the rule for the trade unions in 1825.

But in each of these cases the principle was in some way defective.

The LCS was a radical democratic or 'Jacobin' organisation. For all its democratic aims and its efforts to educate its politically inexperienced and working-class participants in the practice of political discourse, the LCS was never a mass movement, and while it found correspondents across the country, it never became a nation-wide movement. Further, it was more or less confined to debating debate and fell apart in factional dissension within a short span of time. It was also an exclusively male organisation.

The Methodist Church perfected the practice of organising a truly national movement and embedded it in working-class communities, but while it adhered to the rule of majority voting, it was an organisation run exclusively by its full-time officials and Alexander Kilham's proposals to transform it into a *genuinely* mass democratic formation had been rejected by Conference. In a sense, while the Methodist Church demonstrated the strength of bureaucratic organisation it also manifested the dangers to which both the LCS and the trade unions were highly sensitive and endeavoured to avoid.

The trade unions of 1825 adhered to the rule of one-man-one-vote but their ethos was extremely particularistic – each organisation generally covered a single trade in a single locality, women and young people were generally excluded if not actively disadvantaged, and mobility of all kinds was actively discouraged and discipline was enforced by heavy sanctions.

The Chartists not only transcended these shortcomings, but developed a universalist majoritarian ethos and thoroughly embedded it in the mentality

---

1 My principal source for this chapter are Dorothy Thompson (2013). *The Chartists: Popular Politics in the Industrial Revolution.* Breviary Stuff Publications, Janette Martin's PhD Thesis (2010), *Popular political oratory and itinerant lecturing in Yorkshire and the North East in the age of Chartism, 1837–60*, Chase, M. (2007). *Chartism. A New History* and the http://www .chartists.net/website.

© KONINKLIJKE BRILL NV, LEIDEN, 2016 | DOI 10.1163/9789004319639_009

and activity of the 80% of the British population that united behind the Charter.

The English Reform Act of 1832

Prior to the Reform Act of 1832, a population of 14 million was 'represented' by 406 members of Parliament elected by an electorate of 435,000 voters in a notoriously gerrymandered system – one electorate of 7 voters returned 2 MPs and 152 electorates had fewer than 100 voters, while others had thousands of electors. Parliament had become universally regarded as unrepresentative and corrupt. Agitation surrounding the Reform Act had awakened political consciousness among all classes of British society, and it was widely anticipated to produce a much more progressive and representative government.

The truth however turned out differently. Whereas the number of voters was increased by about 50% to 652,000, with resident ratepayers of property worth £10 per annum rental value qualifying for franchise, this still meant that only about 1/6 of the adult male population had the vote. Giving the vote to those owning property worth £10 p.a. neatly selected the class of non-productive exploiters out of a population of about 14 million, while leaving no part in the political life of the nation to the men and women of the working class or their children, many of whom were also at work in the factories. The legislature which now precisely represented the property-owning classes produced a series of Acts which were shocking in the nakedness of their pursuit of class interest.

The Poor Law Amendment Act of 1834 broke up families and consigned them to privately-run workhouses even in the event of distress due to temporary unemployment. The 1833 Irish Coercion Act imposed an horrific regime on to Ireland and denied to the Irish any recognition of national rights. The 1836 Newspaper Act applied a stamp duty to newspapers which put them out of reach of ordinary working class people and would see hundreds of dealers in unstamped newspapers imprisoned over the years to come. The Factory Act of 1833 failed to protect children under 13 or limit hours of work. These provisions were imposed by a Whig (i.e. middle-class) government under conditions where the Conspiracy Laws punished 'seditious' association and meetings of more than 49 people with imprisonment and transportation.

Economic conditions in the 1830s were very tough. Apprenticeship had been deregulated and the trade unions had lost control of their industries, and as a result, had suffered a series of setbacks. So in a kind of mirror image of what the middle-class had achieved with the 1832 Reform Act a conviction arose in the working class that it was only by achieving representation in Parliament that their existing institutions and achievements could be protected from the attacks being mounted on them by the newly-enfranchised employing class.

   The London Workingmen's Association, which we met earlier on our journey back in time was indeed the author of the People's Charter. However, the
LWMA was a relatively conservative, all-male body of skilled artisans, including for example, Francis Place who had been a member of the London Corresponding Society, and William Lovett, a champion of workers' education, and
were broadly sympathetic to the reformist ideas of Robert Owen. This was the
spark that ignited the Chartist movement, but its heartland was not in London
but in the manufacturing districts in the North.

The Charter

The Charter had six points: universal adult male suffrage, protected by secret
ballot, abolition of property qualifications for MPs, the payment of Members,
equal electoral districts and annual parliaments. The six points of the Charter
were popularised by public speakers who introduced the Charter in every public discussion of whatever topic and advocated the Charter as the solution to
whatever social problem was at issue.

   Although the program was thus defined by the Charter in terms of parliamentary representation, Chartism was by no means limited to the question of
the suffrage. Chartism also stood for free, universal school education to be controlled by the communities, state regulation of wages, conditions and working
hours, state welfare to care for people in times of distress, Irish emancipation,
an end to censorship, freedom of association – all the shared aspirations of
the British working class. But the Charter was the *symbol* of this universal program and even the ignorant London costermonger who knew nothing of the
six points would describe him- or herself as a Chartist. In Dorothy Thompson's
words: Chartism was "the political dimension of the way of life of the produc-
ers in early industrial Britain." The Charter united in a single movement all
those who were not represented in Parliament. For working people, there was
no *other* political organisation in which you could take part: you were either
a Chartist or you were not concerned with politics. The various middle-class
reform movements did not seek working-class participation or make room for
it, while a myriad of radical proletarian currents existed together under the
umbrella of Chartism.

Women

Chartism was a movement based in *whole communities*, especially those homogeneous working class towns where most of the population was employed
in a single industry, out of reach the police and with no more than a few shopkeepers and the odd clergyman representing the middle class. Whole communities participated in Chartist activities – men, women and children. The
Chartists themselves unambiguously favoured universal (male and female)

suffrage. The limitation to adult male suffrage in the six points was a concession to 'realism' – they did not think that the English middle-class would *ever* concede female suffrage. But as far as the working-class members of the Chartist movement were concerned, female suffrage was a given.

Dorothy Thompson believes that it was above all the Poor Law Act which projected the women into action, and in the early years, while Chartist activity took on the traditional forms of political activity available to non-electors – processions, demonstrations, riots and other public events – women were well-represented. Over time however, female participation declined until the famous 1848 photograph of the great Chartist meeting at Kennington Common shows a great sea of male faces. Thompson puts this down to two factors: firstly, in its implementation the Poor Law was not as draconian as was at first suggested by the legislation and its severity was ameliorated over time, and as this became clear, the particular motivation for working-class women lessened. But secondly, as it developed, and particularly after 1840 with the formation of the National Charter Association, Chartist activity took on new forms – regular attendance at weekly meetings, with a fixed subscription to be paid, and all the routine business of maintaining a national organisation which Chartist women left to their menfolk. The same practices which militated against female participation also tended to exclude unskilled and migratory workers.

Women do appear on Chartist membership lists and belonged to Chartist classes, but as the formal organisation developed women tended to put their energies into female-only branches, and it was only in these female-only branches that women were elected as office-bearers, and it was rare for women to speak at mixed meetings. One of the reasons contributing to the reluctance of women to participate in organisational meetings is that invariably the only venue available for meetings were the ale houses – church halls not being made available and their homes too small. On the other hand, there are frequent reports of women's full-blooded participation in marches and demonstrations and even rough-and-tumble with the police. Well over 100 female radical associations have been recorded in the first few years of the movement. The active presence of these Chartist women were in direct contrast to the behaviour of even the most radical middle-class women of the time. Interestingly, most of the references to the question of female suffrage which have been recorded come from men – no Chartist woman ever took issue with the exclusion of female suffrage from the six points.

The "Northern Star"
The radicals of the time first came to feel themselves to be part of a national movement through the part they played in distributing Chartist newspapers.

This could be writing, financing, publishing, distributing or selling illegal radical propaganda through unstamped newspapers, and then organising support for other radicals and their families imprisoned for their activity, or acting as a local correspondent or newsagent for the *Northern Star*.

The *Northern Star* was founded by Feargus O'Connor in November 1837, six months before the publication of the Charter. It was the *Northern Star* which was chiefly responsible for disseminating the Charter, hosting the political discussion it generated, speedily transmitting across the country proposals for action and news of related events, giving to Chartism its national character. Dorothy Thompson says that it would be "impossible to imagine Chartism without the *Star*."

Feargus O'Connor (1794–1855) came from an aristocratic Irish Protestant family with a long history of Irish nationalist activity. After publishing a pamphlet called "The State of Ireland," he was wounded in a fight with soldiers, but escaped arrest. Later, he was elected to House of Commons representing County Cork. He was a charismatic leader, a ferocious speaker and a gifted organiser. He became ill in 1852 and died in 1855 suffering from syphilis.

As a legal weekly newspaper, stamp duty put the *Star* out of reach of working-class people. However, this worked perversely for those who wished to suppress political discussion. Because no-one could afford the *Star* on their own, people *joined together* to subscribe to it. It would be passed from hand-to-hand, or one would read it out while others worked, coffee shops and alehouses subscribed to it for their customers, weekly meetings would be organised to read and discuss its contents every Monday. The collective reading of the *Star* was itself a defining Chartist activity.

Also, O'Connor employed workers as local correspondents for the *Star*, who were in effect full-time agitators for Chartism. Add to this the thousands of small businesses of all kinds that secured an income, at the heart of the movement, to workers who were unable to earn a living at their trade because of their reputation as agitators.

The *Northern Star* was the model for the Party newspaper as organiser, 63 years before *Iskra*, but at a higher level, for whereas all the diverse political currents within Chartism had their own unstamped newspapers to conduct their polemics against one another, the *Star* offered a forum in which *all* the tendencies within Chartism could argue their case, including their criticisms of O'Connor! It was thus the voice of Chartism as a whole rather than any particular current within it. The *Star* was by far the most widely-read journal of its time in Britain; its inclusiveness and its continuity (1837–1852, covering the whole period of Chartism as a mass movement) ensured a continuity of organisation and personnel which no European radical movement had achieved. Insofar as Feargus O'Connor pushed his own line in the paper it was for the need for working people to form *their own organisations* – trade societies, schools, reading groups and especially land colonies (a widespread practice at the time), through which they could develop their own ideas, control their own lives and resist the exploitation and the cultural dominion of the upper classes.

But it was only the principle of universal suffrage which could have united such a popular democratic movement.

Chartist Activity

The universal embrace of the Chartist movement was expressed in its combining the complete range of traditional and modern means of political expression, gathering in the streets, at work, in waste land outside of town, in inns, coffee-shops, reading-rooms and newly-built Chartist Halls. Modern rational argument conducted through printed media and in formal meetings and organisational structures, letter-writing, lectures and fundraising, were combined with "exclusive dealing" (i.e. boycott of unsympathetic traders, usually organised by the women, tending towards self-provisioning in preparation for civil war), demonstrations, processions, carnivals, theatrical performances, camp meetings, sermons and services (including 'occupying' the pews at local churches as well as Chartist non-sectarian preaching), picketing, industrial sabotage, strikes, quasi-military drilling and exercises and from time to time localised armed risings, riots and impressive crowd action. British popular constitutionalism existed side-by-side with direct action and ever threatened to pass over into insurrection. The oldest means of legal participation in the political process, that of petitioning Parliament was used to the limit. Open air public meetings as well as indoor meetings and debates, lectures, teetotal tea parties, soirées and balls, educative reading groups and regular readings of the radical press made up the day-to-day life of Chartists. Frequently, instead of just turning up for a meeting, workers would gather outside of town and march into the meeting accompanied by fife and drum, singing hymns, and in between times there were flags, banners, liberty caps, scarves, sashes and rosettes to be sewn, slogans to be composed and inscribed on banners, engaging men, women and children in collective, creative activity. Thousands learnt to read this way. People would sometimes gather together at separate locations and then march to a central point in the regional town, with the separate marches flowing together to build up into an inspiring, noisy and intimidating flood of human beings. The kind of activities chosen by each community expressed their local characteristics, but all were very conscious of participating in and contributing to a national movement. All they had were their numbers, and they sought to utilise this one lever to the greatest possible advantage.

The Petitions

The central, defining activity of Chartism was petitioning, and in particular the three great petitions of 1839, 1842 and 1848 seeking the implementation of the six points of the Charter. However, between 1838 and 1843 alone, a total of 94,000 petitions were delivered to Parliament, so petitioning was an incessant and ubiquitous activity.

The first two great petitions were supported by a Convention of delegates elected by localities which met in London and were charged with presenting the petition to Parliament, and the third was supported by a mass demonstration in Kennington Common.

The first petition was signed by 1,280,958 men and women – twice the number of electors on whose mandate the Parliament rested, and on 7 May 1839 the convention delegates marched two-by-two behind the petition taking it to Parliament where it was presented to two sympathetic MPs. The petition asked only: "That the poor of England shall be heard by Council at the Bar of the House of Commons," but on 12 July a vote on whether to consider the Charter was rejected by 235 votes to 46. The Convention was then faced, as it was on each subsequent occasion, with what to do now that the petition had been rejected out of hand. A 3-day general strike was called but received only a desultory response. Strikes had already been tried, and workers barely had enough to eat and could not afford such gestures. The Convention dissolved on 6 September 1839.

The rejection of the petition was no surprise, and what to do when it was rejected was a constant theme of discussion everywhere. At no time did the Chartist leadership ever take any steps to prepare for insurrection, instead playing a game of bluff with the government, while in towns all over the North workers drilled in uniform and blacksmiths fashioned pikes. The British ruling class – a class which would go on in the decades ahead to rule half the world – never blinked. The delegates went back to their localities and started again.

In the early hours of Monday 4 November 1839, three columns of workers marched down from the Welsh hills and converged on Newport, a town of no particular strategic importance, expecting, it seems, to trigger a nationwide uprising. The uprising, which had been planned by some of the Convention delegates, was bungled and many of the Chartists had been arrested in advance; a contingent of soldiers fired on the crowd, killing 10 and the leaders were subsequently arrested and sentenced to transportation. The planned nationwide rising did not eventuate, but if the Chartists had ever doubted whether British soldiers would open fire on their own people, there was no longer any room for doubt.

The second great petition was 6 miles long and had 3,315,752 signatures – more than one-third of the adult population of the country! and was presented to Parliament by 16 trade union delegates accompanied by five bands on Monday 2 May, 1842. This Charter had a preamble containing specific demands for the repeal of the Poor Law Amendment Act, and of the Union of Britain and Ireland and again asked only that the petitioners be heard at the bar of the House and was again rejected, 287 to 46.

The third national petition was delivered to Parliament on 10 April 1848. This time massive feeder marches flowed from different quarters of London and converged on Kennington Common across the river from Westminster in a vast mass. Police sealed off all the bridges allowing only a small delegation to cross the Thames and present the petition. The petition claimed to have 5,700,000 signatures, but when parliamentary officials scrutinised the signatures it was found to have only about 1,900,000 genuine signatures. The fraudulent signatures reflected the fact that people had lost faith in the petition process and were discounting it with 'Mickey Mouse' signatures. The process had been discredited. This was the last great petition. Hereafter the Chartist movement went into decline.

The eventual and definitive rejection of the Charter exposed the fact that the Chartist leaders had no Plan B in the event of its rejection. This was the contradiction which lay at the heart of the entire project and would lead to the dissolution of the movement. The only alternative means of achieving political change, however, was insurrection, and not only the leaders, but evidently also most of the ordinary working-class members of the Chartist movement were committed to constitutionalism – at the same time that they were demanding fundamental change to the Constitution! If the British working-class was *ever* in a position to make a successful revolution, it was not ready at that time and its leaders knew it. So the Chartists were never defeated – they just abandoned the aim of a constitutional solution to their problems.

Although all the six points of the Charter and all of the other elements of the Chartist program were abandoned, some seeing partial fulfilment only in the post-World War Two period, and others being altogether forgotten, their time was not wasted. The collecting of signatures was an organising and educating practice quite unlike the kind of petition-signing practices of our own time.

The petitions provided not only a voice for the Chartist movement, but a legal means of mass political agitation, propaganda, education and mobilisation in a situation in which the conspiracy laws still made normal political meetings punishable with prison and transportation.

While petitioning Parliament had been the one constitutional opening for non-electors for centuries, it was in 1788 and 1792 during the anti-slavery agitation, that it had been first developed as a vehicle for mass, political agitation and had become an established practice by the time of the 1832 Reform Act.

As described by Janette Martin (2010), itinerant Chartist orators would move across the country, convening public meetings in towns and addressing large crowds on the merits of the Charter. These public meetings were conducted in accordance with formal meeting procedure and a Resolution would be put supporting the Charter and argued according to strict rules of debate, voted on and then everyone would sign the petition and reports of the meeting printed in the radical press. Generally, the meetings would be held outdoors, but could be held indoors providing numbers were limited to 49, but in all cases the meetings were open and public and thereby immune from conspiracy laws. Frequently, the Chartists, whether itinerant professionals or local people, would intervene in public meetings convened for other purposes and propose a counter-motion, indeed a Chartist speaker might follow a religious or liberal speaker around the countryside creating a kind of spectator sport which attracted considerable excitement and generated wide interest in the political issues being debated.

Given that the point at issue was the fitness of the mass of the poor of Britain to participate in Parliamentary politics, the Chartists were always at pains to demonstrate in these public meetings their dedication to the rituals and protocols of fair-play and constitutional procedure in public political discussion and they invariably behaved with restraint, dignity and decorum and minutely observed the rules of order. As mentioned above, during the Chartist period more than 100,000 petitions were signed over and above the 3 national petitions. The elaborate ceremonies around these public meetings not only served to create and express public opinion and demonstrate the readiness of the Chartists to participate in government, but inculcated the practices of reasoned political debate and collective decision making in the mass of working people who were denied the right to participate in politics by the prevailing system of government. They also trained a staff of skilled agitators and organisers, and gave to working people a venue where they could openly challenge and debate their social superiors.

The hustings, that is, public platforms provided for candidates in an election, were also an opportunity for non-electors to engage in political discourse and argument, with Whig and Tory arguing for the vote of a small minority of voters before an audience non-voters who all supported the Chartists! As a venue for deliberation, the hustings deteriorated over time becoming simply an occasion for mass rallies and were abolished as a formal practice in 1872.

Just as we saw how the London Corresponding Society was more than anything else engaged in an educative practice, the Charter and its petitions and
public meetings took this educative work to a mass scale, and created a politically educated and self-conscious working class.

National Charter Association[2]

After the rejection of the first great petition, the Convention's existence in London was in danger of being seen as an alternative revolutionary government,
and the delegates decided to reconvene in Birmingham, and in July 1840 they
founded a formal structure for the Chartist Movement, the National Charter
Association. Despite the fact that hundreds of local Chartist leaders had been
arrested and the movement was disorganised and somewhat disoriented, the
delegates, having been already elected by localities, resolved to constitute itself
as a National Executive and that:

> The basis of the Association was the People's Charter; and it was agreed
> that none but peaceful and constitutional means should be employed for
> gaining that object. All persons might be admitted as members on declar-
> ing that they agreed with the principles of the Association, and taking
> out a card of membership, to be renewed quarterly, for which they should
> be charged two pence.[3]

There were to be local branches – in many cases this simply meant formalising
existing local Chartist Associations, and an annually elected general Convention which could oversee and regulate the work of the National Executive. The
general secretary was to be paid £2 a week, and members of the Executive were
to receive 30 shillings a week while they were sitting, but were given work as
itinerant lecturers when the Executive was not sitting. One half of the money
collected by local branches was to be at the disposal of the Executive generally
for the hire of itinerant lecturers to open up areas where branches did not already exist; and plans were formulated to stand Chartist candidates at the next
general election. The National Charter Association was to be the main vehicle
for Chartism until it was formally wound up in 1860. According to Dorothy
Thompson, the National Charter Association was "the first nationally organised party of the working class to exist in the world."

---

2   In this section I have consulted Yeo, E. (1982). "Some Practices and Problems in Chartist De-
    mocracy," in *The Chartist Experience: Studies in Working-Class Radicalism and Culture, 1830–
    1860*, ed. James Epstein & Dorothy Thompson, London: Macmillan, pp. 360–362.
3   Gammage, R. History of the Chartist Movement, 1837–1854, cited on chartists.net.

The structure of the NCA was modelled on the Methodist Church but adapted to meet their democratic aspirations. At the base were classes, which, like the local branches pre-existed their formalisation in the NCA. Classes were usually of ten people, who met together weekly and elected a leader from amongst themselves to liaise with the next tier of local organisation. Class meetings were particularly useful in times of repression and became widespread from June 1839; they could be held fairly invisibly in people's houses and yet, by means of the leaders' activity as two-way couriers, they could still generate simultaneous action, without public meetings or newspaper advertisements. Classes were also invaluable in collecting money which was otherwise near to impossible given the distress Chartists members were usually experiencing.

The local branch was the organisational bedrock of Chartism, often predating and outlasting regional federations or national structures, always resurfacing whenever repression slackened, although sometimes in camouflaged form. These branches were genuinely autonomous, and some even developed their own by-laws and regulations.

The local branches differed from the model developed by the trade unions in that rather than governing their activity by frequent general meetings, and rotating office bearers, they elected officers to deal with on-going business, and these Managing Committees, typically of ten or twelve members typically met weekly and were subject to quarterly election. Chartists were acutely aware of the dangers of elected officials becoming a bureaucracy, as were the unions, but Chartist members were very diverse and not all had the opportunity to fulfil regular offices. Also, subscriptions were kept very low and the Chartists did not resort to fines to enforce performance of offices. Usually these offices were filled by people whose conditions of life gave them sufficient free time and flexibility to do the work. The Chairman at public meetings was always elected from the floor, thus giving an opportunity to participate for those unable to make a regular commitment.

The local branches sent delegates to District Councils. These had the power to hire, pay and control their own district lecturers, like the Methodist Circuit, while the National Executive used its funds for missionary work to open up new areas. 'Missionaries' were hired for a short term only, which enabled Districts to keep them in close check and dispense with them when funds were short. Delegates from local Associations to the District Councils and Conventions were mandated and had to cast votes as directed by their branch on contentious issues. Some areas published a monthly lecture plan based on the Methodist model of circuit preaching plans, as well as organising debating societies to raise the political level of the whole membership. Some held monthly lecturers' meetings paralleling the Methodists' preachers' meetings.

The Chartists struggled to develop this democratic organisation not only within the spirit of what they took to be the Constitution, but also within the law. The frequency of arrest and the severity of the penalties made keeping within the law not only a matter of principle, but a practical necessity. But the government effectively made internal democracy illegal. The Seditious Meetings Act made illegal the *election of officers*, or committees, or *any kind of representative structure* or *any communication between branches*. The penalty for contravening these provisions was seven years transportation. The ban on communication was overcome by publication in the *Northern Star*. The ban on electing delegates and officials was circumvented by local branches nominating candidates, and then the National Executive appointing the nominated person. A Convention was recognised as legal to the extent that it was a petitioning body, and the election of delegates was supposed to be legal if carried out at public, county hustings, rather than at private meetings of the local Charter Associations. But the government was continuously changing the laws and making new regulations to thwart the Chartists' attempt to organise democratically while remaining within the law and operating openly and in public. Protracted efforts to register the Association as a charity or friendly society, which would have allowed for a branch structure, were thwarted.

Thus in the wake of the rejection of the petition by Parliament and the unavailability of a revolutionary alternative, and in the face of almost insuperable legal and economic barriers, taking John Wesley's model as a starting point, the Chartists created the model for a democratic, national working class organisation based on the principle of majority voting – a model which would endure up to the present times.

The founding of the National Charter Association allowed the Chartists to regroup as manufacturing was hit by the worst depression of the century. Following the rejection of the second national petition, during the summer of 1842, there was a wave of strikes, including the Plug Riots, in which some of the most violent clashes occurred. The Plug Riots got their name from the plugs which were removed from boilers shutting down factories as striking workers marched from one factory to the next, calling out the workers on strike and removing the plugs from the boilers. All the strikers declared that the strike was for the Charter, and although all the workers were Chartists, this demand came not from those who were known as Chartist leaders, but rather from those whose standing was as union leaders. The term "Plug Riots" conveys an image of aimless and uncontrolled violence, but for the middle-class of England the most frightening thing about the Plug Riots was their orderliness and self-control!

It was at about this time that Chartism shed many of its supporters among the radical middle-class. The strikes were defeated, but this moment coincided with the end of all attempts to form an alliance between the more liberal elements of the middle class and respectable Chartists (to be discussed below) and the gulf between the disenfranchised working class and the ruling middle-class reached its apogee.

The Majoritarian Ethos and Class Consciousness
We saw in the chapter on the London Corresponding Society that the radicalism of the 1790s had no notion of class struggle. This was no longer the case by the 1840s. Working-class radicalism had made its appearance and the divide separating working-class radicalism from bourgeois radicalism was an impassable gulf. Radicals among the middle classes never made common cause with the Chartists, and the great majority wanted nothing to do with any kind of independent working-class activity, regarding the working class as their inferiors in every way, for whom their own role was to provide management and control. England has always had a strong sense of class, but the gap separating the 5/6 of the population which made up the poor and disenfranchised working class, on one hand, the professional and landed middle class and gentry on the other, was as sharp as that separating the living from the dead.

The litmus test for the radicalism of the Chartists was trade-union rights and the Poor Law. Francis Place for example, a member of both the LCS and the LWMA, far from fighting against the Poor Law, hoped for appointment as a Poor Law Commissioner. From this time forward the only genuine radicalism was working-class radicalism and all the radical democrats of the time were relegated to the position of apologists for the status quo.

The Chartists leaders learnt from the experience of the petitions and efforts to collaborate with middle-class radicals, that social attitudes were essentially defined by property, so relying on the support of allies and sympathisers among the upper classes was folly. Politics was fundamentally about classes: property versus labour – the axiom of working class politics.

The significance which the question of decision making by majority vote took on amongst the Chartists should be obvious. England was ruled by a *propertied minority*. For the working class of Britain, for the Chartists, the whole problem of their lives of poverty and oppression came down to the question of whether a minority or a majority should rule. To suggest that the minority had rights as against the majority was to justify the ruthless exploitation which was in their face every day. The majoritarian ethos which suffused the lives of the British working class at this time reflected the world view of the 5/6 of the population which laboured in literally Dickensian conditions to support an Austenian life of leisure for the other 1/6. This ethos entered, as they say, into the DNA of the labour movement. Any criticism made of majoritarianism since 1950, since the word 'majoritarianism' entered the language as a pejorative, has to bear in mind the meaning of such criticism to the global poor, the excluded majority, not just in Dickens' England but to this very day.

As it happens, just such a clash of the two paradigms of collective decision making did take place in England in 1842.

Consensus between Majority and Minority?

Joseph Sturge (1793–1859) was a Quaker who had exposed the failure of slavery abolition measures in the Caribbean and led a campaign for complete abolition which had culminated in success in 1838. As an aldermen in Birmingham at the time of the reconvened Chartist Convention in July 1839, he had played a mediating role in clashes between the police and Chartist rioters and may have been instrumental in saving Chartist leaders from the death penalty. After touring the United States in 1841 he was converted to the cause of "the fair, full, and free exercise of the elective franchise" and launched an initiative to win middle-class elements to the Chartist cause and secured the participation of several 'respectable' Chartist leaders like William Lovett.

William Lovett was a cabinet-maker who, as a founder of the London Workingmen's Association, had drafted the Charter and had continued as a leader of the Chartists, unanimously elected secretary of the Chartist Convention in 1839, before his arrest. However, after his imprisonment he had retired from politics and devoted himself to pursuing the Chartist program for education of working-class communities.

After the Plug Riots and events surrounding the foundation of the National Charter Association, Sturge's initiative was aimed at drawing such 'respectable' elements away from the mass base of Chartism into a formation which could bridge the class divide. At a conference convened by Sturge in April 1842, 87 delegates agreed to set up a National Complete Suffrage Union (CSU), adopting all six points of the People's Charter. But when the question of the name of the new organisation arose.

> Lovett and the other Chartists insisted that, having adopted all the points of the Charter, the conference should adopt the name as well; the Complete Suffragists wished some other name to be chosen, regarding the old term as too much associated with the physical-force methods of the past.

The delegates could reach no agreement upon the point, and wisely determined to let the question remain unsettled until December.[4]

Sturge proposed that a second conference be composed of an equal number of delegates chosen from among the electors and non-electors. This proposition was, in all fairness, eminently sensible as the matter at hand was to find a consensus between two parties – the working-class on one hand and the middle-class radicals on the other, and it was a matter of no significance how many delegates represented each party as to whether that consensus existed or did not. This system, William Lovett wrote

> ...was not as might be supposed, approved of by the O'Connorites...who took every opportunity of denouncing it as anti-democratic and unjust. The Complete Suffrage party, however, instead of defending it as a fair and just mode of choosing a deliberative assembly, where reason and argument were to prevail instead of the power of numbers...gave way on this important point.[5]

For the Chartists the question of numbers was the *whole* question. To accept that a delegate representing thousands of working class people was equal to one middle class gentleman would have been to give away the whole question. Equally, to abandon the *name* of the Charter was to abandon the working-class which had gathered together behind that banner.

When it became clear that the Chartist delegates (constituting a majority of the conference) were not going to budge on the question of retaining the name of the 'Charter', Sturge resigned from the chair, left, and the conference collapsed, and there was never again any effort to find support for the Chartists from among the English middle-class.[6]

This incident is the prototype for all those occasions when middle-class people introduce to labour movement events and organisations the suggestion that decisions should be made by consensus, and the shock that they suffer when this well-meaning suggestion is rejected on principle. Nonetheless, the

---

4   Slosson, P.W. (1916). *The Decline of the Chartist Movement*, cited on chartists.net.
5   Lovett, Wm (1920). *Life and Struggles*. G. Bell & Sons, cited by Dorothy Thompson.
6   This is not to deny the privileged family background of Chartist leaders such as Feargus O'Connor and Ernest Jones, but these few Chartist leaders from propertied families abandoned their class roots and outlook in placing themselves in leadership of a proletarian movement.

labour movement has always had its own ways of finding consensus where the will exists.

The Aftermath

After the rejection of the third national petition, the Chartist movement went into decline. Hundreds of Chartist leaders had been imprisoned or transported, thousands more had emigrated. The fading of support for the Chartists in the '50s was a fading of belief in politics as an means of achieving social change. It was this belief, realised in the practice of petitioning, which had not only given unity to the Chartist movement, but a strong sense of the interrelatedness of all the social issues affecting them. Consequently, the loss of this unifying program implied a fragmentation of the movement into the pursuit of partial solutions in more limited projects such as consumer co-operatives, 'new model' trade unions, mechanics institutes, local government, friendly societies, and the various organisations which characterised the life of the skilled workers in the latter part of the nineteenth century.

There had been several attempts to form national general unions in the late 1820s, culminating in the founding of the National Association for the Protection of Labour in 1830; the Grand National Consolidated Trade Union was founded as a union federation in 1834, and the Tolpuddle Martyrs were sentenced to transportation for their efforts to found a friendly society and affiliate to the Grand National. Throughout the 1830s such moves were widespread, including both national or metropolitan alliances of particular trades, and more ambitious attempts to build general unions including skilled, unskilled, female and juvenile labour, reflecting the whole process of working-class formation represented by Chartism. The foundation of the National Charter Association was typical of this process. After 1848 however, these efforts at *general* union organising were abandoned in favour of what the Webbs called 'new model unions'. These were a partial retreat to particularism of the 1825 unions, but incorporating the organisational innovations of the Chartist period. Unions tended to be restricted to individual trades, generally of relatively highly paid skilled trades, with comparatively high subscription fees; their leadership tended to be more conservative, with an emphasis on negotiations and education rather than strike action.

Alongside unionism, they pursued consumer co-operatives, working-class insurance societies, workers' educational institutes and so on. Assistance from the Parliament of the propertied classes, was neither needed nor asked for, provided only that they had the protection of the law.

At the same time, it could not be ignored that in 1846, the Corn Laws had been repealed by a *Tory* government, and an *un*reformed House of Commons also passed the Ten Hours Act – facts which seemed to contradict the dogma that Parliamentary actions were a direct expression of class interest, which had been the lesson of the 1830s, and upon which the Chartists were founded. At the same time, there was an upturn in trade after 1848, employment was more regular, giving better opportunities for the various self-help organisations, and softening the impact of the Poor Law, especially with the transference of poor relief to direct government control in 1847. These experiences all tended towards to conviction that all that was required was *non-interference by the state in workers' self-help* activity, rather than state regulation of wages and working conditions secured by means of universal suffrage.

The move to workers mutual aid, pursued through the kind of bureaucratic structures which workers had learned to build and operate during the Chartist period, however, led to the exclusion from the labour movement of all those for whom participation in such structures was difficult – women, migrants, unskilled and semi-skilled workers, individual home-based artisans like cobblers, tailors, blacksmiths, small printers, as well as radical preachers and other local agitators who had all found a place in the Chartist movement during its heyday.

The revival of general unionism and a new turn to Parliamentary representation and with that a partial recovery of the universalism of the Chartist period would come only towards the end of the century, but before we can move on from the events leading up to 1848, we have one more current of collective decision making which has so far stayed under the radar, and for this we must turn to the secret activity carried on by Chartists, but not reported in the documents of the time.

Insurrectionary Activity during the Chartist Period

Throughout the Chartist period, in all their public activity, all the Chartist leaders played a kind of game of bluff, never actually initiating an armed uprising but leading the middle-classes to believe that such a turn of events was imminent. They knew that if they were to secure political gains by violence then it was only systematic, well-organised, nationwide armed action which would have the chance of defeating the armed force of the Crown. Even the preparatory activity – arming, recruiting, training, drilling, etc. – would bring down the most severe penalties upon them. And yet that program was in action; there was a kind of dualism, with open, legal political activity going on in public, while an underground movement was distributing pikes and training on the moors by night. The more the Chartist masses were frustrated by the rejection of their public, legal activity, the more they turned to illegal and conspiratorial activities. But this activity could never be reported in the press and on the whole was not recorded at all, leaving little information for historians.

During the last years of Chartism, the constitutional road having been definitively blocked, the leadership of the Chartist movement passed to secret societies led by people like Ernest Jones and George Julian Harney, who *did* see the 1848 Convention as a "provisional government" of Britain. The secret societies not only prepared for armed revolution, but also followed events in Europe keenly. After 1848, these secret societies initiated a new line of development, which was no longer exclusively British, and is the subject of the next chapter.

The Communist Secret Societies

Secret societies of all kinds continued to exist from medieval times through the Chartist period and beyond. Given that every effort by the Chartist leaders to find a legal form for their organisation which would satisfy their need for a democratic and participatory structure were thwarted by the English government and courts, some of those aspirations were bound to be channelled into secret societies.

The narrow particularism of trade societies reflected in the union rulebooks examined by the 1825 Select Committee would not be reflected in aims of those secret societies whose objective was pursuit of religious or insurrectionary political objectives. However, in most respects these secret societies resemble all the other societies from trade societies to charitable, mutual-aid, welfare and friendly societies. All elected officials by "plurality of voices," and applied penalties for failure to carry out official duties, made decisions by majority voting and had elaborate rituals and catechisms for the induction of new members.

In the story so far we have already followed the progress of decision by majority voting to its zenith in the Chartist Movement, 1837–1848. All that is required now is to show how the universality of this ethic was recovered from the particularism into which it fell as a result of the frustration of democratic aspirations and was restored to its place as a truly universal principle of radical, progressive politics by the beginning of the twentieth century.

After 1848, the majoritarian principle was retained as a *universal* principle only by those secret societies which plotted insurrection, that is, by the communist secret societies. By their very nature, however, these secret societies were self-isolated minorities.

Central to our concerns are the League of the Just, founded in Paris in 1836, having split from the League of Outlaws, which had been founded in Paris two years earlier. It had set itself up in London in 1846 using the German Workers' Educational Association as a front. In the various countries across Europe they masqueraded as choral societies or gymnastic clubs or whatever suited local conditions. In England, they were represented by exiled German revolutionaries such as Karl Schapper, Joseph Moll and Heinrich Bauer. These emigrés had succeeded in making contact with the revolutionary elements of the Chartist movement led by people such as Julian Harney and Ernest Jones. In 1845, Marx and Engels participated in meetings including both left-wing Chartists and members of the League of the Just.

The League of the Just held a Congress in London in June 1847 in which Frederick Engels participated. Marx and Engels agreed to join the League

© KONINKLIJKE BRILL NV, LEIDEN, 2016 | DOI 10.1163/9789004319639_010

on condition that their rules be re-written so as to eliminate all elements of sectarianism and conspiracy. As a result of Marx and Engels' intervention, the League now agreed to call itself the Communist League and its motto "All men are Brothers!" was replaced with "Working Men of All Countries, Unite!" – replacing an abstract affirmation with a concrete, practical imperative. Its new Rules (*MECW*, Volume 6, pp. 585–588) were circulated and agreed at the June 1847 Congress.

According to the new Rules, the aim of the League was "the emancipation of humanity by spreading the theory of the community of property and its speediest possible practical introduction." A member was required to "conduct himself in a manly fashion," recognise the principles of the League, "give his word of honour to work loyally and to observe secrecy," etc. and adopt a pseudonym. Members were forbidden to belong to any other political or national association and "members are equal and brothers and as such owe each other assistance in every situation."

Following an established model for secret societies, the League was composed of *communities* which were unknown to each other and which adopted a code name for themselves, each community consisting of 3 to 12 members. Communities admit members by unanimous consent following an induction procedure, and elected their own chairman and deputy chairman. The chairman presided over meetings and the deputy held the funds, into which members' contributions were paid. The community would divide when their numbers exceeded 12.

Circles, like the Methodist Circuits, consisted of 2 to 10 communities, and the circle authority was composed of the chairmen and deputies of the communities, which in turn elected a president from amongst themselves. The *Central Authority* of the whole League was at least 5 members elected by the circle authority of the place where it was to have its seat. The *Congress* is the supreme and legislative body of the League and is composed of one delegate from each circle. Decisions by Congress, however, were to be "submitted to the communities for acceptance or rejection." The communities, rather than individual members, pay a weekly or monthly contribution (thus acting like a Methodist class) to be determined by the circle. All elections are annual.

Like with the London Corresponding Society and all secret societies, members were admitted by giving affirmative answers to a series of questions and pledging his word of honour. The five questions were:

a.   Are you convinced of the truth of the principles of the community of property?

b.   Do you think a strong League is necessary for the realisation of these principles as soon as possible, and do you wish to join such a League?

c.   Do you promise always to work by word and deed for spreading and the practical realisation of the principles of the community of property?

d.   Do you promise to observe secrecy about the existence and all affairs of the League?

e.   Do you promise to comply with the decisions of the League? Then give us on this your word of honour as a guarantee!

Its new Rules were agreed, but further modifications were agreed at a Second Congress in November 1847. Marx insisted on the limitation of the provision banning members from belonging to other organisations to apply only to anti-communist organisations, and on the removal of the right of communities to opt out of Congress decisions and put forward a new formulation of the League's aim:

> The aim of the League is the overthrow of the bourgeoisie, the rule of the proletariat, the abolition of the old bourgeois society which rests on the antagonism of classes, and the foundation of a new society without classes and without private property.
>
> *MECW*, v. 6, pp. 633

There was some modernisation of the requirements placed upon members, and the size of communities was increased from 12 to 20, and an additional layer of organisation introduced with one circle in each region to be nominated as the 'leading circle' for that region. Frequency of meetings were regulated and the right of recall of elected officials introduced, and various aspects of the regulations made more concrete.

The procedure for admission was changed. The chairman of the community was to read the entire 49 articles of the Rules to the applicant and give a short speech on the obligations of a new member of the League, and then ask: "Do you now wish to enter this League?" and on the candidate replying "Yes" the chairman takes his word of honour that he will fulfil these obligations, declares him a member of the League and introduces him to the Community at its next meeting.

The rendering of the aims and requirements of the Leagues into practical and concrete (albeit remote) terms and reduction of the usual Q&A induction procedure to a simple pledge to adhere to the Rules represented a significant move away from the former secret society consciousness. However, secrecy was still obligatory given the conditions of the times and the structure of the League reflected this.

The draft Rules and a draft program written by Engels were approved at the last sitting on June 9, 1847. This program is known as the "Communist

Confession of Faith." It took the form of a catechism, with 22 questions and answers not generally limited to "yes," which present the views of communists on a range of issues, though with an historical slant. After the First Congress of the Communist League, the "Draft of a Communist Confession of Faith" was sent, together with the draft Rules, to the various communities of the League for discussion, the results of which were to be taken into account at the time of the final approval of the programme and the Rules at the Second Congress.

Engels revised the "Confession" to the 25-point "Principles of Communism," but on 23 November, before the second Congress had even begun, he wrote to Marx:

> Give a little thought to the *Confession of Faith*. I think we would do best to abandon the catechetical form and call the thing *Communist Manifesto*. Since a certain amount of history has to be narrated in it, the form hitherto adopted is quite unsuitable.... [It] has not yet been submitted in its entirety for endorsement but, save for a few quite minor points, I think I can get it through in such a form that at least there is nothing in it which conflicts with our views.

The Second Congress agreed, and directed Marx and Engels to write a "Communist Manifesto." Marx and Engels began working together on the *Manifesto* while they were still in London immediately after the congress, and continued until about December 13 when Marx returned to Brussels. They resumed their work together when Engels arrived there on December 17. After Engels' departure for Paris at the end of December and up to his return on January 31, Marx worked on the *Manifesto* alone.

The form of catechism was tied to the practice of swearing in new members with an oath of loyalty and secrecy. This was appropriate for a small secret society, but quite unsuitable for an emancipatory mass movement. Delegates were aware of the social explosion approaching in Europe and the *Manifesto* needed to both speak to and give voice to the emergent international proletariat.

Soon after the publication of the *Manifesto*, Marx published the "Demands of the Communist Party in Germany," 17 points which addressed the immediate demands of the movement which was breaking out in Germany, in contrast to the *Manifesto* which continues to express the movement and aspirations of the working class to this day. Thus Marx introduced a practical distinction between agitation around demands which reflected the immediate consciousness of the masses, and a program which spoke to ideals which would guide the workers' movement for generations to come.

The Manifesto declared:

I.   Communism is already acknowledged by all European powers to be itself a power.

II.   It is high time that Communists *should openly, in the face of the whole world, publish their views,* their aims, their tendencies, and meet this nursery tale of the Spectre of Communism with a manifesto of the party itself.

and in its famous concluding lines:

> The Communists *disdain to conceal their views and aims.* They openly declare that their ends can be attained only by the forcible overthrow of all existing social conditions. Let the ruling classes tremble at a Communistic revolution. The proletarians have nothing to lose but their chains. They have a world to win.
>
>   Working Men of All Countries, Unite! (emphasis added)

So while retaining the obligatory structure of the Communist League as a secret society, they "openly, in the face of the whole world" publish their views: "the forcible overthrow of all existing social conditions." This is a fundamental break from the policy of the Chartists to remain within the bounds of legality, no matter what the cost to internal democracy and effective organisation, committing their members to use only 'moral force' and to eschew non-constitutional or illegal means. It is also a fundamental break from the closed, sectarian mentality of the secret society in that the *Manifesto* and *Demands* address themselves to a mass movement beyond their own ranks, seeking to place themselves at the head of a mass movement without trying to swear everyone to an oath of loyalty, etc.

It was not until the 1860s that conditions made it possible for the communists to legally and openly engage in agitation, and this they did through the International Workingmen's Association, which took the form of an international mutual-aid society. For the approximately 8 years of its existence, the International went some way to recovering the kind of universal majoritarian ethos which the Chartists had fostered. What the International could achieve was limited however by underlying changes in the structure of the labour process and consequently in the working class itself. No longer would it be possible to rely on the traditional resources of the artisan class and take for granted the growing mass of unskilled labour.

The General Workers Unions

Skilled workers defended themselves effectively after 1848, and enjoyed a steadily increasing standard of living thanks to the 'new model unions' they built, all of them organised at a national level, with full-time officials and control over their trade exercised by means of strict union discipline and a monopoly of skilled labour.

The Trade Union Act of 1871 and the Criminal Conspiracy and Protection of Property Act of 1875 made it legal for workers to organize trade unions. The Electoral Reform Acts of 1867 and 1884 had broadened the franchise, but lower-paid men and all women were denied the vote until 1918, and women under 30 did not get the vote until 1928.

The progress of the industrial economy coupled with the expansion of the British Empire allowed the British middle class to accumulate vast wealth, out of which it was able to satisfy the demands of the organised skilled workers, but this left behind a mass of absolutely impoverished unskilled workers.

In 1883, Frederick Taylor had carried out his first exercise in "scientific management" at Bethlehem Steel. Taylor redefined what could be meant by "productive labour." Taylor taught that about 25% of employees in large-scale industry ought to be engaged in the science of work: observing, measuring, supervising and directing the work of others. Taylor turned on its head the idea universally held by capitalists at the time that only those who actually work with their hands could be counted as productive workers, and profitability depended on working them as hard and as long as possible, paying them as little as possible, and having the minimum of overheads. Taylor enumerated seventeen different roles in a manufacturing workshop that were formerly performed by a single gang-boss or the 'productive' workers themselves. He proposed that a specific department be established for each of these functions, employing one or a number of functional bosses. Most of these new positions were filled by promotion from the shop-floor, and participation in the new form of management brought wage increases of at least 30%, provided you did not belong to a union. Pay increases were financed by productivity levels up to ten times what they had been previously. The pay of every worker would be set individually according to their level of productivity and responsibility.

The result of this revolution in real political economy was fragmentation of the working class into numerous, relatively distinct strata, and these new strata to a greater or lesser extent shared their boss's social standpoint. Taking a social position between the workers and the bosses brought with it a share of the surplus value extracted from the labour process. Together with the skilled

© KONINKLIJKE BRILL NV, LEIDEN, 2016 | DOI 10.1163/9789004319639_011

workers organised in craft unions, and the workers engaged in retail or home-based shops, the professional and supervisory classes blunted the sharp division of society between propertyless workers and property-owning exploiters, and the professional and small-business petit-bourgeoisie, far from disappearing as some had supposed, actually grew. The binary world of the Chartist years was gone forever.

But there remained a growing mass of absolutely impoverished workers whose conditions of work had hitherto made it impossible for them to organise and gain control of their work. In the late 1880s this situation exploded in a series of great strikes which brought an entirely new section of workers into the trade union movement. These were the personifications of what Marx had called 'abstract labour' and in organising themselves in new General Unions, they restored the majoritarian principle to the place it had enjoyed in the Chartist days, albeit among a more limited section of the population at the very bottom of the heap.

In June 1888, the Matchgirls working in the Quaker-owned Bryant & May factory in Bow went on strike against cruel conditions which exposed them to poisonous white phosphorus and a system of fines for trivial 'offences' which reduced their wages to starvation level and created unbearable pressure of work. They formed their own union with their own leadership and won very considerable concessions. On 27 July 1888, the inaugural meeting of the Union of Women Match Makers was held, and by October, 666 members had been enrolled. By the end of the year, the union changed its name, and became the Matchmakers Union, open to men and women. This set off a series of big strikes which brought all low-paid, unskilled workers into General Unions over the next decade or so.

Next was the Beckton Gas Workers just down the road from Bryant & May, when workers were laid off in March 1889. Gas workers from all over London held a protest meeting on Sunday, 31st March. One of the speakers at the meeting, an illiterate gas worker from Birmingham, Will Thorne, suggested that the gas workers form their own union, saying: "I pledge my word that, if you will stand firm and don't waver, within six months we will claim and win the eight-hour day, a six-day week and the abolition of the present slave-driving methods in vogue not only at the Beckton Gas Works, but all over the country."

Will Thorne, Ben Tillett and William Byford formed a three-man committee and that morning recruited over 800 members to what became known as the National Union of Gasworkers & General Labourers. Elections were held and Thorne defeated Tillett for the post of General Secretary. Thorne argued that "the eight-hour day would not just mean a reduction of four hours a day for the workers then employed, but that a large number of unemployed would be absorbed, and so reduce the inhuman competition that was making men more like beasts than civilized persons." Within a few weeks Thorne had successfully negotiated an eight-hour day and the Gasworkers' Union soon had over 20,000 members.

The conditions of workers in the nearby London docks was described by a docks employer to a Parliamentary Committee in the following terms:

> The poor fellows are miserably clad, scarcely with a boot on their foot, in a most miserable state... These are men who come to work in our docks who come on without having a bit of food in their stomachs, perhaps since the previous day; they have worked for an hour and have earned 5 d; their hunger will not allow them to continue: they take the 5 d in order that they may get food, perhaps the first food they have had for twenty-four hours.

Work was assigned at the docks by throwing tokens into the crowd of workers waiting at the gates and letting them fight for one for admission to a job. The dockers were inspired by the Gas Workers and in 1889 went on strike. They were led by the cooper Ben Tillett, the engineering worker John Burns and the former farm-labourer, Tom Mann, demanding a minimum of four hours continuous work at a time and a minimum rate of sixpence an hour. 10,000 men came out on strike. The employers hoped to starve the dockers back to work but widespread support from the Salvation Army (who had also supported the matchgirls), and trade unions such as those in Australia which sent over £30,000, helped the dockers continue the struggle. After five weeks, the employers accepted defeat and granted all the dockers' main demands. With Ben Tillett as its General Secretary, the Dock, Wharf, Riverside and General Labourers Union had 31,000 members by the end of 1889, and 57,000 by the end of 1890.

The leaders of these new unions were socialists; people such as Tom Mann, Ben Tillett, Kier Hardie, H.H. Champion, Will Thorne and John Burns would go on to become leaders of the Labour Party or the Communist International. The only competition for these workers' jobs was from each other; exclusivity was foreign to them because they had nothing to defend. *Their* aspirations were necessarily *universal* aspirations.

These new General Unions differed from the old craft unions in several respects.

- They were *general*, not exclusive, and actively recruited workers from as wide a range of trades as possible. To encourage more workers to join, they kept their entrance fees and contributions as low as possible.

- They recruited unskilled and semi-skilled workers, such as dockers, seamen, gasworkers and general labourers across *entire industries*, rather than selected membership in a *single trade*.
- They were created by great militant strikes which brought about very significant gains for their members and generated the *solidarity* which made the mere threat of a strike sufficient to maintain their bargaining strength, despite not having a monopoly of skill.

The Rule Books for the Dock, Wharf, Riverside and General Labourers Union and the Workers Union demonstrate the renewed commitment to majoritarianism as a universal principle. The Preamble of the Dockers Union Rules declares:

> Poverty is the curse of mankind; ...To mitigate, aye, to abolish this thrice-accursed Poverty is the work of Trades Unionism. ...obtaining reductions of the normal working day [has] lessened the fierce competition for employment, which, when left unchecked, drives wages down to starvation point. It is the duty now of the Trade Unions to work unceasingly until the evils of Industrial Competition are removed by Industrial Co-operation.... Being called to enrolment in a common Brotherhood governed by self-made rules, it is for us to prove loyal members and at all times assist in the careful administration of such rules.... Heartily wishing every other Union genuine success, we look forward to the time – we trust not very far distant – when the lot of the worker will be free from anxiety as to how to obtain the ordinary necessities, and when the advantages of a thorough education, mental, moral and physical, with work for all and over-work for none, shall be the lot of all...never forgetting that the workers' cause is one and the same the world over, we sincerely wish God-speed to the workers of both sexes in all lands.

The Union's aims included establishing compulsory Courts of Arbitration, providing dispute pay, funeral benefit, supporting legal action, promoting amalgamation or Federation with other Unions and securing the election of Trade Unionists as direct representatives of labour not only to Parliament, but also to County, Borough or other Municipal Councils, Boards of Guardians or School Boards.

Their membership was to be: "any number of male or female workers actually engaged in Dock, Wharf, Riverside, Ship, Warehouse, Copper, Tin, Fuel, and Brick work, and of those engaged in such other trades as shall be recommended by the District Committee and sanctioned by the Executive Council."

There was an entrance fee 1 s., for the book of Rules and contribution card to be held by every member, to be shown to a union official upon demand, and a list of members over six weeks in arrears was to be posted up in the branch room. A new branch could be formed by 60 or more workers and branches could have up to 1,000 members.

Foremen, employers, mastermen, or anyone managing a pub or beer-shop were not eligible to hold office in the union and no meeting was to be held in any place where intoxicants are sold when other places are obtainable at reasonable rates.

A system of fines like that which we saw with the 1825 unions was adopted to maintain discipline among these formerly unorganised workers. Swearing or using bad language at union meetings incurred a fine of 2s 6d, 5s fine and expulsion from room for persistent bad behaviour. Insulting language 20s, divulging union business 2s 6d, insulting an official, 2s 6d, striking another member in the branch room 5s, upbraiding another member outside the union's rooms 1s per offence.

The Branch Secretary was liable for particularly stiff fines and could be removed from office if their conduct was deemed unsatisfactory. The Branch Secretary was paid 5% of all money collected from the members, which was to be shared 50–50 with any Collectors used by the Secretary to collect Union dues.

The Branch Doorkeeper must admit only members on presentation of Contribution Card, and no member "who is the worse for drink." The Branch also elected a Chairman, Branch Auditors, Trades Council Delegates and District Committeemen.

Branches were organised in districts and the District Committee had the "fullest powers of local autonomy subject only to these Rules. ...but under no circumstances shall bye-laws be allowed." Candidates in any election supported by the Union must be members and not connected in any way with the Liberal, Unionist or Conservative Party.

The District Secretary was elected annually by ballot of all members in the District and was subject to dismissal on a month's notice. The District Committee sent delegates to an Executive Committee which met quarterly in London and elected a full-time General Secretary. An Emergency Committee, comprised of the London Delegates, who met with the General Secretary, was empowered to deal with emergencies. Executive Councilmen were fined for lateness or absence from meetings.

The General Secretary and two national organisers were elected annually by a ballot of all members. The Gen. Sec. salary was £186 p.a., the two Organisers £2 10s p.w. Districts with more than 500 members could hire their own paid officials.

All members could have access to the Union's books.

The only two exceptions to decision by simple majority were the 2/3 support required for an amalgamation with another union, and the usual 5/6 required to dissolve the union.

In summary, the Dockers Union was able to implement the kind of structure which Alexander Kilham had wanted for the Methodist Church and which the Chartists had been prevented from building by the State – a Union open to everyone, however poor and disenfranchised, everyone equal, in control of their own Union, access its books, hiring and firing their own officials and making their own decisions on the basis of majoritarianism.

The Workers' Union was founded in 1898, later merging into the Transport and General Workers' Union (TGWU), with about 100,000 members remaining to transfer. Its rulebook reflected the same universalist approach as the Dockers Union as did other general unions founded in this period.

That these general unions were instrumental in raising the living standards of the mass of working class people in Britain over the following century is incontestable. It was not just that this most downtrodden section of the population stood up for itself, but by doing so, they established *universal* rights which were and are still enjoyed by everyone, thus raising the entire level of culture. Essential to this achievement was the majoritarian ethos for which every individual person had an equal voice through which their moral equality was guaranteed.

It is important to recognise that the Rules outlined above, based on Majority, did not only manage personal and episodic differences within the union, but over generations, managed the conflict between opposing social and political currents within the working class and therefore within the union. Thanks to Majority, union members act as one despite often deep political and ideological differences within their own ranks. Respect for the majority and protection of the minority at any given moment is the sine qua non for working class unity in the class struggle. The archetype of the Majority decision in a trade union is not the election of a delegate, but a strike vote. Strike votes are invariably the culmination of exhaustive discussion, but nothing is more alien to the workers' movement than the idea that compliance with a strike vote is a matter of individual conscience. Once the question is put to the vote, Majority decides. Anything else spells the end for a trade union and the working conditions of their members.

As remarked above, beginning from the end of the Chartist period, the labour movement began to fragment, not just because of the political barrier the British government erected against universal, national, democratic organisation, but because of *changes in the labour process itself.* As a result, by the end of World War One, when many social rights were achieved, the labour movement itself was divided between rival parties and factions. This placed insuperable barriers to the realisation of the majoritarian ethos, even though formal political equality was achieved in the form of universal suffrage. Everyone was an equal participant in the political process, but the political state was subordinated to a civil society in which capital ruled. To understand the problems that affected the labour movement and its majoritarian ethos, it is necessary to take a brief detour into the developments on the international arena during the first half of the twentieth century.

The End of Uncritical Majoritarianism

The great strikes which created the general unions in Britain coincided with a revival of economic activity and worker militancy across the world and opened the way for a Second International. Initiated by Marx's supporters to continue the work of the First International, the Second International was based in *national* Social-Democratic political parties, including the British Labour Party, organised around programs as governments-in-waiting, able to contest Parliamentary elections, when legally possible, as well as organise economic and political struggles of the working masses. If the workers' movement was to assume leadership of the whole people, as Marx had prefigured, then it would have to be organised on a national basis, however internationalist its policy.

Socialists had not however fully grasped the implications of the fragmentation which had affected the working class during the latter part of the nineteenth century. Socialist leaders, such as Karl Kautsky, anticipated the ever-increasing size of the proletariat, its ever-growing militancy and organisation, alongside the continued concentration of capital in the hands of great corporations and the eradication of petty-capital, inevitably leading to a polarisation which would place the social democrats in a position to form a government and implement the socialist program with overwhelming numbers on their side.

> We consider the breakdown of the present social system to be unavoidable, because we know that the economic evolution inevitably brings on conditions that will *compel* the exploited classes to rise against this system of private ownership. We know that this system multiplies the number and the strength of the exploited, and diminishes the number and strength of the exploiting, classes, and that it will finally lead to such unbearable conditions for the mass of the population that they will have no choice but to go down into degradation or to overthrow the system of private property.
>
> KAUTSKY, 1892

Engels expressed much the same sentiment in an interview with *Le Figaro* in 1893 (*MECW* vol. 27, p. 543). Not only would economic forces fashion the modern working class and *compel* it to make revolution, they thought there was no need for the working class to seek alliances with other non-proletarian parties or classes.

© KONINKLIJKE BRILL NV, LEIDEN, 2016 | DOI 10.1163/9789004319639_012

> If there is one thing that will rob us of the confidence of all the honest el-
> ements among the masses and that will gain us the contempt of all strata
> of the proletariat ready and willing to fight, that will bar the road to our
> progress, then it is participation by Social Democracy in any bloc policy.
> KAUTSKY, 1909

The most successful social democratic parties, like the German SPD, were the head and heart of a vast social movement which provided education, entertainment, social security, police and legal services to their members and produced great art and literature. It would be wrong to see them as ruling over, dictating to or parasitic off the social movement, because they were themselves its most perfect expression. Kautsky saw no reason to reach out beyond the ranks of the proletariat.

A further change was also overtaking the composition of the working class towards the end of the 19th century, this time on the international plane: the introduction of modern manufacturing plant into countries such as Russia, where there had not already grown up an indigenous bourgeoisie and proletariat, and where the peasantry remained the majority of the people. Also, in countries like Italy where capitalism was endemic, but with large, backward agricultural sectors, leaving the working class in a permanent structural minority. So Kautsky's program of refusing all blocs, and relying solely on the proletariat, became untenable. The proletariat would *not* be pushed into leading the nation to socialism by the action of economic forces alone and *could not* do so solely by relying on their own ranks.

Matters were further complicated with the rise of Fordism in the United States. The truism that the lower the wages you paid, the longer the hours your workers worked and the higher the price you charged for your product, the bigger would be your profits, was turned inside out by Ford who deliberately paid his workers more, gave them shorter hours and sold his cars for less. His highly profitable revolution transformed the world, and also transformed the character and composition of the working class. Fordism created a solid core of the organised working class which enjoyed access to cheap commodities and were not interested in political change.

These changes presaged the end of *uncritical majoritarianism*. No longer could it be taken for granted that the oppressed masses constituted the majority, all sharing the same interests as against a minority of exploiters. Women, or the labouring masses of the East, for example, had in the past presented problems of outreach, but not political and programmatic challenges. Now, the social and ethical basis of the outlook represented by Kautsky's program, and the forms of organisation that went with it, was gone. Any appeal to the rights of the majority was now rendered problematic, and the rights of the working class now appeared as particular rather than universal.

These changes in the labour process transformed social democracy itself. The party of Kautsky ceased to be part of a social movement, and was institutionalised in the bourgeois democratic government of Germany, a fate which had already befallen many leaders of the First International in Britain, and would characterise later 20th century Social Democracy generally. The trade union leadership joined those new layers of workers created by Taylorism as part of the administrative apparatus of capitalism.

The Russian Social Democratic Labour Party differed somewhat from its partners, as a result of working under conditions of illegality, within a young working class surrounded by a mass of peasantry. The privileges on offer to the leaders of British trade unions were not available to the leaders of Russian social democracy. When, on the eve of the Revolution, Lenin proclaimed the "April Theses," (1917a) we see a classical social democratic vision, a direct expression of the ideals which had inspired the Paris Commune – "Abolition of the police, the army and the bureaucracy. The salaries of all officials, all of whom are elective and displaceable at any time, not to exceed the average wage of a competent worker, etc." A Supreme Soviet was set up in the wake of the February 1917 Revolution, and despite being in a minority in the Soviets, the Bolsheviks agitated for the Soviets to form a government and overthrow the Provisional Government of Kerensky. Thanks chiefly to the leadership of the Bolsheviks, this came to pass. But unlike the Paris Commune, the Soviet Republic was not overthrown after two months, and as the social movement which had made the revolution ebbed, its leaders took on administrative roles in the Soviet Government.

The Soviet Government rested on the Soviets, or workers' councils, and the echoes of them in Soldiers Soviets and Peasant Soviets. As is well-known, after an exhausting and devastating civil war in which the leaders of the workers movement suffered terrible losses and the Soviet Union was wracked by famine and disease, blockaded by the West and under attack from all sides, the Soviet government degenerated into a centralized administrative apparatus.

At the same time, they did inspire support from workers all over the world, and through the Communist International, founded in 1919, Communist Parties were created in every country, competing with the parties of the Second International for the loyalties of the working class.

Collective decision making procedures in the Soviet Union and in the Communist International remained formally majoritarian, but in reality had degenerated into the worst form of top-down line management. This cannot be seen as in any sense an outcome of the majoritarian ethos itself. The majoritarian ethos carries with it the right of a minority to express its view, conditional upon the acceptance by the minority that the view of the majority will carry the day. Indeed, the struggle between opposing political parties in the working class continued to be effectively regulated within the trade unions by Majority.

The sickness which affected the Soviet Union was not majoritarianism, but an *intolerance* towards the manifestation of any minority view, that is to say, *enforced consensus*.

Europe between the Wars

The socialist ideal had been awoken in a proletariat convinced that capitalism could only swell the ranks of the exploited, and confident that solidarity could secure a better future. But the world had changed. I will briefly review the issues posed by these changes, and the methods of organisation devised to respond to them, through the ideas of Lenin, Luxemburg and Gramsci.

Lenin had a somewhat 'algebraic' formula, throughout the years leading up to the October 1917 Revolution, for the relationship between the future dictatorship of the proletariat and the peasantry, loosely talking about a "the revolutionary-democratic dictatorship of the proletariat and the peasantry," (1905) or "an alliance between the workers and the working and exploited peasants" (1917), but once the Revolution happened, he described it as a "dictatorship of the proletariat which *led* the peasantry behind it" (1921). By expropriating the landlords, bearing the greatest sacrifices in the Civil War and providing industrial products which the peasants needed, the workers made it worthwhile for the peasantry to support the Revolution. That is, Lenin proposed that the revolution be based on a *class alliance* in which one class played the leading role due to its unique social position in being able to overthrow the "general stumbling block," and resolve the problems of the entire nation. This was in line with the general formula which Marx (1843, p. 184; 1845, pp. 60–61) had outlined, but posed in conditions not anticipated by Marx.

Rosa Luxemburg was the first to warn of Kautsky's error in waiting for economic forces to prepare the conditions for socialism. Proletarian self-consciousness was not fully formed in the economic struggle, but required political and ideological *formation* and this had to be a specific element of the socialist programme. Luxemburg shared Kautsky's conviction that the working class would make the revolution alone, but challenged Lenin's conception of a party able to represent and *direct* the class struggle on its behalf, constantly emphasising the self-organising capacity of the working class on the one hand and political and ideological direction of the social democratic party on the other.

Antonio Gramsci was the first to theorise the new political landscape, adapting the concept of *hegemony*. Like Luxemburg, Gramsci rejected Kautsky's politics of class *representation* for a politics of *class formation*. Gramsci welcomed the Russian Revolution in 1917 as a break from an economic-determinist conception of history, but at the same time criticised Luxemburg for underestimating the depth of the defences of bourgeois society, likening it to the trenches of contemporary warfare, against which a frontal assault was foolhardy.

In his understanding of the concept of *hegemony*, Gramsci recognised that the entry of the broad masses into political life of the nation required specifically political and ideological struggle to win them over and integrate them. Specific mechanisms were required to extend and concretise the class alliances first elaborated in Lenin's policy of a class alliance between the working class and the peasantry.

> The proletariat can become the leading and the dominant class to the extent that it succeeds in creating a system of class alliances which allows it to mobilize the majority of the working population against capitalism and the bourgeois state.
>
> GRAMSCI, 1926

The concept of hegemony is essentially as proposed by Lenin and indeed just what it meant in ancient Greece: one class plays the role of hegemon, wielding overall power, in exchange for the absolute support of other powers, and achieves this by delivering to the other powers a share of the proceeds of power. What Gramsci proposed was a *counter-hegemony* led by a proletariat which addressed itself to the problems of sections of the population currently in the camp of the bourgeoisie.

These suggestions were the first steps in trying to resolve the problem presented by the crisis of majoritarianism.

The differentiation which had been introduced into the working class by changes in the political economy, would now be aggravated by the political rivalry between the Parties of the Socialist International and those of the Communist International. The problems arising from this rivalry came to a head in the 1930s.

The Front

The 1930s saw the emergence of a new social formation, the Front. The Front could claim to speak for the majority, while one or two or more political parties were actively promoting and directing the activity of the movement, and competing for allegiance, and cooperating on the basis of agreements made *between the party leaders*. The term 'front' implied a kind of façade presenting a unity to the world, behind which tactical differences were talked through.

There were competing concepts of the Front. Trotsky's definition of the 'United Front' is based on a *public* agreement between the leaders:

> No common platform with the Social Democracy, or with the leaders of the German trade unions, no common publications, banners, placards! *March separately, but strike together!* Agree only how to strike, whom to strike, and when to strike! Such an agreement can be concluded even with the devil himself, with his grandmother, and even with Noske and Grezesinsky. On one condition, not to bind one's hands.
>
> TROTSKY, 1931

But this ideal was very rarely achieved, and then only briefly. By contrast, the Comintern's later Popular Front policy aimed at uniting everyone to the right of the Communist Party but to the Left of Fascism, based on a *secret* pact between the leaders. Trotsky criticised this policy in the following terms:

> The political alliance between the proletariat and the bourgeoisie, whose interests on basic questions in the present epoch diverge at an angle of 180 degrees, as a general rule is capable only of paralysing the revolutionary force of the proletariat.
>
> TROTSKY, 1938

The so-called "united front from below" (Dimitrov, 1935) was just a polemical device by means of which one party leadership appealed to the ranks of another party over the heads of its own leaders, with the aim of subduing the opposing party.

It became common practice for the Party to submerge its identity altogether in the Front. The Front was then not so much a means for broadening the social movement but of gathering a periphery around the Party while the Party leadership remained behind the scenes. The Front was a failed attempt to respond to social movements following the changes that had taken place in the labour process and the resulting divisions within the working masses, a failure which flowed directly from the degeneration of the Soviet Union which spread to every country through its impact on the parties of the Comintern.

As the world descended into the hell of World War Two, the majoritarian ethos still held sway among the working masses. Even under German occupation and in the immediate wake of the War, workers in Europe still organized their Councils using the traditional methods of Majority voting and elected delegates to central committees. But the meaning of the principle of Majority had become corrupted by internal differentiation within the working class and the masses generally – economic differentiation separating relatively privileged workers from the poor, national differentiation separating the workers in the imperialist countries from the colonial masses, political differentiation separating workers loyal to rival factions within the workers' movement, and social differentiation separating the bureaucracies administering the workers' movement and the Soviet Union from the mass of ordinary union members or Soviet citizens.

Majoritarianism did not provide any guidance for the resolution of these contradictions. We turn now to an investigation of the origins of Consensus and this line of enquiry will later return us to the Post World War Two conjuncture.

PART 2

Consensus

∴

During the twenty years I spent in England, I was involved in labour movement organisations and a left-wing political group, and never during that time came across consensus decision making (Consensus). It was only after I returned to Australia in 1986, and began reading more widely, that I first read about Consensus. The book was "Resource Manual for a Living Revolution. A handbook of skills & tools for social change activists," (Coover et al, 1977) published by the Movement for a New Society. Most of the material – group bonding exercises, role playing games and so on, which seemed to me like mind control techniques, and ideas for planning campaigns and so on, which looked like corporate management techniques to me, was quite unattractive. However, the short section on Consensus seemed eminently useful. But because no-one I knew had ever read such material, it went nowhere. Participation in some student campaigns at the University of Melbourne exposed me to some of these methods in practice, but being a staff member and over 40, I was an outsider in these campaigns and was never comfortable with the group hugs and so on.

It was in 1992 that Consensus entered my life. The small Trotskyist group of which I was a member at that time took an initiative to establish "Socialist Alliance" (SA). SA was to unite all the left-wing groups in Melbourne into an Alliance for the purpose of coordination and mutual support in the various campaigns and discussions towards mutual clarification. It was never the idea that it would become a new party, but the crisis created by the collapse of the Soviet Union had created opportunities for overcoming past animosities.

The aim was to bring the range of small Trotskyist groups together with the anarchists and Stalinists. The Stalinists refused to participate from the outset, but for a while we had a group of anarchists participating along with all the Trotskyist groups. There was discussion about the role SA was to play and its constitution. The anarchists proposed that decisions should be made by Consensus. This made abundant sense to me, because it was blindingly obvious that as soon as any one of the participating groups were to be out-voted on a matter of principle they would simply withdraw from the project. All the Trotskyist groups had their own organisations, generally including a regular magazine and their own network of interstate and international affiliates; SA for its part offered absolutely nothing other than the opportunity to cooperate with the other participants, none of whom were potential recruits for anyone. Furthermore, in terms of interpretations of history, we all had great differences with each other, even if, in day-today political activity we all tended to do the same things. Also, the meetings of SA were effectively delegates meetings; that is, the participating organisations sent different numbers of delegates to these meetings according to their level of interest in the project. A vote taken in an SA meeting would be meaningless.

So I argued that the SA should be based on two principles: That all decisions (1) must be made on the basis of consensus, and (2) were binding on all participants. Consensus was necessary because only a decision to which a delegate had consented could have any binding force on them, whatever we wrote in the rulebook, and binding decisions were necessary because 'non-binding decision' is not a decision at all. By making clear that decisions were binding meant that only those decisions which genuinely expressed a consensus would ever be made.

To my dismay both (1) and (2) were rejected by all the Marxists and (2) was rejected by the anarchists. I was quite unable to convince any of the participants of either principle and the anarchists soon stopped participating.

The Marxists' hostility was equally strong in relation to both principles. Many argued that they had had enough of 'democratic centralism' which they associated with top-down direction by the Party leadership and the suppression of internal dissent, and were not going to have anything to do with binding decisions. It quickly transpired that, in fact, nothing the SA ever decided was ever carried out.

Hostility to Consensus was expressed by the claim that decisions could never be made because differences between participants were so great that a consensus could never be found. This was demonstrated by obstinate refusal to consent to Consensus. It seemed to me at the time that opposition to Consensus was not genuinely based on practical considerations – it was an irrational hostility to a principle which was foreign to the labour movement. I might just as well have proposed that voting should be based on a property qualification. Once majority voting and non-binding decisions were adopted as norms, SA rapidly folded.

In 2001, delegates from the various Trotskyist groups again met and established a Socialist Alliance that would have included many of the same people that had participated briefly in the earlier Socialist Alliance. The aim of this formation was to provide an electoral front to allow the Left groups to register and participate in elections. A platform was readily agreed 'in committee' by simply omitting areas where the affiliates disagreed. Despite the objective being limited to electoral work, the SA provided a pole of attraction for activists who did not want to join any of the affiliates; individuals were allowed to join side-by-side with affiliated organisations, and by 2003, when the activity and strength of the SA was at its peak, SA was controlled by branches, in which delegates from affiliates simply functioned as individual members alongside others.

The SA always adhered to Majority voting for decision making, though this functioned effectively as a form of Consensus. 'Binding decisions' would have been rejected here as well, should it ever have been raised, because this would have been interpreted as obliging members to actively and publicly support policies with which they did not agree, even though they had no objection to others doing so.

The most contentious decisions would involve the drafting of flyers and electoral documents, which would be done in committee, avoiding contentious issues, and members were free to set up an 'interest group' or 'task force', effectively affinity groups, in which they could work with other SA members of like mind, provided they didn't do anything under the SA banner which others would find positively offensive. They could also cooperate outside the SA banner. On rare occasions when an affiliate would propose an action which was objectionable to other affiliates, the proposal would be withdrawn rather than pressing the point. Differing points of view were tolerated then on the basis of laissez faire, rather than attempting to achieve consensus.

Over time, the superior ability of the two main affiliates, and then just one of the affiliates to provide resources and activists to the SA led to that one affiliate effectively controlling SA, and SA becoming more 'majoritarian' as the views of minorities on any question were given less and less attention by a majority which owed loyalty to the program of an affiliated organisation. The SA went into decline and is currently simply a Front for one of its original affiliates to offer 'part-time' membership.

My next encounter with Consensus was in 2000 at the protest at the World Economic Forum held on 11–13 September that year, known as S11 and modelled on the events the previous year in Seattle. It was the anarchists who had taken the initiative to organise this event and mass meetings were being held to plan the protest for many months leading up to the day. The anarchists were by far the majority in these planning meetings and decided on the agenda and norms for these at their own meeting held elsewhere beforehand, so a fully developed form of Consensus predominated at all the planning meetings. The various socialist groups participated by sending delegates to the planning meetings and thanks to their participation there was a substantial participation by the trade union movement.

While Consensus was accepted as the norm for the large planning meetings it was very clear that this event was an alliance between two parties – the young anarchists who used Consensus and the labour movement (i.e., the socialist groups and the trade unions) who operated by majority vote. All the labour movement participants learnt how to work within the norm of Consensus, but it was always clear that neither side was comfortable with the modus operandi of the other. Throughout the planning, the event itself and the discussions which took place in the months following, this mutual antipathy, though contained, was evident. So long as everything went according to plan, Consensus worked fine.

It was as a result of this experience that I became interested in the question as to when and under what conditions is one or another combination of Consensus and Majority appropriate, and as a step towards understanding this question: what was the origin of Consensus?

At that time, I made a presumption which turned out to be quite mistaken. It was obvious that Consensus had come to Australia from the US. Given what I had read in the *Resource Manual* I presumed (correctly as it happened) that it had come via the Peace Movement in the U.S., but where did the Peace Movement get it from? I was familiar with the work of Kurt Lewin in the interwar years and his involvement in coping with inter-communal tensions in American cities. I was also familiar with the work of John Dewey on "group cognition" and his study of problem-solving groups. I had also read the work of Jane Addams in Chicago and her work in conflict resolution. I presumed that the neighbourhood organising work in which these and people like Saul Alinsky (1971) had been involved had been the origin of Consensus.

This turned out to be quite wrong. None of these writers had developed a theory of Consensus. Jane Addams' approach as expressed in "Democracy and Social Ethics," (1902) is not at all concerned to modify the mechanics of the political democracy of America, but rather to attend to the social conditions which allow political democracy to be perverted. Likewise, in his political writings, John Dewey opposed laissez faire capitalism and the individualist ideology which underpinned it, but did not advocate for or against Majority or Consensus. Kurt Lewin's study of decision making in small groups was predicated on the leadership of a facilitator. He agreed that the 'democratic leader' would seek consensus in a group, as opposed to the laissez faire leader or the autocratic leader, but he never considered Consensus as a formal procedure. Saul Alinsky was not a consensus person either. Everything written in this genre was based on the model of *a professional organiser/facilitator and a group to be organised.*

For example, The Adams Morgan Demonstration Project, administered by American University, would have been informed by all the latest theories of conflict resolution and collective decision making. It was an effort to stimulate community development in a Washington D.C. housing project in 1958, in which Eleanor Garst (who I will come to later) was employed as a Community Organiser. But the community was encouraged to make all its decisions by majority voting. If Consensus had been developed in neighbourhood organising then it would certainly have been considered for this high-profile project. Nonetheless, the US in the 1950s seemed to be the place to look, given its evident embrace by the US Peace Movement. I noted in fact that the word "majoritarianism" had entered language as a pejorative only in 1950. So I turned to the *Resource Manual* and checked up on the biographies of the authors, and while I was at it, I checked the biographies of other notable figures in the American Peace Movement.

Of the authors of the *Resource Manual*, Ellen Deacon was a Methodist who converted to Quakerism in the 1960s, Chuck Esser and Chris Moore-Backman were Quakers, and members of the Movement for a New Society, which had published the *Resource Manual*. MNS was founded in 1971 by George Lakey who was a Quaker, Bill Moyer who was not a Quaker but acknowledges that he learnt nonviolence from the Quakers in 1966, Lawrence Scott converted to Quakerism in 1939, and George Willoughby was a Quaker. Civil Rights leader Howard Thurman studied under the Quaker Rufus Jones. Looking through other figures in the Peace Movement I found that Joan Baez's family converted to Quakerism while she was a child, Howard Brinton was a Quaker, and the leader of the 1963 March on Washington, Bayard Rustin, was a Quaker, as was his mentor, the one-time Trotskyist, A.J. Muste. Muste converted to the Quakers in 1918 and became a Trotskyist in 1933 and from 1940 to 1953 was executive director of the Fellowship Of Reconciliation, an international Peace organisation which united Lutherans, Quakers and others to work for Peace during the Second World War. Later I found that Julian Bond, one of the Atlanta students who attended the training course in nonviolence run by James Lawson in 1959 attended a Quaker prep. school, and Quakers Dr. Nelson Fuson and his wife, Marian had some connection with the Highlander School. The anarchist writer Andrew Cornell in fact credits the Movement for a New Society, successor to the Quaker Action Group, as the source of Consensus for American anarchists of the post-1968 generation.

This suggested that Quakers may have been the source of Consensus, but it was not decisive. With the assistance of Jo Freeman, who was an activist in the 1960s, I was able to make contact by email with a number of people who were activists in the early 1960s and before. Asking people to recall the circumstances under which they first came across Consensus, I was led back to two distinct moments at which it was introduced into the Peace Movement and Civil Rights Movement in the US in 1959–61.

I arrived at two names: *James Lawson* who introduced Consensus to the Civil Rights Movement in 1959 and *Eleanor Garst* in 1961, who independently introduced Consensus into the Peace Movement in 1961; Garst was a Quaker convert and although a Methodist, as a Conscientious Objector Lawson had had contact with the Quakers. There is a third figure, *Myles Horton*, but his name did not surface till later.

Although Quakers are strongly implicated in the introduction of Consensus to social change activism in the US in the 1960s, the most prominent coalitions in which they collaborated with non-Quakers – the Fellowship Of Reconciliation (FOR) and the Draft Resistors' League – are not mentioned by *anyone* as locations where Consensus was practised. Also, most of the people who figured in the introduction of Consensus to the wider movement were ex-Quakers or Quaker converts, rather than people who had been raised as Quakers.

I will return to 1959–61, but I had formed the view that it was the Quakers who were the origin of Consensus in the Peace and Civil Rights Movements (both of which significantly predate the Student Protest and the Women's Liberation Movements). So at this point I terminated my search back from the present, and went back to the English Revolution to find the origins of the Quakers and their decision making process, before returning to the Peace and Civil Rights movements in the 1950s and '60s.

English Revolution and the Quakers[1]

The Quaker method of making decisions takes us back to the origins of the Quakers themselves and the conditions which led them to develop their procedure for making decisions. The Quakers have their origins in the aftermath of English Revolution of 1642–1649. This same Revolution was the birthplace of modern ideas of egalitarianism and the rights of the individual which are in play whenever a group of people discuss collective action, so we should widen our lens somewhat to look at the range of ideas about collective decision making which appeared during the Revolution, and how the Quakers resolved problems arising from these ideas.

After this historical excursus, I shall follow Quaker decision making to modern-day America and how the Quakers see what we call Consensus.

The English Revolution

Civil War broke out in England in 1642 when the king entered the House of Commons accompanied by 400 soldiers to arrest five members of Parliament. Parliament refused to give them up and the country rapidly descended into civil war and a New Model Army was raised by Cromwell to fight for Parliament against the king's forces.

The population of England expanded rapidly during the 16th and 17th centuries, while arable land remained locked up for the benefit of the gentry. London became a refuge for victims of enclosure, vagabonds and criminals. Discontent was rife, bitterness and contempt for the nobility was all-pervasive, exacerbated by the royal obsession with costly military adventures. The economic hardships of the years 1620 to 1650 were among the most terrible in English history. By 1640, censorship and the authority of both government and Church had completely broken down.

The growth of a stratum of people without land or master had given birth to guilds in late Anglo-Saxon England. The continuing growth of trade, urbanization and technical innovation had in turn gradually eroded the authority of the guilds, and it was now undermining the stability of the entire kingdom, its economy and its system of rule.

---

1 A principal source for this section is Hill, C. (1975). *The World Turned Upside Down: Radical Ideas During the English Revolution.*

Beneath the stability of rural England, then, the vast placid open fields which catch the eye, was the seething mobility of forest squatters, itinerant craftsmen and building labourers, unemployed men and women seeking work, strolling players and jugglers, pedlars and quack doctors, vagabonds, tramps: congregated especially in London and the big cities, but also with footholds wherever newly-squatted areas escaped from the machinery of the parish or in old-squatted areas where labour was in demand.

> HILL, 1972, p. 39

Widespread economic distress, the breakdown of social support as well as law and order, the end of censorship, giving rise to an outpouring of political and religious pamphlets, inflamed political and religious dissent among the large mass of individuals who were no longer tied to any plot of land nor owed allegiance to any master. The king was losing control of the land and the Church had lost control of the people's souls. The Puritans, who no longer looked to the church for moral guidance, could only look into their own heart or to their local preacher to know what was right.

Not only was the growing number of masterless forest-dwellers and slum-dwellers undermining England's political economy – it was also nourishing the growth of Puritan religious consciousness and was to fill the ranks of the New Model Army.

The Levellers and the New Model Army[2]

The New Model Army was no mere mercenary army; it was the common people in uniform, moving back and forth across England for a decade overturning the power of the local landowners and the royalist clergy, and stimulating political discussion under conditions in which every utopian dream seemed to be a real possibility. Free discussion within the ranks of the Army itself led to a rapid development of political ideas.

In these times, political discussion was inseparable from the religious questions which were the subject of passionate debate, and indeed, for the majority, the religious problems would have been primary, as political principles were derivative from religious principles.

The numerous religious sects were strongest in the towns, where religious communities provided comfort for itinerant and displaced people, including

---

2 My principal source for this section is Baker, P. (2007). Ed. *The Levellers. The Putney Debates*, including an introduction by Geoffrey Robinson.

poor relief and all manner of social support. Here voluntary ties were formed on the basis of shared religious sensibilities which rejected the need for any mediator between the individual person and God. Meanwhile, itinerant preachers were subject to the same harsh penalties for vagrancy as any tinker, unemployed tradesman or beggar. These were the social strata which signed up to fight the king, and as soldiers in the New Model Army, the boot was on the other foot.

The leaders of the Army – Oliver Cromwell, Henry Ireton and Sir Thomas Fairfax – did not share the political perspectives which came to be widely embraced by the soldiers, but they did share many of the religious precepts which underlay the democratic political ideals that the soldiers were developing. That soldiers could be and were convicted of offences, even including *lèse majesté*, committed while acting under orders during the Civil War, illustrates the social gulf separating the rank and file from their generals. The world had never before seen such a politically self-conscious army as this one; the soldiers knew what they were fighting for even better than their generals, and the New Model Army soon began to inflict defeats over numerically superior Royalist forces staffed by professional soldiers and the military elite.

Cromwell did not set out to dethrone Charles I, far less put him to death. After Charles had surrendered in June 1646, he was allowed to remain free while Cromwell 'negotiated' with him. Keeping in mind that, as a proportion of the population of England, twice as many people had died in the civil war as would die during the first world war, this refusal to deal decisively with the enemy was intolerable for the soldiers. At the end of March 1647, the rank and file took matters into their own hands calling on their officers "to go along with us in this business, or at least to let us quietly alone in this our design."[3] The troops elected Agitators, two for each regiment, starting with the cavalry, and by the middle of May, "every soldier gave four pence apiece" towards the expenses of meetings. The troops wore a red ribbon on their left arms, as a symbol of solidarity till death.

The Agitators called on Fairfax to order a general rendezvous, otherwise, "we…shall be necessitated…to do such things ourselves," a warning which the Army leadership took seriously and acted upon. On 3 June 1647, the day before the rendezvous, on a plan initiated by the Agitators without the authority of Cromwell, Joyce, a junior non-commissioned officer and "a party of horse sent from the committee of troopers" arrested the king.

It was this situation that gave rise to the Putney Debates, in which elected representatives of the soldiers, the Agitators, debated with the generals

---

3   *An Apologie of the soldiers to all their Commissioned Officers*, anon, 1647, cited in Hill 1972,
    p. 49.

in what was called the Army Council. The Agitators presented their arguments in a series of pamphlets which they had printed in large number in London, and circulated widely among the troops and citizens. At stake was the form of government to be instituted by the Army following their victory over the king.

The term 'Leveller' was invented by their opponents to describe the political sentiment which permeated the New Model Army and spoke through its elected Agitators. They were not 'levellers' in the sense of being advocates of economic levelling, but they were consistent advocates of a thoroughgoing *political* egalitarianism based on universal adult-male suffrage. While a much wider program is reflected in their manifestos published at Putney – an end to the monarchy, complete freedom of religion and an end to all tithes, annual parliaments, reform of the judicial and education systems which discriminated against the poor – the debate with Cromwell and his generals never got past their demand for one-man-one-vote. The Levellers reasoned that since the state had broken down, a state of nature existed and military force could justly be used only to hand power back to the people, from whom it had been stolen by William the Conqueror and his heirs. Although the Levellers had no shortage of supporters amongst the civilian population, and indeed some of the Agitators were civilians, the Levellers essentially expressed the political aspirations of the rank and file of the New Model Army. All the dissident religious sects of the period were represented within the ranks of the Levellers: Everard the Digger, and the Quakers James Nayler and William Dewsbery among them, and probably John Bunyan.

Charles I was executed on January 30 1649, but in April/May 1649, the Leveller leaders were arrested, and the radical regiments provoked into an unsuccessful mutiny, which was crushed at Burford leaving Cromwell in undisputed power. Army democracy was finished, and so were the Levellers.

We have no record of the discussions which led to the formulation of the Leveller demands and the election of the Agitators. Notwithstanding the bewildering diversity of religious views, all the religious sects supported the political program of the Levellers, which after all, expressed nothing more than the basic principles underlying bourgeois democratic society today, even if more honoured in the breach than in observance.

Although we have no record of the camp-fire discussions which formulated this program, much of the formal debate at the Army Council between the Agitators on one side and Cromwell, Ireton and Fairfax on the other was recorded verbatim. The aim was to come to an agreement on the form of the new government, but the debate could not get past the Levellers' demand for universal adult male suffrage, with the Generals continuing to insist on the vote being restricted to property-owners.

In the immortal words of Colonel Thomas Rainborough:

> For really I think that the poorer he that is in England has a life to live, as
> the greatest he; and therefore truly, sir, I think it's clear, that every man
> that is to live under a government ought first by his own consent to put
> himself under that government; and I do think that the poorest man in
> England is not at all bound in a strict sense to the government that he
> has not had a voice to put himself under; and I am confident that, when
> I have heard the reasons against it, something will be said to answer those
> reasons, in so much that I should doubt whether he was an Englishman
> or no, that should doubt of these things.
>
> BAKER, 2007, P. 69

The Levellers compromised on this point, eventually granting that those of
weak mind or in prison should not have the vote and finally conceding that
beggars and servants should not vote, on the basis that they were not *independent*. However, Ireton and the others continued to insist on a property qualification and no progress was made beyond this point. Facing an impasse, General Ireton said:

> I am agreed with you if you insist upon a more equal distribution of elec-
> tions; I will agree with you, not only to dispute for it, but to fight for it
> and contend for it. Thus far I agree with you. On the other hand, to those
> who differ in their terms and say, 'I will not agree with you except you go
> farther', I make the answer, 'This far I can go with you: I will go with you
> as far as I can'. If you will appoint a committee of some few to consider of
> that, so as you preserve the equitable part of that constitution that now
> is, securing a voice to those who are like to be freemen, men not given up
> to the will of others, and thereby keeping to the latitude which is the eq-
> uity of constitutions, I will go with you as far as I can. And where I cannot
> I will sit down, I will not make any disturbance among you.
>
> BAKER, 2007, P. 91

Ireton thus raises the *paradox of the status quo* in which one partner consents
to the status quo but the other does not, and the status quo is taken to be the
default position in the event of failure to agree. This is a paradox because consensus is pre-empted by the status quo. Thomas Rainborough responded:

> But the end wherefore I speak is only this: you think we shall be worse
> than we are, if we come to a conclusion by a sudden vote. If it be put to

the question we shall at least know one another's mind. If it be determined, and the common resolution known, we shall take such a course
as to put it in execution. This gentleman says, if he cannot go he will sit
still. He thinks he has a full liberty to do so; we think we have not. There is
a great deal of difference between us two. If a man has all he does desire,
he may wish to sit still; but I think I have nothing at all of what I fight for,
I do not think the argument holds that I must desist as well as he.

> BAKER, 2007, PP. 91–92.

The question was ultimately resolved in the Generals' favour by force. And our
review of collective decision making procedures has to encompass this situation: sometimes there is simply no agreement, and if the status quo is not in
itself an agreed position, and the default position is the status quo, then there
is no justice. No vote, no amount of discussion or communal prayer could have
persuaded Cromwell and Ireton to concede. However, it is evident that Cromwell took the debate seriously and negotiated in good faith at the time.

One important fact which comes through in the debates at Putney is that
the soldiers and their generals shared the conviction that their victory against
the monarchy which had ruled England since the Norman Conquest was solely
thanks to the fact that God was acting through them, that they were the instrument of Divine will. So it is not surprising that they saw their debates in
the same terms, that is, that when they spoke at the Army Council, *God spoke
through them*, and a resolution to the debate, if achieved, would express the
Divine will.

Accordingly, at Cromwell's suggestion, each session of the debate was pref-
aced by a morning spent in silent prayer, "to seek the guidance of God, and to
recover that presence of God that seems to withdraw from us."

In the last recorded session of the debate on 29 October 1647, Cromwell said:

> Truly we have heard many speaking to us, and I cannot but think that in
> many of those things God has spoke to us. I cannot but think that in most
> that have spoke there has been something of God laid forth to us, and
> yet there has been several contradictions in what has been spoken. But
> certainly God is not the author of contradictions. The contradictions are
> not so much in the end as in the way. I cannot see but that we all speak to
> the same end, and mistakes are only in the way.
>
> BAKER, P. 100

So if God is speaking through us, and since we all share the same end, how can
it be that there is contradiction? Anticipating Immanuel Kant, he is sure that

"*God is not the author of contradictions.*" Cromwell's resolution of this problem was this:

> Thus far I find us to be agreed; and thus far as we are agreed, I think it is of God. ...and truly when we have no other more particular impression of the power of God going forth with us, I think that this law and this word speaking within us, which truly is in every man *who has the spirit of God*, we are to have regard to...
>
> BAKER, P. 100–101, emphasis added

But on the other hand, Leveller John Wildman held that:

> I observe that the work has been to inquire what has been the mind of God, and every one speaks what is given in to his spirit. ...consider what is justice and what is mercy, and what is good, and I cannot but think that *any one* does speak from God when he says what he speaks is of God.
>
> BAKER, 2007, PP. 102, emphasis added

Oliver Cromwell was an Independent, that is, one of those Protestants who held that each congregation should have control over church matters affecting them, and were therefore opposed to a state church, but were not Dissenters in theology. The Royalists were High Anglicans, and the majority of Parliamentarians were Presbyterians, both of whom favoured a state church, though they contended on which it should be; Anglicans were to be found on both sides of the Civil War, and among the rank and file as well as officers. The Levellers, however, were mostly Dissenters. In terms of the problem of collective decision making, the question which separated the Dissenters from all the others was this: does God speak through *every* believer, or only *some* believers? And if, as the Dissenters believed, the Light shone within every heart, how was contradiction to be understood theologically and how was it to be dealt with in practice?

With the king executed and the Levellers suppressed, in 1653, Cromwell established himself as Lord Protector of the Commonwealth. After his death in 1658, his son, Richard, took control, but at the end of the next year instability threatened again, and the English ruling class called an end to its experiment in republicanism and invited Charles's son to return from exile in Holland and restored the monarchy in 1660. Charles 11 was suspected of being a Catholic, and when his Catholic son, James, assumed the throne in 1685, England was faced with a return to religious warfare. Parliament invited the Dutch Protestant William and his wife Mary (James' daughter) to invade England, overthrow James and to jointly assume the throne of England, Scotland and Ireland, thus in 1688 returning England to Protestantism and securing the supremacy of Parliament forever after. The period from the Restoration of the monarchy in 1660 to the Act of Toleration in 1689 was a period of severe repression for the Dissenters. It was during this period that the Quaker movement took shape, and the development of dissenting religions during this period is the main line of my narrative. However, I cannot continue our narrative without first pausing to look at Gerard Winstanley and the Diggers, or 'True Levellers'.

Gerard Winstanley and the Diggers[4]

Gerard Winstanley had had little education was a small tradesman in the clothing trade and had probably been a member of one of the London Companies discussed in an earlier chapter. He fell on hard times and in 1649 he was eking out a precarious living pasturing his neighbours' cattle.

The Levellers had been political liberals. Winstanley, on the contrary, was a communitarian, adopting mutual aid and cooperation as his principle. Whereas the Levellers idealised Anglo-Saxon England before the Conquest, as he wrote to Lord Fairfax, Winstanley's aim was:

> not to remove the Norman *Yoke* only, and to bring us back to be governed by those Laws that were before *William the Conqueror* came in, as if that were the mark we aime at. No, that is not it; but the Reformation is according to the Word of God, and that is the pure Law of Righteousnesse before the fall, which made all things, unto which all things are to be restored...
>
> WINSTANLEY, 1965, P. 292

The Fall, according to Winstanley, made "one part of Mankind to be a Taskmaster, and to live Idle; and by the beast-like power of the sword, does force another part of Mankind to work as a servant and slave," (p. 423) whilst Winstanley held that "Israel shall neither take Hire, nor give Hire." (p. 161) Everyone would work the earth.

And further, "Shall we have no lawyers? There is no need of them, for there is to be no buying and selling; neither any need to expound laws, for the bare letter of the law shall be both judge and lawyer, trying every man's actions. And seeing we shall have successive *Parliaments* every year, there will be rules made for every action a man can do." (p. 512) So, no lawyers or judges (because

---

4   My principal source for this section is Winstanley, G. (1941). *Works*, with an introduction. Ed. G. Sabine. Cornell U.P.

laws would be framed in terms which would be clear to the common man) and no buying and selling. Goods would be supplied to stores from which people could take what they needed, without buying and selling.

But despite the utopian character of this program, it was not based on an idealisation of human nature: the law would be enforced ruthlessly. After a first warning, transgressors would be dealt with harshly, punished by overseers with anything from hard labour to the gallows. Persistent buying and selling was punishable by death and anyone wishing to escape justice would be hunted down and put to death.

According to Christopher Hill:

> The whole Diggers movement...can be plausibly regarded as the culmination of a century of unauthorised encroachment upon the forests and wastes by squatters and local commoners, pushed on by land shortage and pressures of population...by lack of employment for casual labour in the depression of 1648–1649. Winstanley has arrived at the one possible democratic solution which was not merely backward-looking, as all other radical proposals during the revolutionary decades – an agrarian law, partible inheritance, stable copyhold – tended to be. (1972, p. 104)

Winstanley believed that half to two-thirds of England was not properly cultivated, and despite the confiscation of Church and Crown lands, "though there be land enough in England to maintain ten times as many people as are in it, yet some must beg of their brethren." Throughout 1649 and 1650 the price of land was discussed frequently in Parliament, the misery and discontent among the poorer people being a manifest threat of disorder and rioting, not to say of insurrection. The danger posed by the Diggers was that they called on the poor not just to vote, but to organise themselves and take *direct action* to remedy their situation.

Winstanley's vision came to him in a trance in January 1648.

> I heard the words, Worke together. Eat bread together; declare this all abroad. Likewise I heard these words. Whosoever it is that labours in the earth, for any person or persons, that lifts up themselves as Lords & Rulers over others, and that doth not look upon themselves as equal to others in the Creation, The hand of the Lord shall be upon that labourer: I the Lord have spoke it and I will do it; Declare this all abroad.
>
> WINSTANLEY, P. 190

He claimed that he received inspiration from no man and no Book. God had spoken directly to him, and he believed that this direct access to the Word of God, unmediated by priest or Bible, was available to every man and woman.

He announced his project and on 1 April 1649 half-a-dozen men began digging in waste land at St. George's Hill, about 30km from London. The Settlement at St. George's Hill was broken up by local landowners with assistance from Fairfax. Still, the settlement grew to 45 by June. As a result of continued harassment by local landowners assisted by a magistrate, they moved to land owned by the wife of a sympathetic clergyman about 30km away in West Horley. By April 1650, more than 50 men were cultivating 11 acres of grain and had built 6 or 7 houses. There were sympathetic colonies in Northampton, Buckinghamshire and Kent, but in April 1650 all were driven out by landowners and hired thugs. All that is known of Winstanley's life after the writing of the *Law of Freedom* in 1652 is that he became a Quaker and was living at Cobham in 1660.

The only insight we have into Winstanley's approach to decision making is what is set out in his utopian writings, most particularly in *Law of Freedom*. Such utopian proposals do not usually count even as norms. It is worth noting though that Winstanley shared the view of all the Dissenters that God spoke directly and truthfully to every man and woman, were they to listen to that Spirit within them. This view was associated in the instance of the Levellers with a relatively liberal, individualist position in politics, so it is noteworthy that Winstanley saw no incompatibility of this idea with his extreme communitarianism. Direct unmediated access to the Spirit may be consistent with strong communities as well as individual rights, for as Cromwell himself had said: "God is not the author of contradictions."

Winstanley and the Diggers are of interest in a history of communism, but are a footnote in English Revolution and in British history altogether. However, taking Winstanley as a representative of the extreme Left of the Revolution, he can shed some light on our theme in two respects.

Winstanley was himself a member of a London guild at a time when they were still at the height of their powers. Of interest, firstly, are his views on the guilds, given the part they played in the history of Majority; secondly, his views on how Parliament can legitimately make decisions on behalf of the whole country. Finally, Winstanley's fellow Diggers did not have the same sense of history as Winstanley himself, but the views of an anonymous Digger on decision making are enlightening.

The abolition of wage labour which Winstanley advocated entailed the preservation of apprenticeship and management of the labour process along lines modelled on the London Companies.

> And truly the Government of the Halls and Companies in *London* is a very rational and well ordered Government; and the *Overseers of the Trades* may very well be called *Masters*, *Wardens*, and *Assistants* of such

and such a Company, for such and such a particular Trade. Onley two things are to be practised to preserve the peace. The first is, *That all these Overseers shall be chosen new ones every year*. And secondly, the old Overseers shal not chuse the new ones, to prevent the creeping in of Lordly Oppression; but all the Masters of Families and Freemen of that Trade, shall be the chusers, and the old Overseers shall give but their single voice among them.

WINSTANLEY, P. 549

His ideas for discipline were even more draconian than those of the guilds:

If any refuse to learn a trade, or refuse to work in seed-time or harvest, etc., reproved openly...if he still continues idle, he shall then be whipt, ... if still he continue idle, he shall be delivered into the taskmasters hand, who shall set him to work for twelve moneths, or till he submit to right Order. (p. 593)

The "agricultural trades" would be organised along parallel lines and:

Likewise this Overseership for Trades shall see That no man shall be a House-keeper, and have Servants under him [i.e. run a workshop], till he hath served under a Master seven years, and hath learned his Trade. (p. 550)

So we see that the extreme left wing of 17th century England had no trouble with the structure of the guilds and with making decisions by majority voting – only that elections had to be annual and that provisions for rotation of offices had to be strictly adhered to, so as to avoid the formation of cliques, hereditary succession and hierarchy. Even the restriction of the franchise to Masters he approved of.

Winstanley did not foresee that there would be fundamental divisions within the Parliament of his Commonwealth, and he gives us no particular guidelines about Parliamentary debate. His concerns were in relation to consultation with the electorate:

It is now the work of Parliament to search into Reason and Equity. How relief may be found out for the people in such a case, and to preserve a common Peace; and when they have found out a way by debate of Councel among themselves, whereby the people may be relieved, they are not presently to establish their Conclusions for a Law. But in the next place, they are to make a publicke Declaration thereof to the people of the Land who chose them for their approbation; and if no Objection come in from the people within one moneth, they may then take the peoples silence as a consent thereto. And then in the third place, they are to enact it for a Law, to be a binding Rule to the whole Land. (p. 559)

All Overseers and State-Offices shall be chosen anew every year, to prevent the rise of Ambition and Covetousness; for the Nations have smarted sufficiently by suffering Officers to continue long in an Office, or to remain in an Office by hereditary succession. (p. 596)

So much for Winstanley's vision which we can see was consonant with that of the politically conscious of tradesmen of his time. Winstanley was indeed a 'true leveller'. The harsh labour discipline of this utopia can only be reconciled with with what Winstanley evidently imagined prevailed "before the Fall" and the institution of class society, if we accept that this reflects an element of realism, and that it would take discipline and time for these habits to be normalised.

A hint as to how Diggers *actually* made decisions is suggested in the utopian vision in the anonymous Digger pamphlet, *Light Shining in Buckinghamshire*:

The government to be by Judges, called Elders, men fearing God and hating covetousnesse; Those to be chosen by the people, and to end all controversies in every Town and Hamlet, without any other or further trouble or charge.

This sounds like the witenagemot of Anglo-Saxon England: decisions to be made by *wise men*, so that there should be no controversy and dissension – dependent of course on the prior eradication of all class differences. Winstanley knew better than this, but the anonymous author may reflect how the Diggers actually made their decisions, an approach no doubt similar to those described by St. Benedict.

After this digression, we now return to the main line of our narrative, the development of the Dissenting sects in England after the crushing of the Levellers in 1649.

Ranters and Seekers[5]

Like Gerrard Winstanley, the leader of the Quakers, George Fox, was a relatively uneducated man who experienced what he took to be a Divine revelation,

---

5 My principle source for this section is Hill, C. (1975). *The World Turned Upside Down: Radical Ideas During the English Revolution.*

which he genuinely believed came from neither person nor Book. Our narrative requires us to follow the emergence of the Quakers out of the milieu of dissenting sects in England following the Revolution, following the inner logic of that development, and the subsequent development of the Quakers themselves. However, the features of Quaker practice and belief which interest us were not fresh creations, but were to be found in embryo in pre-Revolutionary England.

The first Baptist congregation was founded in Holland in 1609 by the English pastor, John Smyth, and from there reached England and America prior to 1642. They were called "Baptists" because they baptised only adult converts who could make their own confession of faith, not infants. Although Protestant in origin, the English Baptists were heavily persecuted by both Catholic and Protestant regimes. Many Baptists emigrated to America where they could worship free of persecution, and flourished up to the present day. The Baptist ministers in England did not settle and foster a congregation in their community, but travelled incessantly, thus enhancing the authority of the local deacons and the relative autonomy of the local congregations. Unlike in any previous denomination, women were allowed to preach as Baptists.

The Quaker writer Robert Barclay (1640–1690) describes a business meeting of a Baptist congregation, in which all those present "had free liberty of voting decisively, and of debate," yet "nothing must go by *number or plurality of voices*, and there must be no moderator, or prolocutor, for the order of their action." (cited in Sheeran, 1996, p. 127) The Baptists introduced the idea of Divine guidance for communities seeking God's will together. The idea of a 'Light within', which we came across in connection with the debates at Putney was introduced to England by a Baptist sect known as the Family of Love, or the 'Familists'. Although we may recognise in all these features of Baptist practice elements which would come to be seen as distinguishing features of the Quakers, there is no evidence that the founding fathers of the Society of Friends knowingly appropriated Baptist meeting procedures. All these ideas would have been in circulation among those who were later to become Quakers.

Among the dissenting sects abounding in England at the time, the line of religious development I am following runs in succession through the Ranters, the Seekers and the Quakers. Most of the early members of these currents had been either soldiers in the New Model Army between 1642 and 1649, or were sympathetic to the political program of the Levellers. Once all hope of political reform faded, the ideas which had motivated the Revolutionary Army moved from politics into religion, from whence they had come, in the Dissenting congregations of England.

The period of the Civil War saw an upsurge in millennial enthusiasm but as the possibility of political liberalisation receded, a conviction that the end of the world was near came to be widely accepted. If the New Model Army could not deliver freedom, one could look forward to the Final Judgment.

At one time, only a few gentlemen would perceive the Light within, and this posed no danger to the social order; now any artisan or labourer was as likely to receive the Divine Light, throw away their Bible, denounce their pastor and follow their own Light, rather than a theology of sin and hell-fire fashioned for the purposes of social control.

> The world exists for man, and all men are equal. There is no after-life: all that matters is here and now. 'In the grave there is no remembrance of either joy or sorrow after... Swearing i'th light, gloriously', and 'wanton kisses', may help to liberate us from the repressive ethic which our masters are trying to impose on us – a regime in which property is more important than life, marriage than love, faith in a wicked God than the charity which the Christ in us teaches.
>
> HILL, 1972, P. 273, glossing Lawrence Clarkson, 1660

In harsh times, rather than discipline and self-control, the Ranters (as they came to be called) emphasised love and pleasure. But the Ranters posed no *political* threat, because they never formed a sect and had no motivation to risk their life in political contention.

The Ranters' ideas did pose a threat to labour discipline and law and order however. Nothing was sinful to Ranters, if only you truly followed what God spoke to you. But the Ranters were very difficult to suppress, because they would not hesitate to compromise or recant, and yet silently remained of the same opinion.

The logic of the Ranters stands up well to criticism. If a person requires no mediator – neither priest nor Bible – to hear the Word of God, if every person has an equal claim to know what God wills, then why not do whatever brings pleasure? The end of the world is coming anyway, there is no afterlife and no eternal damnation. At that time, no great feats of oratory or evangelism were required to convince a person of this doctrine.

The harshness of the times began to re-assert itself. The masses were forced by economic discipline back into a life which brought little pleasure, leaving Ranterism the privilege of a few gentry, and there was nothing to fill the void. For a Ranter there was no point in risking persecution by publicly preaching their beliefs. And in any case, proselytising made no sense if *every* person had access to God's will.

The Ranters were gradually displaced by the Seekers. Since the end of the world was probably near anyway, a resigned withdrawal from sectarian controversy and a rejection of all sects, and of all organised worship made more sense. Among the Seekers were the Leveller pamphleteer William Walwyn (whose views were close to Winstanley's), the poet John Milton and according to Hill (p. 154), possibly Oliver Cromwell himself. They held that no true Church existed in their age, and worshiped together in silence awaiting a new Revelation.

With no clergy, no Bible and no doctrine beyond the anticipation of a second coming, this movement had a limited life expectancy. As time went by, no Saviour came nor any new Revelation, the social order re-stabilised and even the king was restored to the throne. Not only was the entire established church discredited, but even the Bible was widely regarded as neither the Word of God nor historically truthful. Sin and the afterlife were no longer believed in, but life brought little pleasure and little light of any kind. People needed comfort and they needed social support and they needed something to believe in and above all, some guidance as to how to live a good life.

But so long as every individual had their own unmediated access to the true Word of God, it was impossible to embark on any collective venture or construct a community of faith.

The Quakers[6]

George Fox (1624–1691) came from a moderately well-off family in Leicestershire and was apprenticed to a local shoemaker and grazier. He had only basic schooling but as a youth formed a very low opinion of the churchmen of his time. Between 1643 and 1647, he travelled through civil war torn England, meeting with the various Dissenting preachers in search of answers to the religious questions which troubled him. In the course of this search Fox heard a voice speak within him. He took this to be the voice of Jesus and with the continued guidance of this inward voice, he developed his own teaching.

Any man, woman or child can understand Scripture and preach, *provided only* that the Spirit guides them; all the rituals of church life, ornate church buildings and costumes were meaningless; all that mattered was that one experience God's presence. The book which you should read was not the Bible, but the Book within your own conscience.

---

6 My principal source for this section is Sheeran, M.J. (1996). *Beyond Majority Rule: Voteless Decisions in the Religious Society of Friends.*

Fox began preaching publicly in 1647 and soon gathered a following of 60 converts, who toured the Dissenting communities across England, and in 1652, he met James Nayler, who had experienced his own revelation. Though Fox is rightly remembered as the founder of the Society of Friends, in the early days, Nayler would have been seen as as much a leader as Fox, and played an important role in the early years. Fox and his Friends opposed tithes and all the privileges, doctrines, pretensions and immorality of the clergy of the established church and they were formidable orators, denouncing their religious opponents, and stalwartly standing up to the sometimes violent reception with which they were met.

The practices and beliefs of the Quakers underwent a development, driven by the contradictions within this central idea of the Light of Jesus within every person, at the time by no means unique to the Quakers, and the changing social context in which they lived.

Politically, Quakers were radicals in the 1650s, and Friends would generally have supported Parliament in the civil war. Even apparently innocent eccentricities, like refusing to remove their hat or to use the second person plural before social superiors, confirmed suspicions that they harboured radical political designs. Winstanley had done likewise. In 1656, the Leveller hero "Freeborn John" Lilburne himself became a Quaker. Quakers were also suspected of being immoral Ranters disguising themselves as upright citizens.

The early Quaker movement was, in fact, far closer to the Ranters in spirit than its leaders liked to admit, and a great deal of effort was expended distinguishing themselves from Ranters. However, unlike Ranters who would recant under persecution, the Quakers' principles led them to declare their faith openly, in public, and stand by that faith. Consequently, they were very vulnerable to persecution by the magistrates.

Although Fox believed his revelations to come direct from Jesus, he did not discount Scripture. As the Familists had held, the Quakers believed that it is only thanks to the spirit of Christ within that the believer can understand the Scriptures. Fox reported, for example, that "Yet I had no slight esteem of the Holy Scriptures, and what the Lord opened to me I afterward found agreeable to them." Thus a Quaker could give his own sense to the stories in the Bible.

This mode of thought of which the Quakers were a part was not necessarily anarchistic and individualist. It had two sides to it: on one hand the reliance on *experience*, referred to at the time as "experiment," and on the other hand, reliance on the holy spirit within one's *own* heart, as opposed to traditional or institutional beliefs and book knowledge. These same authorities marked the development of secular philosophy and natural science at the time, transposing struggles between empiricism (Bacon) and rationalism (Descartes) into the domain of religion. As such, it was cutting edge at the time.

In 1651, Fox toured the North of England meeting congregations of Ranters, Seekers, Anabaptists, Familists and other displaced persons who had been left without hope following the defeat of the Levellers and he met with outstanding success. Fox and the other Friends continued to gather converts, and Quakers reached one per cent of the population of England before emigration to America to escape persecution began to reduce their numbers.

To understand the development of the Quakers and the particular features of their practice which are of interest to us, we have to consider the "James Nayler Crisis" of 1656. This event precipitated processes to which Fox had already begun to turn his attention and the contradictions within the Quakers' founding principle would have manifested themselves sooner or later and been resolved in much the same way, whoever had been in leadership at the time.

Quakers believed, like the Ranters, that any believer could receive the Word of Jesus. But the Quakers did not hear a voice leading them to follow their own desires, but rather actions which were difficult and contrary to desire. In 1656, to make the point that every believer could hear and give witness to the Word of Jesus, James Nayler rode into Bristol – the second city of the Kingdom at that time – on the back of a horse, with women strewing branches before him. Nayler had made no secret of his eight or nine years' service in the New Model Army, and at this point, the Quakers were sweeping up recruits among Dissenters and former Levellers across the country. This was not some eccentric preacher who needed to cool his feet in prison for a few weeks! Nayler's gesture was a provocation of the first order. A frightened Parliament spent six weeks debating what to do with Nayler before having him savagely flogged through the streets of London, his forehead branded, his tongue pierced with a hot iron and then sent to Bristol for a further flogging and flung into prison. Unlike the adoring crowd which had sustained Lilburne through his flogging in 1638, Nayler's punishment was observed by a hostile crowd. He bore his ordeal with fortitude, but he never recovered. He was imprisoned for three years, released in 1659, but was attacked on his way home and died. The fear and vitriol which had been sparked by Nayler now fell upon the entire Society of Friends.

This incident confronted Fox with the fact that individual believers *could be mistaken* in their perception of the Light within, and not just trivially so, but to an extent which had the potential to destroy the Society, and in particular to expose them to prejudice and persecution. Secondly, it demonstrated just how vulnerable they were to persecution whilst congregations remained autonomous and had no check on individual 'leadings' and no structure to offer guidance or support to Friends.

Fox was doing one of his innumerable stints in prison at the time and when he was released he toured the country and became alarmed at the intensity and frequency of negative reactions to such Quaker ways as refusing to show conventional deference to social betters, refusal to take oaths and refusal to pay tithes whilst denouncing the immorality and deceit of clergymen and public officials. And over and above these routine Quaker provocations to authority, one could never foresee when some Friend might be led to emulate James Nayler's provocation. Fox urged "patience" and a less "aggravating" public witness and asked that firm guidance be exercised by more mature Friends over those who may "go beyond their measure" and suggested monthly and later quarterly regional meetings with the specific aim of discovering and dealing with "disorderly walkers" and promoted the dissemination of "reliable" books and generally a campaign of consolidation and unification of the Society. (Sheeran, p. 12–13)

Despite their vulnerability though, the Quakers did not cease advocating social reform. The Levellers, Ranters and Seekers who had been recruited to the Society were the most individualist of all nonconformists. How was Fox to impose discipline in such a Society? For they could not otherwise survive.

Quaker ministers had already been making a practice of checking their 'leadings' (or revelations) with fellow ministers. These cautious measures were all very well, but what Fox was faced with was a fundamental challenge to the basic principle of his ministry – the reliability of the voice of Jesus within every believer. Practical measures were one thing, but the crisis also posed a problem for Fox's teaching.

The reliance on the Light within was not unique to the Quakers. It was shared to one extent or another by all Protestants. But other denominations had Scripture, as interpreted for them by an educated clergy, and an institution – buildings, rituals, a hierarchy, moral proscriptions – 'objective religion' which acted as a check upon and a guidance for the 'subjective religion' of the heart, and a history which included precedents and 'inherited wisdom'. The Quakers were new, they had little traditional knowledge to fall back upon and in any case eschewed tradition; they held the Scriptures to be open to interpretation by the believer themself; rituals and trappings were discounted. How was Fox to form a disciplined, united sect out of this rabble of ex-Ranters without the objective guidance normally provided by the Church? It could no longer be maintained that the Spirit of Jesus spoke to each Friend independently.

Letters from the Quaker writer Edward Burrough in 1662 describe how Quakers were urged to conduct their business meetings:

First, that the meeting do consist of just and righteous men...not limited to a number of persons; but freedom for all friends... But if any person out of the Truth, and of another Spirit, contrary to the faith of Christ professed and practised by Friends, come to the meeting, such are not members thereof, but are excluded from having their advice and judgement taken...

Secondly, ...to hear and consider, and if possible to determine the same, in justice and truth. *Not in the way of the world*, as a worldly assembly of men, by hot contests, by seeking to outspeak and overreach one another in discourse; as if it were controversy between parties of men, or two sides violently striving for dominion, in the way of carrying on some worldly interest for self advantage; *nor deciding affairs by the greater vote or the number of men*, as the world, who have not the wisdom and power of God: that none of this kind of order be permitted in your meeting. But in the wisdom, love and fellowship of God, in gravity, patience, meekness, in unity and concord (submitting to one another, in lowliness of heart and in the Holy Spirit of Truth and Righteousness,) *all thing coolness, gentleness and dear unity*, I say, as one only party, all for the truth of whatsoever ability God hath given. And to determine of things by a general mutual concord, in assenting together as one man, in the spirit of truth and equity, and by the authority thereof, *in this way and spirit all thing are to be amongst you, and without perverseness in any self-separation, in discord and partiality*. This way and spirit is wholly excepted, as not worthy to enter into the assembly of God's servants, to give an judgment or counsel amongst them, in any case pertaining to the service of the Church of Christ: in which his spirit of love and unity must rule.

Thirdly, if at any time, any matter or occasion be presented to the meeting *which is doubtful, or difficult, or not within the judgment of friends then assembled* (they not having full knowledge or experience of the matter depending) that then, on such occasions, *the judgment be suspended...*

Fourthly, But if at any time any strife or division shall happen to fall out amongst friends, ...to seek mediation, ...etc.

BURROUGH, 1834, P. 137–138

This is historically the first formulation of Consensus, clearly distinguished from Majority, Counsel and Negotiation. These practical directions urged upon Quakers brought about a modification in the Quaker teaching on the Light within. The Spirit's voice could be reliably heard only when Friends were gathered together *with an awareness of the presence of God in their midst*. Individual leadings had to be subordinated to the Spirit's voice in the gathered community, only then could it be heard reliably. By the zealous observance of the practical directions as outlined in Burroughs' letter, fostered by silent communal prayer, Friends could indeed feel the presence of the Spirit covering them. Through this practice, Quakers would be led to consciousness of the "sense of the meeting."

Thus every person did have direct access to the Word, but only on condition that they sought divine guidance in the humble presence of a community of believers. This provided the check upon the anarchy of every individual having an independent access to the Truth, so long as the Quakers lacked the structure, rituals, full-time clergy and sanctions available to the state church.

Whereas in the early days, revelation for Quakers entailed challenge and trial, now the touchstone of right guidance was the "presence of inner peace," fostered by quiet undemonstrative speech, and protracted silences in meetings.

The decisions made in such meetings carry a great deal more conviction and engender more commitment than the individual intuition. Meetings were not *just* silent prayer, but entailed giving reasons and discussion, so the voice of Jesus comes to function very much like Reason. But whether you believe Reason or Divine Light is at play, decisions arrived at by participation in a group carry considerably more commitment and legitimacy than an individual intuition, and prepared the Quakers to withstand the heat of persecution with fortitude.

And amongst already like-minded people, in those times, God did in fact say similar things to the members of the same congregation. Further, according to Christopher Hill:

> In time of defeat, when the wave of revolution was ebbing, the inner voice became quietist, pacifist. This voice only was recognised by others as God's. ...Once the group decided this way, all the pressures were in the direction of accepting modes of expression not too shocking to the society in which men had to live and earn their living. ... [and] asked only to be left alone.
>
> The openness of the religion of the heart, of the inner voice, to changes in mass moods, to social pressures, to waves of feeling, had made it the vehicle of revolutionary transformations of thought: now it had the opposite effect. The 'sense of the meeting' accepted the 'common sense' of the dominant classes in society.
>
> HILL, 1972, P. 299–300

The second line of action by Fox to ensure the unity, solidarity and coherence of the Society of Friends was the institution of regular quarterly and yearly meetings of representatives of each of the local communities. Once ad hoc, now the very regularity of these meetings soon raised them to a position not unlike the structure of the mainstream churches.

Nonetheless, not only were Fox's measures successful in curbing disorderly behaviour, the Friends proved able to withstand the persecution that came down on them, and even their enemies noted with admiration their stoutness under persecution. Furthermore, the Quakers continued to hold their meetings publicly and openly, with unflinching tenacity and calmness. The local Quaker communities continued to flourish in spite of the persecution and on the whole congregations maintained their autonomy.

However, the persecution had an impact on the development of the Quaker faith. In the estimate of Christopher Hill, the intensification of persecution as the Restoration approached and the singularly brutal suppression of the Quakers under Charles II, persuaded Fox to adopt a public stance of unambiguous pacifism and non-participation in politics. Ten leading Quakers wrote to the king:

> All Bloody principles and practices, we as to our own particulars, do utterly deny, with all outward wars and strife and fightings with outward weapons, for any end or under any pretence whatsoever.
>
> Cited in SHEERAN, 1996 P. 14–15

Sheeran points out that at least two of the signers had advocated the use of force as late as 1659. He goes on to demonstrate that in order to defend the Society against persecution by discreet lobbying of parliamentarians and magistrates, the Committee of Sufferings, established to care for the dependents of Friends in prison, had morphed into a national coordinating committee controlling the activity of local congregations. Sheeran says that this went much further in displacing the Divine guidance of sovereign communities with a central polity, but claims that this move did not follow the Quakers into emigration in America where persecution continued, but was bearable. (p. 15)

The first serious schism took place in the 1670s over these measures, with what is known as the Wilkinson-Story separation opposing subordination of the individual Light within to the sense of the meeting, and objected what they saw as an hierarchical structure. Over the succeeding centuries there were a number of schisms, and in any case, the local communities always retained a degree of sovereignty, and while there remained little in the way of theological doctrine, over time the Quakers did accumulate a considerable body of traditional wisdom.

Many left the Society under the weight of persecution. They despaired of seeing the political reform to which Friends had once been devoted, but with their communal solidarity and reputation for uprightness and honesty, despite repression, they did prosper. With a ban on exogenous marriage, their numbers declined, and the Quakers became a self-selected elect.

What the Quakers created was not a new doctrine or theology so much as a *practice*, a practice of conducting meetings, whether for worship or to make decisions. And what made a Quaker a believer was not the satisfactory answers given to theological questions, but the *experience* of discovering the Spirit within together with others.

Neither George Fox nor John Wesley sought to convince converts of a theological argument or system, but offered *organisational* innovations which met the needs of their times which in both cases have proved to be of enduring value irrespective of religious or metaphysical conviction.

Like other Dissenters, many Quakers fled persecution by emigrating to America in the 1650s, establishing Quaker communities in Rhode Island, Massachusetts, New Jersey and Pennsylvania. While they remain a tiny minority, there are today over 100,000 Quakers in North America, mainly concentrated in New England alongside the descendants of other Nonconformist immigrants from Restoration England. My theme leads me to follow the Quakers to Pennsylvania where I will rely on Sheeran for a description of how Quakers made decisions in twentieth century America, and on Barry Morley for a defence of Quaker decision making as opposed to how Consensus is practised among non-Quakers.

The Quakers in Twentieth Century Pennsylvania

In 1983, Michael Sheeran made an extended study of the Pennsylvania Yearly Meeting, that is, the Quaker community in Pennsylvania, of which the annual meeting is the peak body. This is the largest Quaker community in America, being founded on land owned by the Quaker William Penn in 1681. Sheeran is a Jesuit, and his account is that of a sympathetic outsider which has been received with approval by the Quaker community.

The Quaker historian at the University of Birmingham, 'Ben' Pink Dandelion, confirmed to me that there is no difference in the practice of 'sense of the meeting' between England and America:

> Quakers have practised this method from the beginning and it is still one of the shared practices worldwide today. I have not heard of any...distinction between US and British Quakers on this. Only very exceptionally have Quaker Meetings voted on a matter and it would not be seen as theologically appropriate. (personal email, 11 Feb. 2014)

Sheeran's report confirms that the practice of collective decision making has been transmitted from 17th century England to 20th century Pennsylvania essentially intact. Here is a Quaker overview of the conduct of meetings, from the London Yearly Meeting's 1960 *Book of Discipline*:

> As it is our hope that in our meetings for Discipline the will of God shall prevail rather than the desires of men, we do not set great store by rhetoric or clever argument. The mere gaining of debating points is found to be unhelpful and alien to the spirit of worship which should govern the rightly ordered Meeting. Instead of rising hastily to reply to another, it is better to give time for what has been said to make its own appeal, and to take its right place in the mind of the Meeting.
>
> We ought ever to be ready to give unhurried, weighty and truly sympathetic consideration to proposals brought forward from whatever part of the Meeting, believing that what is said rises from the depths of a Friend's experience, and is sincerely offered for the guidance of the Meeting, and the forwarding of the work of the Church. We should neither be hindered from making experiments by fear or undue caution, nor prompted by novel suggestions to ill-considered courses.
>
> Neither a majority nor a minority should allow itself in any way to overbear or to obstruct a meeting for church affairs in its course towards

© KONINKLIJKE BRILL NV, LEIDEN, 2016 | DOI 10.1163/9789004319639_014

a decision. We are unlikely to reach either truth or wisdom if one section imposes its will on another. We deprecate division in our Meetings and desire unanimity. It is in the unity of common fellowship, we believe, that we shall most surely learn the will of God. We cherish, therefore, the tradition which excludes voting from our meetings, and trust that clerks and Friends generally will observe the spirit of it, not permitting themselves to be influenced in their judgment either by mere numbers or by persistence. The clerks should be content to wait upon God with the Meeting, as long as may be necessary for the emergence of a decision which clearly commends itself to the heart and mind of the Meeting as the right one.

SHEERAN, p. 48

The Quaker way of doing meetings generally depends on having a group of limited size who know and respect each other. Members of this group must be willing to listen to each other with open minds and to learn from each other. After an individual has stated his or her own insight, his responsibility is over. On the other hand, the Pennsylvania Yearly Meeting has 1,100 people making collective decisions together, made possible because all of them believe in and are committed to the process. The Quaker Stuart Chase lists nine principles of Quaker decision making:

1. unanimous decisions – no voting;
2. silent periods – at start of meeting and when conflict arises;
3. moratorium – when agreement cannot be reached;
4. participation by all with ideas on the subject;
5. learning to listen – not going to meeting with mind made up;
6. absence of leaders – the clerk steers but does not dominate;
7. nobody outranks anybody;
8. factual-focus – emotions kept to a minimum; and
9. small meetings – typically limited numbers. (Sheeran, p. 51)

The normal way discussion proceeds is as follows (Sheeran, pp. 66–70):

· the clerk states the question to be discussed;
· there is a preliminary phase which resembles what non-Quakers often call "brainstorming," where proposals are put up merely as possible starting points for discussion;
· there is a transitional phase in which participants "test the waters" to see if a proposal is going to "float" as we say, before
· the "serious" discussion gets going;

- participants may express their "unity" with a proposal or may express shades of dissent which Sheeran listed as follows:
  "I disagree but do not wish to stand in the way"
  "Please minute me opposed"
  "I am unable to unite with the proposal"
  Absent from the meeting.
- the clerk attempts to enunciate the 'sense of the meeting'.

"It is the clerk's task...either to find a resolution with which the assembled Friends can largely agree to follow the Quaker rule, 'when in doubt, wait'. ... if the tide is running in one particular direction...propose a tentative minute embodying the agreement as the clerk understands it from listening to the discussion." (Sheeran, p. 65, quoting Douglas Steere) ...the clerk will either again propose the original minute or offer a substitute. And finally, the *paradox of the status quo*: no change is made until agreement is reached. (p. 50)

It is very clear from this that the success of the meeting and the long-term maintenance of the culture in which trust is vested in the process depends on the clerk. The meeting chooses the clerk in advance of the meeting date from among those Quakers known to be 'gifted' as clerks. The clerk's ordinary duties include the following, all potential levers of power (Sheeran, p. 91):

- compiling the agenda;
- stating the questions;
- evoking comments from the silent;
- maintaining discipline;
- diplomacy dealing with difficulties;
- judging what is important;
- judging the sense of the meeting;
- neutrality and self-restraint.

The clerk's role begins prior to the meeting as items for the agenda are brought to their attention and may involve other preparatory work, as well as side-discussions and problem-solving outside the meeting and in follow-ups. Claims for the special qualities of the Quaker way of running meetings clearly hinge on the whether or not the clerks use these levers of power strategically. It is clear that the Clerk acts as a facilitator, not a Chief. Together with the commitment to equality this marks Quaker Consensus off from Counsel.

Sheeran's investigation showed that there were only minimal formal constraints on the clerks' exercise of their responsibilities but that "abuse of power seems curiously rare" (p. 97). Further he found that the clerks themselves "exhibited an impressive sensitivity to the clerk's possible abuse of power" (p. 98). While there were "horror stories" about previous generations where such abuses did occur, it seems that accounting for the character and success of Quaker meetings requires us to take account not only of the high level of mutual trust among members of the community, but the raising of a stratum of people possessing the admirable qualities demanded of the clerks, and the recognition of those qualities by others in the community, such that clerks deservedly enjoy the unqualified trust of participants in the meeting.

Sheeran's report also dealt with the belief systems underlying Quaker decision making. We have seen that Quakers are not united by a theological doctrine, but rather by the *practice* of Quaker worship and communal decision making and the *experience* of that practice. Without a full-time clergy and the rest of the paraphernalia of an 'objective religion', Quakers have been free to develop divergent theological and metaphysical views. Decision procedures which are reliant on participants having a shared metaphysical belief cannot meet the demands of 'public reason', to use John Rawls' terminology, or of discourse ethics, to use Habermas's terminology.

Sheeran found that Quakers had a variety of interpretations of what in Quaker discourse is referred to as the voice of Jesus and the idea of awareness of the presence of God in a 'covered' meeting, that is, of God 'leading' a meeting or of a 'gathered' meeting.

For a start there were different senses in which Philadelphian Quakers spoke of Jesus. For some, he was the historical Jesus who died two millennia ago, and for others 'Jesus' was another name for the Creator and had the capacity to be really present in a meeting. For others, however, the presence or voice of Jesus was simply taken as a metaphor which could mean simply the *feeling* derived from a successful meeting and a good decision, or could refer to the impersonal force manifested by the joining of minds, without ascribing any extra-mundane significance to it.

Sheeran also found that many (including those who for whom 'Jesus' was involved in Quaker decisions) understood the Quaker practice in terms of the Society of Friends being 'democratic', that is, in terms of the will of individuals being moderated by organizational practices, rather than in terms of a Spirit or any such religious conception.

Sheeran found that these differences in metaphysical belief had no impact on the way Quakers participated in meetings or related to one another. The main difference which could be seen between Quakers relevant to the quality of their participation in meetings was that some experienced the condition of the 'gathered meeting' and awareness of the presence of a Spirit in the meeting, and some simply didn't. And this difference cut across differences in metaphysical belief. During Sheeran's investigation, he did witness meetings in which that special quality was experienced, but the "great majority" did not reach the "gathered" condition (p. 88). At the same time he found that negotiated compromise, as opposed to the achievement of a genuine and fully satisfactory unity, was the "occasional exception to the rule" (p. 54).

From what has been said already it will be very clear that the style of meeting which is nowadays generally known as Consensus decision making is not the same as the Quaker meeting. I think it is an entirely open question as to whether any of the paradigms of decision making – Counsel, Majority and Consensus – can achieve creative decisions which provide a genuine basis for unity to which the Quaker meeting aspires. In my experience, under the right conditions and with skilled leadership, chairmanship or facilitation, *any* of these paradigms can produce very satisfactory and creative decisions. Quakers, however, invariably insist on the distinction between 'sense of the meeting' and Consensus, though what Quakers refer to as 'Consensus' is what I have called 'Negotiation'.

The Quaker Critique[1]

A defence of the Quaker way is given by Barry Morley (1993). Morley says that "Sense of meeting is a gift. It came to Quakers though their commitment to continuing revelation. They discovered that the Light which had come to teach the people could lead them to revealed corporate decisions," and regretting the extent to which young Quakers have accepted the identification of sense of the meeting with Consensus, he says: "I don't know how or when Quakers came to believe in consensus, but it happened recently and has spread across us like an oil slick" (pp. 1–2).

Morley explains the difference as follows: "consensus is achieved through a process of reasoning in which reasonable people search for a satisfactory decision. But in seeking the sense of the meeting we open ourselves to being guided to perfect resolution in Light, to a place where we sit in unity in the collective inward presence...we turn our decision making over to a higher power. Consensus is the product of an intellectual process. Sense of the meeting is a commitment to faith" (p. 5).

As is common among Quakers, 'Consensus' is understood in a very impoverished sense, what I call 'Negotiation' or 'bargaining', as "a process in which

---

1   My principal source for this section is Morley, B. (1993). *Beyond Consensus. Salvaging Sense of the Meeting*, Wallingford, PA: Pendle Hill.

adjustments and compromises are made for the purpose of reaching a decision that all of us can accept. It brings us to an intellectually satisfactory conclusion. But sense of the meeting reaches beyond that. ...It is a process that cares for the whole of the corporate body" but by contrast, "because everyone has given up something to attain consensus, commitment to the conclusion is often shallow. In one way or another we make decisions by 'going along'.... Sense of the meeting, on the other hand, fosters powerful commitment." (p. 6) As I remarked above, my experience has been that the achievement of a genuinely creative and satisfying decision depends more on the mutual trust between participants and the skill, insight and patience of the facilitator(s) or principal protagonists. Unfortunately, many non-Quakers mistakenly refer to the process of striking a bargain as 'consensus', so it is hardly surprising that Quakers should form such a low opinion of it.

Morley points to three components which he sees as essential to revealing a sense of the meeting:

1. Release. After an issue has been presented to the business meeting, Friends should allow Friends whose feelings have been aroused to release those feelings....
2. Long Focus. ...we should focus our attention beyond the immediate discussion *toward* the sense of the meeting.... Sharp edges are blurred.... A period of silence is sometimes suggested when discussion gets difficult, angry, or competitive.... Contention and compromise, though sometimes appropriate in early stages of discussion, narrow our focus.
3. Transition to Light. ...as we lay aside any need to win, as we turn increasingly inward in order to transcend differences, long focus brings us to the Source of resolution and clarity.... Silence is an inward and outward sign that the process has been completed. A sensitive clerk will allow the silence to linger. (pp. 16–19)

I suggest that we accept the Quaker view that Sense of Meeting is a distinct paradigm of collective decision making, marked by its Quaker origins, with silence rather than dialogue as its mark. This does not contradict the possibility that the Quaker Sense of the Meeting may have been the *inspiration* for the invention of the practice of Consensus amongst social change activists in the USA in 1959–61. The Quaker Sense of the Meeting relies upon the mutual trust fostered between members of the Quaker community and the raising of Clerks who have confidence in this process and are skilled in facilitating it – conditions which may not exist among the broad population of participants in social change activism.

New England Town Meetings[1]

The New England Town Meeting is widely regarded as a surviving early historical exemplar of deliberative democracy and is often taken as a reference point
for the design of processes for public consultation. So the question arises: is
there a relation between the Quaker emigration to America and these para-
gons of democracy.

The short answer is "no," as New England was settled by Puritans seeking
freedom to practice their religion during the period before the English Civil
War, i.e., between 1620 and 1642 when emigration was temporarily halted, *before* the Quakers were formed.

The Puritans who settled in Plymouth in November 1620 and with the
Massachusetts Bay Company in 1631, and later in Connecticut and New Haven
were Congregationalists. That is to say they were broadly Calvinists in their
theology, but unlike mainstream Anglicans and Catholics whose churches
were governed by a top-down hierarchy (called an Episcopacy), and the Presbyterians, whose ministers met in synods who had authority over their congregations, Congregationalists held that congregations had to right to hire and fire
their ministers and were subject to no other power.

In the words of Rev. John Cotton, the leading minister of the colony: "it is better that the commonwealth be fashioned to the setting of God's house which
is his church, than to accommodate the church frame to the civil state" (1636).
By 1643, 56 English towns had been founded, each with their town meetings.
Based on the congregational principle of Puritan church government, the town
meeting gave all the adult male members of the church of each new town a
chance to take an active role in local government. The overall governance of
the colony was effected by transforming the charter under which the *trading
company* which had been given rights to land in the New World by the English
king into a *government*. The Massachusetts Bay Company (the largest colony)
did this by granting to every resident the right to elect the officers of the Company, formerly reserved for *shareholders*. The Massachusetts Bay Company referred to its board as a "court," its elected members as "assistants," and its members as "freemen," thus adopting the terminology of the medieval companies
or guilds, not that of Parliament. The first democratic government in America
grew out of the board of directors of a *company* whose constitution had its
origins in the medieval guilds.

---

1 For this section I have relied mainly on Daniels, B.C. (2012). *New England Nation. The Country
   the Puritans Built*. Palgrave Macmillan.

Thus the principle of congregational autonomy within the Puritan church led to its secular equivalent, the New England town meeting. Newtown (later renamed Cambridge) was the first new settlement to hold town meetings. In 1632, the male heads of households began to meet monthly to pass bylaws and issue administrative orders. By 1635, most towns had followed suit. The town of Dorchester codified and described the process and met weekly for the first few years. "Agreement made by the whole consent of the plantation [i.e., town] ... and every man to be bound thereby without gainsaying or resistance." (1633) Congregationalists just like Quakers did not understand their election and decision processes as manifestations of the human will, but rather as God working His way through the actions of church members.

In 1642, Thomas Lechford described the congregational church at work: "Every church hath power of government in and by itself... In Boston, they rule, most an-end by unanimous consent, if they can. ...In Salem, they rule by the major part of the Church; You that are so minded hold up your hands; you that are otherwise minded, hold up yours. In Boston when they cannot agree in a matter, they will sometimes refer it to some select brethren to hear and end.... Some churches have no ruling elders, some but one teaching Elder, some have two ruling and two teaching elders..."

Rhode Island was the colony where Puritan Dissenters were banished and when they formed their first governments, they adopted nearly universal, white male suffrage; they required written, private ballots as opposed to the customary public voting. They also codified and defended three great principles – liberty of conscience, separation of church and state and participatory democracy. Rhode Island secularized at an earlier time than its neighbours as well as pursuing a most aggressive form of capitalism.

Despite this belief in localism, the Puritans did strive for uniformity, hoping that education and persuasion could give them the cohesion that English monarchs and Roman popes had tried to impose through bishops, magistrates and armies. However, a synod met in Cambridge in 1646–48 and issued a comprehensive code, the Cambridge Platform, which become effectively a constitution for church government for the rest of the century: congregations could elect and dispose of their ministers and eligible voters must be adult male church members. But it did impose on all residents of the colony a strict Puritan orthodoxy which left no room for Anabaptists, Quakers, mainstream Anglicans or indigenous people not wishing to become Puritans. The Indians were subject to genocide, while the migrant ships kept bringing in emigrants of all the faiths to be found in England.

The first Quakers known to set foot in the New World were Mary Fisher and Ann Austin. They made converts but all were subject to severe repression until

1664, when Charles II issued instructions that Dissenters be allowed to worship unmolested in New England. The Quakers were still ostracized however.

In 1691, a property qualification for voting was substituted for the previous religious qualification and all laws could be appealed to England. Religious toleration continued by a thread in New England, but the tradition of local self-government continued up to the present day, on the basis of *majority voting*, notwithstanding the obligatory effort to achieve unanimity.

The New England Town Meetings are widely held up in the Deliberative Democracy movement (Gastil & Levine, 2005) as a model of non-adversarial democratic deliberation. The considerable social homogeneity of these communities of independent farmers and the long history of practice in deliberation ensured that majority voting was no barrier to finding consensus.

One is reminded of that other outstanding example of faith-based settlement, the Kibbutz movement in Israel. Here the smallest details of an individual's life may be governed by collective decisions of the whole community. And here again, it is majority voting which is the rule. Majority rule is by no means necessarily divisive, oppressive or adversarial.

The Peace and Civil Rights Movements

I return now to my search back to find exactly where Consensus entered the Peace and Civil Rights movements in the 1950s and '60s.

In my search for the earliest appearance of Consensus in the social movements of the 1960s, I found that people who were active in those movements in the early '60s tended to *merge* four distinct concepts together, viz., Nonviolence, Civil Disobedience, Participatory Democracy and Consensus decision making. As important as are each of these concepts are and as closely interconnected as they may be, it is important for my theme that I clearly distinguish Consensus from the other concepts with which it may be associated.

Civil disobedience is the active refusal to obey certain laws, norms, and lawful commands. It is not necessarily non-violent, and even when non-violent it can be confronting, provocative and even aggressive. For example, mounting a picket line, when, as is often the case, it is unlawful to do so, usually means actively deterring or obstructing others from entering a workplace. In the eyes of many this is a violent act. Nonviolence is a strategy which does not necessarily entail disobeying a law or although it certainly may, but it would not sanction mounting a picket line which actively obstructed people from passing.

It was Gandhi who developed nonviolent civil disobedience to a *science*, and is unquestionably the main source and inspiration for its practice in the US. And as is well-known, Martin Luther King was one of the many African-Americans who visited India to study Gandhi's methods. King adopted Gandhi's philosophy of nonviolence while at Crozer Theological Seminary between 1948 and 1951, and used it in the Civil Rights Movement during the Montgomery bus boycott in 1955. King was further confirmed in his belief in nonviolence during a visit to India in 1959. James Lawson had independently met students of Gandhi earlier while in India and returned to the US in 1955. He immediately joined King and became his leading 'theorist'. Based in Nashville, Lawson became a teacher of Gandhi's nonviolence strategy and, with Ella Baker and others, initiated the Student Nonviolent Coordinating Committee.

An email from Casey Hayden, who had been a participant in Women Strike for Peace (WSP), Students for a Democratic Society (SDS) and the Student Nonviolent Coordinating Committee (SNCC) from very early on in each case and of the Second Wave of the Women's Liberation Movement from its beginning, forwarded to me by Jo Freeman in February 2014, turned out to be decisive.

> The consensus decision making style came to SNCC I think, via the Nashville group. Direct influence of Fellowship Of Reconciliation and C.O.s

© KONINKLIJKE BRILL NV, LEIDEN, 2016 | DOI 10.1163/9789004319639_016

from WWII...included Nashville advisor Jim Lawson, who was also influenced by Gandhi and a stay in India. Bayard [Rustin] was part of that group, and the editor of *Liberation*, which published the second women's paper Mary [King] and I wrote.

I experienced it in Women Strike for Peace most forcefully, actually, in Ann Arbor. They were heavily influenced by the Quakers, I think.

The general idea during this time in all sectors of the '60s uprisings, in my experience, was that we were organizing outside citadels of power, and the most important issue was to be open to broad recruitment and to hold together. More important than theory about how to achieve power was the impetus to speak to and organize the powerless, and to speak to power...all influenced by peace movement orientation. Also influenced by the Y (part of the Student Christian Movement, allied with Catholic Workers, East Harlem Protestant Parish and so on) which operated in small groups, achieving consensus all the way up the before moving forward with action ...

I don't think there is much understanding of the broad ethical non-violent coalition which passed away when young black activists chose a more separatist and militant stand (reflecting the Marxism which also dominated the women's groups seeking theoretical and strategic agreement (I assume viewed as necessary to militant struggle against an agreed upon enemy) above other values).

I think Consensus in SNCC grew mostly from the idea that if folks were going to risk their lives they had to be able to do it for something they agreed with. And the ethical notion that if one disagreed with a plan, one might have to leave as a matter of conscience. And all that stuff about holding together and avoiding splits, the curse of the left. It's quite true that the talkier folk tended to dominate, but if one disagreed with any given outcome, you could just do something else, at least up until Waveland [in November 1964] and the hard liners... Then entered trashing.

I viewed organizing as expanding our counter communities of resistance until we were so large we overcame the powers that be...no need for theoretical and strategic agreement (which implies voting and/or throwing out anyone who disagrees...), only agreement on broad principles: (mine being segregation is wrong. war is wrong, women and children first) and willingness to die for it...or, perhaps more appropriate for today than back then when we were actually risking our lives...willingness to live it. (ellipses in original)

Mary King, who worked for SNCC for two years, was close to Martin Luther King, still collaborates with followers of Gandhi in India, and James Lawson to this day, responded on 14 April 2014:

> ... Casey is dead right in saying that the commitment to consensus came from the Nashville group [of SNCC]. They were the largest delegation to the Shaw University conference at Easter 1960 and reports have said that they were the most 'coherent'. At any rate they had been working with James M. Lawson in weekly workshops in autumn 1959 and with strong support from various local clergy had begun test actions aimed at discrimination in downtown stores.
>
> ... Jim also told me that the actual origin [of SNCC] was from the Nashville group's Central Committee during 1960–62. There was C.T. Vivian, and students and adults managed things jointly, but the committee always was chaired by a student. Initially they had 2 from each campus that had participants in their campaigns: 2 Fisk, 2 Tennessee State, 2 American Bible College, and, later, 2 from Vanderbilt or Peabody. Jim proposed for the structure of the Nashville movement that they reach consensus, seek a common mind. Jim said that they felt that they needed come together in a common place. They had no conversations on parliamentary order. Jim proposed a central committee as 'a structure to facilitate the operation, evaluation, and planning of the Nashville movement'. They decided to work at an issue until they could come to a common place. 'In creating a new kind of scenery for ourselves, if the questions were compelling, then we ought to be able to reach common decisions, and not have power plays'. In the committee, very often the major decisions were made from that spirit. It was part of the Nashville group's vitality.
>
> As to Jim's personal roots for this consensual search, he said it was the Methodist Youth Fellowships with which he grew up, and that this is how they had made decisions. He said that in all of his churches he had tried as much as possible to search for a common mind.
>
> Casey may well be right about Bayard, but this doesn't 'feel' right to me. I don't remember him as being intent on process, rather 'what' instead of 'how'. But I bow to Casey if she has exact recall. Jim told me that some had attributed it to Miss Baker, but he said that he had no evidence for that.
>
> At Shaw, consensus took. SNCC's 'Statement on Nonviolence' is attributed to Jim. But he says that he was recruited in the [April] 1960 meeting to be the 'drafter'. The whole group talked about it at great length. Eventually two different drafts emerged, as they tried to capture 'the mind of

the attendees'. He says it was the wishes of the group and was approved by the entire gathering by consensus. He recalled that subsequent reports had said that the Nashville group at Shaw had a 'common sense of commitment and passion', and that this was because they had been preparing themselves four months in the workshops and working together in the central committee, managing direct action. He also said that Diane [Nash]'s emergence as the leader was also consensual.

[Minor corrections have been made to this message, in the light of an interview King conducted with Lawson in June 2014, in which Lawson confirmed King's recollections as recorded here.]

Subsequent investigation confirmed that Eleanor Garst independently introduced Consensus to WSP in September 1961, but there remained some doubt in my mind about just how it appeared in SNCC in April 1960. But it is clear that there were two distinct, almost contemporaneous origins for Consensus in the social change movements about to break out in the US in 1960. I had a number of leads to follow up. There remained some doubts and alternative hypotheses, so before focusing on James Lawson and Eleanor Garst's stories we must review ten possible contributors: (1) Mahatma Gandhi, (2) SDS, (3) Ella Baker and (4) Bayard Rustin. No-one I have spoken to suggests that it was Martin Luther King who introduced Consensus. Though a charismatic and gifted orator, King was more of a follower than a leader in matters of policy and theory.

After telling James Lawson's story, I will also look at (5) the students who attended James Lawson's workshop and the founding meeting of SNCC in April 1960 and their prior experiences at (6) the Highlander Folk School in Tennessee and its prototypes, (7) the Danish Folkehøjskole, and failing all these ask whether Consensus was *invented* by (8) SNCC itself. Then I will tell the story of Eleanor Garst.

I have found no evidence that prior to 1971 there was any connection between the use of Consensus in social change activism and the small US Anarchist movement, but by 1971 it was already well-established in the Civil Rights, Nuclear Disarmament, Anti-War, Anti-Draft and Women's Liberation movements. It seems that the American Anarchist movement learnt their Consensus from (9) the Movement for a New Society, formerly A Quaker Action Group, after 1971. (10) The Anarchists and their tradition of decision making stretching back to the nineteenth century will be dealt with later.

Did Lawson learn Consensus from Gandhi? Dozens of leaders of the Civil Rights Movement visited Gandhi between 1935 and 1959. He was a huge influence. Gandhi had a superb political sense and continuously consulted the mood and aspirations of the Indian masses and tested out his estimation of their readiness to struggle with *experiments* in nonviolent struggle. This continuous, practical attention to the people is essential to nonviolent struggle, as it is to all social change activism. But he was no advocate of Consensus. In fact, so far removed from Consensus was he that it is almost necessary to define a new category of collective decision making especially for Gandhi. In brief, his method was "My way or the Highway." He often abandoned campaigns as soon as violence took place. When delegated by the Indian Congress in January 1930 to lead a campaign of civil disobedience in support of national independence, he went into *seclusion* for several weeks and then *announced* the Salt March. This campaign united the masses and marked the beginning of the end of the British Raj.

Although Gandhi took upon himself absolute control of any action he was involved in, in advance of any action he *consulted the masses* and his political sensibilities were so sharp that activists grew to trust his judgment, even when he seemed to fly in the face of reality. Gandhi consistently went over the heads of his closest comrades and took his advice from the masses. He was however acutely aware of the need for trained cadre of activists of sufficient number to be able to lead a mass movement, and would launch no action unless such a cadre was ready for it.

The Indian Congress used majority voting in the normal way, but Gandhi operated as a force unto himself, but when necessary he also used voting in order to gain commitment to a course of action. It was by force of his own personality that he maintained the unity and discipline of the movement.

According to Mary E. King: "Gandhi deserves the sole credit for persuading the Congress Party that nonviolent resistance could be effective. There was nothing inherent in India for this. The majority of the working committee of the Congress Party did not believe in nonviolence as a creed." (private email from Mary King, 14 April 2014.) If Gandhi had sought consensus on a strategy for Independence, it would not have been for non-violence.

Did the SDS introduce the idea of Consensus? 'Participatory democracy' was the ideal pursued by the Students for a Democratic Society, founded in 1962 by Casey Hayden's partner, Tom Hayden and others. Consensus was already firmly implanted elsewhere by that time, but further, the ideal of 'participatory democracy' as defined in the Port Huron Statement, took Majority for granted: it is about the *who* and *what* rather than the *how* of decision making.

According to Alan Haber, who was a founder of SDS in 1962, participatory democracy "goes beyond voting, although voting is crucial. It goes into birthplace democracy and neighbourhood democracy and community councils and community empowerment." (Hayden, 2012, p. 92) However, the definition given of participatory democracy (p. 132) was all about removing the distortion of public democratic life in America by the power of money and the insulation of important spheres of public life, such as business enterprises, from democratic decision making. It was very much based on the ethic of majoritarianism – the right of the mass of ordinary workers to out-vote the capitalists – and had nothing to do with Consensus, even if, as Casey Hayden reports, the sds itself realized participatory democracy "in sncc's consensus-style self-government" (p. 64). sds was converted to Consensus, but it did not originate it.

Did Ella Baker introduce Consensus to sncc? Ella Baker was advocating "participatory democracy" long before the founding of sncc or sds, but her concept of "participatory democracy" was something else again. At the time of the founding of sncc in April 1960, Ella Baker was 57, 25 years older than James Lawson, and 40 years older than most of the young people who would carry out the sit-ins. She was a gifted and seasoned organizer who described herself as a backroom person. She opposed the type of charismatic leadership practiced in the Black churches, and is remembered as an advocate of 'participatory democracy'. What this meant to Baker is nothing to do with Consensus or Majority. Rather, her credo was the active involvement of the base membership of any organization and their active control over the leadership. In relation to society at large, it meant relying on street-level activism to bring about change, rather than lobbying government or seeking to elect favoured candidates. There was not a shred of utopianism in her concept of participatory democracy, but rather it represented a practical approach to the struggle for social justice.

Baker attended the Easter 1960 meeting at which sncc was founded, resigned her position with the sclc (Southern Christian Leadership Conference) and became the much-admired and much-loved "Godmother of sncc." But Consensus was already established among the young members of sncc before the Easter 1960 conference, so Ella Baker cannot be credited with its invention or introduction.

Did Bayard Rustin introduce Consensus to sncc? Bayard Rustin was born in 1912, and raised in Pennsylvania by his maternal grandparents, a Quaker and a Methodist, educated at a African Methodist Episcopal Church (amec) college, and trained as an activist by the Quaker American Friends Service Committee (afsc). In 1936, he joined both the Young Communist League and the Fifteenth Street Meeting of the Quakers. He learnt nonviolence from the Fellowship Of Reconciliation (for) and worked with Congress of Racial Equality (core) on the 1947 Freedom Ride and in 1948 visited India to study Gandhi's methods of civil disobedience. He also helped organize the sclc and became a leading strategist for Martin Luther King 1955 to 1968, and King insisted on keeping him in this role despite attacks on Rustin as a Communist and an openly gay man.

Rustin was not involved with SNCC until July 1960. A scandalous attack on him by an NAACP official led to his withdrawal from SNCC in September 1960. So Rustin's involvement was too late and too short for him to be attributed with the introduction of Consensus.

James Lawson[1]

Via the Free African Society (FAS) the Methodists had recruited freed slaves in Philadelphia in 1787, but as a result of a racist incident, some left to found the African Methodist Episcopal Church (AMEC). Nonetheless, many African Americans stayed with the United Methodist Church. The AMEC split started in Philadelphia and the AMEC Zion Church was a split that came out of New York. It was to AMEC Zion, James Lawson was born in 1928. However, Lawson returned to The United Methodist Church, created by a 1939 merger of several branches of the Methodist Church, which set up five regional 'jurisdictions' of Methodists in the US, organized to maintain regionally identity and a sixth, called the 'Central Jurisdiction' which combined the Black annual conferences, thus building segregation into the constitution of the Church. The Methodists went through a long and painful process, carried out in accordance with the Methodist Code of Discipline, which mandates the principle of Majority, to re-integrate the white and Black, but it was not till after 1964 that Black conferences started to merge into white conferences. At the local level, congregations continued much as before. So it was within the Black section of the segregated United Methodist Church, that James Lawson became a Methodist.

James Lawson was born in 1928, in Uniontown, Pennsylvania. His father, James Snr., was the grandson of an escaped slave, and a Minister for the African Methodist Episcopal Zion Church in New England. James Snr. was a militant preacher; he packed a 38 pistol and set up branches of the NAACP wherever he was assigned to preach. After serving at St. James AMEZ Church in Massillon, Ohio, he transferred to the Lexington Annual Conference of the Central Jurisdiction of the United Methodist Church. James Snr. was no pacifist and according to Lawson he "refused to take any guff from anyone, particularly on the point of race" and "insisted that he was going to be treated as a man."

---

1 My principal sources for Lawson are "James M. Lawson, Jr.: Methodism, Nonviolence and the Civil Rights Movement," Dickerson, D.C. (2014), *Methodist History*, 52:3 and King, M. (1999). *Mahatma Gandhi and Martin Luther King Jr. The power of nonviolent action*, as well as private email messages from Mary King. All quotes in this section are Lawson's own words.

Lawson's mother, Philane May Cover, on the other hand, was decidedly non-violent. Lawson's challenge, which was to form his character, was to reconcile his father's militancy with his mother's nonviolence. Lawson grew up in Massillon. One day, at the age of 10, Lawson was asked by his mother to run an errand:

> A little white child in an automobile yelled 'nigger' out the opened window. I walked over...and, since I was in a hurry running my mother's errand, I smacked the child and went on my way. When the Lawson kids got called 'nigger' on the streets or at school, we usually fought. I don't know where we got that from, except that we figured that it was something to fight over.
>
> LAWSON, cited in King, 1999

On the return trip home, aware of possible repercussions, Lawson tried to find the parents of the offending child, to talk to them, but the car was gone. Once home, he told his mother of the incident. Lawson's mother replied, "Jimmy, what good did that do?"

> She talked about who I was, the fact of God's love, that we were a family of love and that such an incident could not hurt me, because of who I was. I don't remember anyone else being around, but a stillness took over my being at that moment. It was, as I realized much later on, a mystical experience. In a very real way, my life stood still. I realized in that stillness that I had changed forever. One of the phrases my mother used in her conversation with me was that 'there must be a better way'. I determined, from then on, that I would find the better way.
>
> LAWSON, cited in King, 1999, pp. 187–188

He first became acquainted with Gandhi's experiments in nonviolence as a child, thanks to the African-American press which the family discussed around the dinner table, and had read Gandhi's autobiography as a teenager. At Baldwin Wallace College, a liberal arts Methodist college in Berea, Ohio, he studied Thoreau, Gandhi and Tolstoy, and the pacifist theologians Dietrich Bonhoeffer and Reinhold Niebuhr. At age 19, he became a draft resister, refusing service in the Korean War. Executive director of Fellowship Of Reconciliation (FOR), A.J. Muste, frequently visited to lecture at the College:

> All of us in history classes were required to hear Muste. I was thrilled. He made me realize that I was not alone in my experimentation, that there

was a world movement, and a national movement. ... He acquainted me
with the Fellowship Of Reconciliation, which I joined on the spot in 1947.
That meant that I got exposed to their book list.

After hearing a lecture by A.J. Muste, he joined FOR and CORE. Muste was instrumental thereafter in strengthening Lawson's nonviolent orientation, directing
him towards Gandhi and later facilitating his entry into the sit-in and boycott
movement beginning in the South. In the late 1940s and early 1950s Lawson had
organized sit-ins and protests directed at establishments that discriminated
against blacks in Massillon, long before the Montgomery bus-boycott.

He was also active with the National Conference of Methodist Youth. Although a member of a segregated Methodist Church, he found plenty of support for his stands against racial discrimination and war from his white col-
leagues and church fellows. While he was in prison serving thirteen months
of a two and a half year term for draft resistance in 1952, he was re-elected as
Vice-President of the NCMY.

Wesleyan Methodism was central to Lawson's outlook. Just as John Wes-
ley had sought to cleanse individuals of iniquity, so could society be purged
of the social sins of slavery, segregation, poverty, and war. Generations of
African American Methodists from Harriet Tubman (AMEZ) and Henry
M. Turner (AME) in the nineteenth century, to Rosa Parks (AME) and James
Farmer (MEC), were led to social justice activism by this Methodist heritage.

Lawson used his prison time to read and think. Writing from prison in 1952
aged 23 years old and yet to enter the seminary, Lawson said he aspired to emulate "the life of Jesus, St. Francis, George Fox, Gandhi, Buddha…and other great
religious persons." These figures attached little importance to "theology but (to
their) experience with God." Further, he noted "religious failures today are in
(the arena of) experience and practice, not theology." When Lawson entered
prison, he was a Christian pacifist. He told Mary King however, that his "first
commitment was to work on race," and conscientious objection came second.
By the time of his release, he had advanced to Gandhian nonviolence. He won-
dered "why can't a mass non-violent revolution be staged throughout the South
where the segregation pattern is much like the 'untouchables' of India? Such a
movement would have to start with one person who had the Christian vision to
make such a revolution a reality in his own life." Gandhian nonviolence became
the synthesizing factor for Lawson's religious thinking: the militancy of his father's Methodism and the Christian pacifism that he drew from his mother.

Muste arranged for Lawson to visit India after his release from prison with a
letter of introduction to activists in the Gandhian movement, and he remained
in India from May 1953 to 1956, working at Hislop College in Nagpur, reading

Indian literature and working with Gandhi's movement. Lawson's practice would remain deeply religious; his nonviolence was saturated with the message of Christian love, and blended with principles synthesized from a broad range of religious and secular sources, both Eastern and Western. His aim was the "mass education and training of people in the use of nonviolent direct action techniques." Lawson insisted that "you are fighting a system, not an individual, not a race, or not the people of another country, but a system."

He continued his study of pacifism and Gandhian nonviolence at Oberlin College, Ohio. While still in India, he had read about Martin Luther King and his successful leadership of the Montgomery bus boycott. King's lecture at Oberlin on February 6, 1957, fortified his long-held intention to work in the South for transformative social change. After King's lecture to a packed audience, he and Lawson talked together at dinner. Though Lawson was contemplating study for a Ph.D., King told him "don't wait, but come south now!" adding that there was no one else like Lawson. Muste arranged for FOR to hire Lawson as southern field secretary to be stationed at Nashville in January 1958. Upon his arrival, he found that Glenn Smiley, national field director of FOR, had arranged for Lawson to run a full schedule of workshops – including one to take place early that year at the first annual meeting of the SCLC in Columbia, South Carolina.

At the SCLC meeting, King made an exuberant introduction of Lawson as FOR's new regional representative and discussed the organization's role in Montgomery, telling delegates to be sure to attend Lawson's workshop on nonviolence. King took his seat in the first pew, waiting for the three-hour session to start:

> Martin did that at every SCLC meeting as long as he lived. He would ask me to conduct an afternoon workshop, usually two or three hours, and he would arrange for it to be 'at-large' so that everyone could attend, with nothing else to compete. He put it on the schedule himself. A few minutes early, he would show up and sit alone, as an example, in the front row.

Back in Nashville, Lawson continued with Monday evening workshops during the autumn of 1959 in which he trained the students who were to be the core of the Nashville sit-in movement. As a result of his involvement with the sit-ins Lawson was expelled from Vanderbilt, but he enrolled with Boston University to finish his degree in theology, while continuing to work with the students. Several professors in the School of Theology resigned over his expulsion.

The techniques that the students deployed were drawn from Lawson's workshops. In 1958 and 1959, Lawson mobilized all that he knew about Christian pacifism, Gandhian nonviolence, and Methodist social ministry and blended

them into an unprecedented curriculum that influenced the civil rights movement in Nashville and beyond.

Blending Christianity and interreligious sources, he did not present its philosophy and practice as a secular doctrine, but as the essence of religion itself.
Core to nonviolence was mirroring God's love for humankind and exhibiting
it through concrete relationships of human solidarity and community. "Nonviolence," Lawson taught, "is the aggressive, forgiving, patient, long-suffering
Christ-like and Christ-commanded love or good-will for all humankind even in
the face of tension, fear, hatred, or demonic evil." Moreover, "it is the readiness
to absorb suffering with forgiveness and courage rather than to inflict suffering
on others."

Lawson divided his instruction into four modules: how nonviolence reacts,
training for nonviolence, the virtues of nonviolence, and the methods of nonviolence. Practitioners prepared themselves by jettisoning anger, hostility and
fear thus "minimizing the effect of an attack," valuing love, courage, fearless-
ness, and forgiveness, and pursuing redemptive suffering which "releases unknown elements for good." Preparation included meditation and prayer, study
of the scriptures, practicing nonviolence through challenges to segregation in
bus transportation and in other public facilities. The practical steps included
fact-finding, negotiation, education of the community, and various methods
of nonviolent direct action including sit-ins, boycotts, strikes, and civil disobedience. Lawson provided an extensive bibliography including relevant verses
from the Bible, the Bhagavad Gita, and from the Chinese philosopher, Mo Ti
and the Hebrew prophet, Isaiah.

The Nashville sit-ins and those led by students in other southern cities convinced Ella Baker of the SCLC to call a conference in April, 1960, at Shaw University in Raleigh, North Carolina. Out of this meeting emerged the Student
Nonviolent Coordinating Committee. Lawson delivered an opening keynote
address that helped to frame SNCC's nonviolent trajectory. Later, Lawson sum-
marized discussions and the consensus that emerged out of the conference,
and his synopsis received the approval of everyone there. Lawson's overall
comments said that "nonviolence as it grows from Judaic-Christian tradition
seeks a social order of justice permeated by love."

It was Lawson who delivered the keynote address and framed SNCC's nonviolent orientation.

> The whole group, perhaps 120 participants, all in the room, asked me to
> draft a statement. Eventually, three different drafts emerged. The Nashville
> group was cohesive. The extant draft was the third, influenced by the Nash-
> ville group, after two earlier conversations.
>
> Interview with King, June 2014

Lawson's synopsis was approved by the Conference.

In a private email message Mary King told me:

> He [James Lawson] was reading from the FOR booklist from a young age, but I don't think that he was influenced on notions of Consensus by Quakers, because the connection was too abstract. Let me underscore that he says it was for him Methodist origins.
>
> Private email, 15 April 2014

In his interview with Mary King, Lawson confirmed that the origin of Consensus in SNCC was the Nashville Central Committee, confirming what Mary King had told me in April. As to the roots Consensus in Lawson's own experience, he emphasized that:

> It was the Methodist youth and student movements with which I had grown up, and this is how they made decisions. They knew the rules of parliamentary procedures, but they wanted to find a common mind.
>
> Interview with King, June 2014

The Methodist Church to this very day still mandates Majority decisions, but this would never have entailed children voting – in general youngsters in these organizations were simply told what to do. The Black congregations had operated separately for more than a century, so there was some room for Lawson to develop a consensual model of collaboration in working with young people. It is also possible the Black congregations, like other Black Churches in America, drew on other traditions of decision making. We will return to this problem later.

Had the students who attended Lawson's workshops in nonviolence already adopted Consensus? They had all previously attended a course at the Highlander Folk School in Monteagle, Tennessee, modelled on the Danish Folkehøjskole. Here is Angeline Butler's report of the nonviolence training workshop in the Autumn of 1959.

> I began attending the Nashville Friends Sunday morning discussions and other informal meetings and events at the home of Quaker faculty member Dr. Nelson Fuson and his wife, Marian. Discovering the larger world outside the small world we had known, we began to open our minds to new ideas regarding American politics and race relations. Here we began the process of intellectual and spiritual exploration that led us into social activism.

The Fusons were connected to Highlander Folk School in Monteagle, Tennessee. Founded in the thirties, Highlander was a centre for exchanging ideas related to making social change. The centre encouraged labour organizing and civil rights efforts among both black and white southerners. In the spring of 1959 the Fusons took a group of Fisk students to Highlander. There we discussed the South, race relations, and the change that needed to come to the South and met long-time activists... In the company of these older activists, we held informal self-exploratory discussions that allowed us to see ourselves in the larger scheme of things in the South and the world. We also discussed more democratic ways of organizing. The central idea of Highlander was that people needed to talk and listen to one another until they could discover some common ground, some agreement on what changes needed to be made. Once a consensus was reached, only then could a method be applied.

Highlander provided an opportunity for black folks and white folks to sit down together, to experience communication as human beings. We had dinner together, washed dishes together, slept in bunk beds in the same room side by side, laughed, and shared humorous stories. We were able to touch one another and to see up close the obvious differences. We had to realize we each had God's light within us, that we were all from the *same* source and deserved to share the same opportunity in life.

In the fall of 1959 also through the Fusons, I heard about the workshops on nonviolence at Clark Memorial Church. With the help of members of the Nashville Christian Leadership Council – ... Rev.C.T. Vivian and others – Rev. James Morris Lawson Jr. organized and conducted the workshops. Lawson was a divinity student at Vanderbilt University and a field worker with the pacifist organization called the Fellowship Of Reconciliation. He had travelled to India to study the philosophy of Mahatma Gandhi and had already served time in jail as a Conscientious Objector to the Korean War. I recruited other students from Fisk to attend the workshops: Peggy Alexander and Diane Nash were among the female students who responded. Mary Anne Morgan from Meharry Medical College in Nashville came also.

In these workshops what we were all talking about was our future. A new phase of my life began as we addressed the truth about our place in the society and how the society looked upon us as a people. We studied Mahatma Gandhi, the life of Jesus Christ, and Thoreau. Pretty soon we applied their teachings of nonviolence and civil disobedience to the fundamental inequality of people in Nashville's segregated society. We began to define clear targets that needed changing. We wanted access to

all services in establishments where we spent money – lunch counters
in five-and-dime stores, department stores, bus stations, and drugstores.
HOLSAERT ET AL, 2012

So, according to Angeline's testimony, she learnt consensus at the Highlander
Folk School, *before* attending Lawson's workshops on non-violence. Before
looking in more detail at Myles Horton and the Highlander School, I asked: *did
the Highlander acquire Consensus from its model in Denmark?*

The Danish Folkehøjskole

Myles Horton had visited Denmark in 1931 in search of a model for commu-
nity education which would promote social change. He visited a number
of folkehøjskoler, but he was particularly impressed with the International
People's College (IPC) at Elsinør. The folkehøjskoler were created in 1867 by
Danish Lutheran Bishop N.F.S. Grundtvig and IPC was founded in 1921 by Peter
Manniche. During the Great War, Manniche had visited the Woodbrooke
Quaker Study Centre in England, and he was struck by the tranquillity and
spirit of peace activism and became a Quaker. Manniche developed the idea
that people from countries that had been former enemies should have opportunities to live, work and study together at a folkehøjskoler. So here was another Quaker connection! Further investigation brought to light an exercise used
at the IPC in 1996, which was a kind of consensus decision making exercise.
I further learnt that Denmark is widely held to have a consensus style of
politics – they even have a board game called Konsensus.

However, all of these leads proved to be false.

Whatever Manniche brought back from Quaker Study Centre, he did not
introduce the Quaker way of running meetings at IPC. The exercise proved to
be an exercise in multi-party Bargaining, in which a group of people have to
collectively prioritise a set of valued objects. Like the game of Konsensus, this
exercise does model Danish political life, but Danish political life is as fragmented and conflict-riven as that of any country.

Ever since the ancient Folketing (equivalent to the Anglo-Saxon witenagemot), was recreated in 1849 as the lower house in a bicameral legislature within
a constitutional monarchy, Denmark has been governed by a minority government. The situation of minority government obliges the parties to makes deals
and bargain to achieve what they want. When mutually independent parties
strike a deal, this is *not* Consensus, because Consensus presupposes the joining
of the wills of all participants in a single project; in the case of the bargaining
which goes on in a Parliament where there is minority government, the parties
to the bargain *retain their mutual independence* and there is no shared will.

Denmark is marked by highly developed practices of conflict resolution, achieved by means of Negotiation. As a small trading nation, on the crossroads between powerful and warlike neighbours, the Danes learnt how to strike a deal. But the practice of bargaining is by no means unique to Denmark, and nor is the tendency to refer to this deal-making as "consensus." In both Japan and Denmark, for example, the process of negotiating business contracts and settling labour disputes is referred to as "consensus," and I have found that some labour educators in the US also refer to the process of union-management bargaining as a process of finding "consensus."

This practice of trading off your wish-list to strike a bargain is not what is meant by Consensus decision making, and Myles Horton, for example, specifically rejected this approach to fighting for social change, and nor was this the type of decision making practiced in SNCC. The Highlander Folk School, however, was not a false lead.

Myles Horton and the Highlander

Myles Horton was the first of four children, born in 1905 into a poor white family at Paulk's Mill outside of Savannah in West Tennessee. His parents were former school teachers and Presbyterians, both from families who had lived in Tennessee for many generations. Myles's father, Perry, having had a grammar school education, had secured a job as a county official, while his mother, Elsie, was a respected and active member of the community. Myles attended the elementary school at nearby Brazil, and completed eighth grade, which was as far as the school went. Thanks to help from a family friend he was able to enter the nearby Cumberland Presbyterian College in the autumn of 1924, where he would receive religious training. It was here also that Horton read Shelley. From Shelley, Horton learnt that it was right to stand up to authority in support of social justice, and never to be afraid of punishment or to submit to the temptation of rewards. While still working his way through college, he came under fire for agitating amongst factory workers and was involved in a number of social justice issues. He also read Marx.

> It was then that I discovered about Marxism and analysis of society on a class basis. ... So I found from Marx that I could get tools, not blueprints, tools that I could use for analyzing society. That helped me to analyze. Then I had to get a synthesis of my religious background and my understanding of economic forces.
>
> HORTON, 2003

During the summer breaks, Horton had been running a Bible class for children for the Presbyterian Church in Ozone, Tennessee. In 1927, he expanded his class to include adults, and attracted an ever expanding crowd to a program of community education in which he encouraged participants to share their problems and through discussion and talks by invited experts, seek solutions to these problems. The residents of Ozone appreciated him so much they urged Horton to forego his last year of college and stay on teaching at Ozone. But Horton was well aware of his own limitations, and promising the community that he would return, set off on a journey to discover how real social change could be achieved through education.

First came his own education. A local Congregationalist minister, Abram Nightingale, helped Horton work his way through a reading program covering the history and culture of the South, the social problems of Appalachia and the moral issues of modern capitalism. In the summer of 1929, Nightingale

© KONINKLIJKE BRILL NV, LEIDEN, 2016 | DOI 10.1163/9789004319639_017

persuaded Horton to apply to the elite Union Theological Seminary in New York. To his own surprise, Horton was accepted. Here he came under the radical socialist theologian Reinhold Niebuhr who was to become his lifelong friend, mentor and supporter.

After completing his course at the seminary in 1930, he attended the University of Chicago where took classes with Robert Park and learned about group problem solving and conflict resolution and acquainted himself with the ideas of John Dewey. Horton continued to read and toured the country, studying utopian communities, community education projects and Native American communities. He became convinced that utopian communities which cut themselves off from the wider community were of little value in achieving social change. He also visited Jane Addams at Hull House on several occasions, but nothing he saw satisfied him. He completely rejected the conception of vocational education, which, like school education, was intended only to fit people into the status quo, and he was hostile to programs which served to "educate people out of their class." None of these projects had any potential to effect social change.

He had read about the Danish folkehøjskoler, and in 1931, travelled to Denmark with Don West to see if these Folk Schools lived up to their reputation. He was disappointed, partly because he felt that the spirit which had animated the early folkehøjskoler had been lost, and partly because he realized that the folkehøjskoler belonged to a certain times and a certain culture and could not be transplanted into twentieth century America. Nonetheless he noted with approval the following features of the folkehøjskoler all of which he was later to adopt at the Highlander Folk School:

> Students and teachers living together;
> Peer learning;
> Group singing;
> Freedom from state regulation;
> Non-vocational education;
> Freedom from examinations;
> Social interaction in non-formal setting;
> A highly motivating purpose;
> Clarity in what for and what against.
>> HORTON, 1990, p. 52–53

Before returning home he wrote to himself:

> What you must do is go back, get a simple place, move in and you are there. The situation is there. You start with this and let it grow. You

know your goal. It will build its own structure and take its own form. You can go to school all your life, you'll never figure it out because you are trying to get an answer that can only come from the people in the life situation.

HORTON, 2003, p. 3

Horton returned to Tennessee and was given a farmhouse in Monteagle, in Grundy County – one of the poorest counties in the USA, where he established the Highlander Folk School in 1932, in the depths of the Great Depression.

Highlander

Horton was clear from the outset about the motivating purpose of his project:

From the start it was aimed at reaching southern workers who would be willing to build a new social order. We wanted to use education as a tool to bring about social change in the South. ... I thought there ought to be a revolution in this country. (2003, pp. 8 & 125)

There were three components to Highlander's programs. Firstly, they delivered community education, much like what he had been doing in Ozone years before, for the local community in Monteagle. As a result of this service he earned the loyalty of the community, and when Highlander was firebombed, raided by the police or the Ku Klux Klan, witch-hunted in the press, shot at and subject to all manner of slander and legal attack, the community stuck by them. But this component was never going to bring about social change.

The second component was the residential program. Horton actively engaged with organizations in the region, in the early days, mainly the labour unions, and encouraged them to send to Highlander emerging grass-roots leaders – not people who were on the union payroll and owed allegiance to the bureaucracy, but shop-floor people whose loyalties remained with their peers. Students would come typically for two or three weeks and over time they built up to classes or 20 or 30 students.

The third component was what he called the extension program. This entailed taking the Highlander staff and students out to picket lines or whatever struggles were going on at the time and doing whatever they could to help. This included actively participating in picketing, research, fund-raising and publicity as well as running Highlander-type courses on the picket lines, including singing and dramatics as well as discussion groups. Workers from these struggles would then be selected on the same kind of criteria as for the residential courses, and brought back to Highlander for a few days or longer if possible.

When students left Highlander, and went back to their organizations, in 90% of cases they took up full-time leadership positions. Highlander maintained contact with them and continued to help them work through the problems they were dealing with. By this means, Horton and the Highlander built up a network of support which could be called upon when required. They knew everyone and everything that was going on in the South, and their reputation in the labour movement grew accordingly.

Highlander also had at any given time some graduate students, typically from Northern universities, working with Highlander for research or practicum. Everyone at Highlander, without exception, participated in every activity on an absolutely equal footing with everyone else. This included both the manual work needing to be done about the farm (money was so short, growing their own food was obligatory and there were no salaries paid), discussion and participation in struggles during the extension program.

The history of Highlander is marked out by a succession of projects. At a certain point, Highlander let go of a program that they had been running, and handed it over to the organizations to run on their own behalf, rather than by sending recruits to Highlander. Then Horton would intensively research a new domain of activity, often leaving Highlander for extended periods to go and live and work and organize in an area, before launching a new project. Horton was able to anticipate with remarkable success the emergence of new social movements and the fact is that his programs could only work in close connection with a growing social movement.

The first project, beginning in 1932, growing slowly under terribly difficult conditions, was work amongst the poorest stratum of workers in the labour movement. The CIO (Congress of Industrial Organizations, originally Committee for Industrial Organization – dedicated to general unionism as opposed to craft unionism) was founded in 1935, and Highlander was subsequently accepted as their official educational arm. That is, Horton started working with the hitherto unorganized sections of the working class just as the move towards industrial unionism was emerging, and three years before the American Federation of Labor set up the Committee for Industrial Organization.

In the mid-1940s, Horton began to hand the union education program back to the CIO unions and turned to the poor farmers in the South in collaboration with the National Farmers' Union, 90% of whose members were in the North. In the late 1940s and early 1950s he turned to the movement against racial segregation, a few years before the *Brown vs. Board of Education* case was heard in the Supreme Court, and their unanimous finding announced on May 17 1954 triggered the school desegregation struggle.

The Civil Rights Movement grew out of this struggle, and well before the Birmingham Bus Boycott in 1955, Highlander was deeply involved with all those who were to become leading activists. In the mid-1960s, they handed their education program back to the Southern Christian Leadership Conference to run themselves and turned back to where they had started from, to address the problems of poverty in Appalachia, and an array of cooperative ventures emerged as a result of their work.

The program which Highlander ran for the labour movement in the first years had something approximating to a curriculum. The core curriculum was labour economics, labour history, public speaking, union tactics, dramatics, labour journalism and what they called 'parliamentary law', i.e., formal meeting procedure. From 1937, they used the ACWA (Amalgamated Clothing Workers of America) rule book and a mock AFofL Convention held at the end of each term to teach meeting procedure. Myles Horton ran classes on union problems, including organizing methods, strike tactics and race relations. Participants would write and produce a short play on a labour theme and role-play negotiating a union contract.

However, Horton became dissatisfied with this program: "We were giving answers to questions they didn't have," and went on to develop the unique approach which led to Highlander becoming arguably the greatest force for social change in the South.

Horton realized that people were coming to Highlander looking for experts who would give them the answers to their problems. But this was never going to work. They had been habituated to regard their own experience and that of their peers as worthless, and yet it was only by analyzing their own experience and taking their own experience as a starting point that they could resolve their problems and learn from it. But they were the experts in their own experience. Horton believed that adults learnt through experience and every adult had something like the same amount of experience: but they needed to learn how to analyze that experience. The staff at Highlander might indeed have a lot of knowledge and solutions to offer, but unless this knowledge arose out of the workers' own experience, it would mean nothing to them. The first task was to get people to voice their problems and talk about their own experience, together with others, including their peers as well as the staff. Very soon others would chime in with similar experiences and people would begin to search for further information about these problems – where they may have arisen in the past, how others had resolved them, and so on as well as seeking background information, such as the relevant legal codes, underlying economic conditions, and so on. Horton said that once people learn to analyze their own experience and that of their peers, ninety per cent of the time they find that what they thought was their problem was not at all, and they begin to dig deeper. Staff were then able, as equals, to share their experience, suggest books where answers may be found, invite experts to come and answer questions which had arisen in the discussion the answers for which were not readily available.

Experts were invited to address classes to provide information about specific problems when the students requested it, but often they were sent home again if their input was not specifically requested by the students. No material was ever introduced except as it arose from a life situation presented for discussion by the students. The students tended to remain convinced that they would have to get the answer from an expert, but even when staff or invited experts believed they had the answer, it would not be provided, nor any suggestion given that they had a solution. The workers had to find the solution to their own problems by analyzing their own experience and pursuing questions that arose out of the analysis of their own experience. Sometimes staff would put questions to the group, so as to focus the discussion and help the discussion move in a productive direction, but never provided answers; sometimes they would help manage domineering personalities or other difficulties that might put up barriers to discussion, that's all. And of course their experience with running such workshops allowed them to prompt participants in profitable directions with well-aimed questions.

This reliance on the experience of poor people as the source of solutions to their own problems, experience which was as valuable as the experience of any expert, was crucial to the egalitarianism which prevailed at Highlander. People learnt not only to value their own experience and that of their peers but they also came to feel comfortable interacting with middle-class people, academics and so on, as equals, confident in their own knowledge.

Decision Making

Horton found that poor people, especially uneducated or young people, or people in minority groups, not only regarded their own knowledge and experience as worthless, but had become habituated to having every important decision in their life made for them, and being told at every point what they should do, to the extent that they were quite incapable of making a decision for themselves, let alone as part of a group. And yet the ability to make a decision, and even more importantly, to make a *collective* decision together with their peers was the very essence of liberation – taking charge of their own lives. Collective decision making was also central to the very meaning of learning.

> Learning and decision making are inseparable. People learn from making decisions and learning helps them make decisions. The motivation

for decision making, like the motivation for learning, comes through genuine involvement in an undertaking considered worthy of the effort and possible to achieve. ...significant learning proceeds *in the process of shared decision making.*

HORTON, 2003, pp. 246–7

The day-to-day running of the school would be placed in the hands of the students. At the beginning of each residence, the staff would inform the students about what previous students had done and then it would be left to the students to decide everything. The students usually found this situation distressing at first, but staff would refuse to give directions or make suggestions. The same applied to the problems which workers brought with them to Highlander for resolution. There is a story told in which a group of workers involved in a difficult strike had come to Highlander for a weekend residence to discuss their strike, but at a certain point found that they did not know what they were going to do, and demanded of Horton that he tell them what they should do. Horton refused, and a worker put a gun to Horton's head saying that if he didn't tell them what to so he would shoot him. Still Horton would not give way.

So this is what Highlander was doing: teaching poor people to trust their own experience and that of their peers and helping them learn how to analyze that experience and forcing them to take charge of their own lives by participating in the process of collective decision making and taking responsibility for those decisions.

During the first phase of Highlander's work, with the CIO, collective decision making meant forming committees, having meetings and so on and making decisions the way decisions have always been made in the labour movement, by Majority. Horton said that he never agreed with majority voting, but this is what the workers needed to take charge of their lives in and through the union movement.

Segregation

In the South, segregation had the force of law. Not only that, union activists in the South might even be Klan members. Nonetheless, Horton always made it known to the unions sending members to Highlander that Highlander was an integrated school. Racial segregation increasingly became a barrier to Highlander's objectives, however. Whenever they had tried to build unions, coalitions or virtually anything else, they eventually came up against the barrier of racism. Highlander always stood firm against the pressure to segregate, but for a number of years the unions selected segregated groups to send to Highlander.

On one celebrated occasion, Horton invited a black worker to a union class and a member of the KKK whose union was paying for the course objected and demanded that the black worker be excluded. Horton refused and said that if he didn't like it he (the Klan unionist) could leave. Objecting that he had paid for the course, he grumbled, but stayed, and he learnt from the experience; as a union official he later included black members in the groups he sent to Highlander from his own union. Over time, the people coming to Highlander just accepted it. Horton did not make integration a topic of discussion, but people just learnt through the experience of learning together, and as Angeline Butler related, eating and working together and sharing bedrooms and bathrooms together, and working towards common goals, that it wasn't so terrible after all.

Between 1932 and 1947, 6,800 students had participated in Highlander residences and over 12,000 workers had participated in extension classes. This work transformed the labour movement in the South, the more so because Highlander graduates invariably moved into leadership positions representing the lowest grades of the proletariat in the South, and they remained in touch with Highlander afterwards. Despite the progress Highlander had made towards integrating the unions, few Highlander graduates believed that integration could be extended beyond the union movement.

The relationship with the conservative CIO leadership was becoming untenable however. Anyone who openly advocated political action beyond the narrow pursuit of union wages and conditions faced expulsion. The CIO responded to the House Unamerican Activities Committee witch-hunt by demanding their affiliates, including Highlander, make declarations of opposition to and dissociation from Communism. Highlander's refusal to comply meant parting ways with the CIO. The responsibility for union education was handed back to the CIO to run for themselves, but the methods developed by Highlander which was encouraging initiative from the ranks of the union movement, were not continued by the CIO. Highlander had gone as far as it could in organizing the lowest ranks of workers in the South into unions; it was time to move on.

The war had created demand for farm produce and the end of the war only increased demand, and Horton determined that it was time to turn to the poor farmers of the South. The next phase of their work was directed at educational work amongst farmers, both black and white, assisting them in developing cooperatives and encouraging the growth of the National Farmers Union.

Highlander was able to use the contacts they had made through their union work to make new contacts with farmers, and after 5 or 6 years working amongst farmers they had built up a broad layer of support amongst both black and white sections of the rural poor in the South and a large number of cooperative ventures were being operated by farming communities, giving them a degree of independence from the agribusinesses which had always exploited them.

Until 1954 only 10 to 15 percent of students at the school were black, but during the summer of 1954, in the wake of the Supreme Court finding on school segregation, about 50 percent of the workshop participants were black. For the next decade, a majority of those coming to Highlander would be black as Horton became convinced that a social movement was building up in the South.

Horton did not attempt to suppress racial conflict within the school, but the experience of living together and working towards a common goal invariably led to participants accepting the egalitarian and integrated regime at Highlander and they were invariably full of praise for these practices by the time they left.

The Civil Rights Movement

A one-week workshop for the United Furniture Workers of America held in May 1954 included 35 blacks and whites from 16 locals. The course covered the use of formal meeting procedure and all the usual topics of interest to unionists, but they also discussed the importance of union participation in the drive for school desegregation.

At that time, there was a lot of interest in the UN and the new world situation following the end of the war, and Highlander held workshops where people could learn about the United Nations and the progress being made by the National Liberation Movements around the world. Horton particularly sought out blacks who were relatively free of pressure from white people, either because they ran their own businesses serving the black community, or were preachers in the black churches which were all owned by their black congregations.

In August 1954, the bus owner/driver, Esau Jenkins, and the retired schoolteacher, Septima Clark, attended one of these workshops. They came from Johns Island, one of the Sea Islands of South Carolina, one of the most deprived and marginalized areas in the country, where people spoke a dialect incomprehensible to outsiders. Jenkins drove the bus that took people to work on the mainland every day and he had been trying to teach people to read while driving his bus, so they could register to vote. According to the Constitution of South Carolina, poor black people had to prove they could read by reading the Constitution, before they were allowed to vote.

A two-week summer workshop on school desegregation in May 1955 attracted 50 teachers, unionists, students and community leaders, among them Rosa

Parks, whose fare to Monteagle had been paid for by the Alabama branch of the NAACP. A July 1955 workshop on the UN was attended by a young beautician, Bernice Robinson, who was inspired to help her cousin, Septima Clark, promote community activity on Johns Island.

The visit of Esau Jenkins, Septima Clark and Bernice Robinson to Highlander led to Highlander's most successful program – the Citizenship Schools, and within a few months of attending Highlander, Rosa Parks triggered the famous Montgomery Bus Boycott, conventionally taken as the beginning of the Civil Rights Movement. Rosa Parks had made no plans while at Highlander, but she went home with a different spirit. According to her own testimony Rosa Parks's decision to refuse to give up her seat to a white man and to force the police to arrest her was because at Highlander she had found respect as a Black person and white people that she could trust. This gave her the courage to insist on being treated with respect and confidence in eventual victory.

After Esau Jenkins raised the problem of voter registration in the Highlander workshop, Highlander took on this project, and Horton spent several months, on and off, in Johns Island, learning the dialect and familiarizing himself with people's lives there. A room was hired and Bernice Robinson was appointed teacher; Bernice was given no direction as to how to teach and had no teaching experience. All she had was what she had learnt at Highlander about treating people with respect and as equals, beginning from their experience and responding to people's problem as they saw them. On 7 January 1957, she stood nervously before her first class and said "I'm not a teacher. I really don't know why they wanted me to do this, but I'm here and I'll learn with you. I'll learn as I go along." She pinned up a copy of the Universal Declaration of Human Rights on the wall and told her students that by the end of the term she wanted them all to be able to read it. She had brought with her reading material from her local elementary school but immediately realized that these were inappropriate for her adult class. Allowing the problems raised by the class to set their program, they worked on writing their own names and moved on to reading the labels on supermarket cans, filling out work dockets, filling in the blanks in a mail order catalogue – all those practical everyday tasks which frustrate the illiterate person. In two months the enrolment increased from 14 to 37. The final exam was to go down to County Hall and register to vote. Throughout the program, approximately 80% of the class passed the exam at the end of the approximately three-month term.

Septima Clark was appointed director of the program, which became known as the Citizenship School, and rapidly spread across the South. New teachers were apprenticed to Bernice by observing her at work in the classroom, and these new teachers in turn trained others. By 1961, over four hundred teachers had been trained, and there'd been over four thousand students. By 1970, approximately 100,000 illiterate black people had learnt to read and had registered to vote, and many hundreds of black people, none of them with teaching credentials of any kind, had been trained as teachers by the former beautician Bernice Robinson and her apprentices. Very many of these teachers would go on to become activists in the Civil Rights movement. The program, together with Septima Clark as Director, was subsequently handed over to the Southern Christian Leadership Conference to run as their own program.

The runaway success of the Citizenship School was possible only thanks to the fact that there was a revolutionary situation in the South. Horton was able to detect this in its earliest stages and provided the kind of education which not only gave black people the confidence to stand up to the system and offer leadership to their communities, and the knowledge that there were elements of the white population who could be expected to support them, but also the means to analyze their situation and draw on the experience of the black communities in the South to overcome the barriers erected against them.

The first lunch counter sit-in was staged by four black students from North Carolina Agricultural and Technical College at the Woolworth lunch counter in Greensboro, North Carolina, on 1 February 1960. On 1 April 1960, Highlander held its seventh annual college workshop entitled "The New Generation Fights for Equality," the focus of which was demonstrations, college students, and the civil rights movement. Two weeks later, sit-in leaders, many of whom had participated in the Highlander workshop, met in Raleigh, North Carolina, to form the Student Nonviolent Coordinating Committee (SNCC).

Here are some of Horton's own words on these events. On nonviolence:

> Education per se is nonviolent. ... Our whole approach to life is an educational approach. We can't beat things into people's heads, so in that sense we predate the nonviolent advocacy. ...
>
> The student leaders were influenced primarily by Martin Luther King and people like the Reverend James Lawson, who has been conducting workshops in Nashville. But the first meeting of the sit-inners, which later became the SNCC, was at Highlander, and I remember the discussion very well. In fact, I have some written records of it. On tape I have a speech I made to them at the time. I said: 'I am convinced that these spontaneous student protests mark the beginning of a sustained effort which will lead to fuller participation by Negroes in all phases of economic and political life'. My observation then was that 15 or 20 per cent of the students espoused nonviolence philosophically and for the

rest of them it was a matter of going along with what seemed to be the best procedure.

HORTON, 2003, p. 148–9

In relation to formal meeting procedure and majority voting, he made the following criticism of officials of the Democratic Party who effectively excluded black people from participation in the Party:

> They never examined their racism which showed itself to me in their assuming that all the structures that white people hold so dear, parliamentary law, majority votes, what I call procedure sort of claptrap, should be held dear by Negroes also. ... Negroes have never mastered that way, their churches don't act that way. The civil rights movement taught white people not to act that way. In the mountains poor people got together and they don't have any Robert's Rules of Order, don't have any procedure. They get together and talk. None of your poor people, Negroes or whites, fit these categories.

HORTON, 2003, p. 180–1

According to Horton, Majority was the mode of decision making used in the American political system and in the labour movement, but it had no inherent virtue. For those excluded from these institutions, which meant not only blacks but also the poor white famers of Tennessee, these procedures made no sense. Consequently, in implementing Highlander's approach to education which hinged on collective decision making, during the civil rights period, Horton did not use voting and formal meeting procedures, but began from the experience of his students, developed in accordance with strict egalitarian principles and relations which prevailed at Highlander.

> At Highlander, we frequently recruited people for workshops on the basis that they had problems in their community and had expressed the desire to talk with other people who had similar problems. Staff members would be available to help, for example, with techniques of keeping discussions properly focused or with bits of factual information. ... In each case significant learning proceeded *in the process of shared decision making*. The participants themselves, in effect, were inventing alternate channels for their own education. ... The civil rights movement in the South demanded precisely this kind of learning made possible by democratic decision making of the type described. Every time people decided to ride a Freedom Bus, or to sit in at a lunch counter, or to march down a

highway, individual learning and conscientization takes place. If they had not, there would have been little determination, little staying power and (probably) insufficient courage. The people would not have developed the sense of potency and worth necessary for sustained militant action.

HORTON, 2003, p. 245–6

Not only were black people and poor whites educated in the use of this kind of decision making, a kind of decision making which arose naturally as an extension of their own experience, but the young white college students who came down to work in solidarity with the black people putting their lives on the line in the sit-ins and Freedom Bus rides, were also trained in this type of decision making which would have been equally novel for them.

Horton does not necessarily have the last word on this. It cannot be assumed from the absence of formal procedures and voting that these poor communities normally practised Consensus. Prior to their experience at Highlander, most of these people would have found making decisions in such a way extremely difficult. Generally speaking deference to one's elders and one's social superiors, both within their own community and at large, would have ruled out the kind of open and egalitarian consensus-seeking which we associate with SNCC-style Consensus. The kind of decision making which was manifested in SNCC was an *extension* of the experience black people had had in their own communities, but it was not identical to it. It was an *invention* marking the transformation of formerly oppressed people into political actors in the life of the nation.

As I see it, when the students went from Highlander into the nonviolence workshops with James Lawson and on to the founding of SNCC, they freely made the decisions, as Mary King reports, about the delegate structure of SNCC and continued on with the decision making practices that they had learnt at Highlander. Lawson immediately recognized that this mode of operating was entirely appropriate to the extremely dangerous nonviolent actions they were planning and continued to foster the practice of Consensus with the students.

SNCC[1]

After the success of the Montgomery bus boycott campaign 1955, and the publicity it received, students in black colleges and universities in the

---

1   In addition to the personal recollections of Mary King and Casey Hayden, I have used numerous sources for the SNCC, including *Many Minds, One Heart: SNCC's Dream for a New America*, by Wesley Hogan.

South – generally in isolation from each other or in small groups of threes and fours – began to consider what to do next. In 1958–59, the Nashville Christian Leadership Conference, the first affiliate of the SCLC, undertook a nonviolent direct action campaign aimed at downtown stores and restaurants. Extensive preparations had begun, including workshops at Highlander, and in the autumn of 1959, James Lawson began his weekly Monday-evening meetings in Gandhi's theories and techniques. Experiments were carried out, including small sit-ins for practice and role-playing. These workshops lasted for several months in the autumn and winter of 1959.

In February 1960, a successful sit-in at Woolworths in Greensboro by four Black students from the North Carolina Agricultural and Technical State University, triggered the coalescence of these groups. When news broke of the Greensboro sit-ins, 75 Nashville students began the largest, most disciplined and influential of the sit-in campaigns in 1960.

The Student Nonviolent Coordinating Committee (SNCC) was founded at the Easter 1960 conference at Shaw University, North Carolina, attended by 126 student delegates from 58 centres in 12 states where sit-ins had already begun, as well as Martin Luther King, Ella Baker, Howard Zinn, James Lawson and delegates from FOR and CORE. The conference was convened by the SCLC, and Ella Baker gave up her job at SCLC to join SNCC, which remained independent of the SCLC. Even though all the participants were now already experienced activists, the Nashville group – with the extensive collective reflection and training that they had undergone with Lawson – were the decisive influence in forming the character and nonviolent orientation of SNCC, and all of this group went on to play leadership roles in the movement throughout the South.

It seems that the Nashville students had acquired powerful skills in Consensus from two independent sources – Myles Horton and James Lawson – before they led the founding of SNCC as an autonomous organization and their Consensus practice began to change the face of America. But according to Horton, Consensus is not foreign to the practices of African American Churches which were the central institutions of the Black communities.

The evidence that SNCC practiced Consensus decision making is clear enough and acknowledged by all. Here is a recollection by Wesley Hogan.

> Casey [Hayden] often acted as recorder for the SNCC meetings at B.B. Beamon's restaurant on Auburn Avenue in Atlanta. The discussions, as Charles McDew noted, could ramble – 'Somebody may have spoken for eight hours, and seven hours and fifty three minutes was utter bullshit, but seven minutes was good'. Casey's dexterity in human relations was

evident in these meetings as she became skilled in the development of consensus – an absolutely critical component of SNCC's functioning at that time. Majority rule would not suffice: 'Consensus was important in nonviolence, because the final arbiter of one's behaviour was one's conscience'. Whoever lost in a vote, therefore, following their conscience, 'might have to leave the group'. So in SNCC, unity came first. Yet it was hard to achieve. Black Mississippian Joyce Ladner said that the staff meetings in which she participated sometimes lasted days. 'You'd think you're going to arrive at a decision after all this dialectical stuff goes on, and then someone jumps up and says, "Well, who gave you the right to decide?" and then you start all over again'. Casey recalled that 'it took real effort to find the line of thinking, and make it clear without distorting anything. If I could do that, I could assist in the development of consensus'.

HOGAN, 2009, p. 107

Note that as Hogan points out, the term 'unity' was often used at that time, rather than 'consensus'. On Mary King's home page we find the following description:

In SNCC, we tried to make all decisions by consensus... In SNCC it meant discussing a matter and reformulating it until no objections remained. Everyone and anyone present could speak. Participants included those of us on staff (a SNCC field secretary was paid $10 weekly, $9.64 after tax deductions), but, as time went on, an increasing number of local people would participate as well – individuals whom we were encouraging and coaching for future leadership. Our meetings were protracted and never efficient. Making a major decision might take three days and two nights. This sometimes meant that the decision was in effect made by those who remained and were still awake!

When building a nonviolent movement, one cannot order another to take a public stand or break the law. Individuals must decide for themselves whether they are ready to make the sacrifices entailed and pay the penalties that civil disobedience requires. The experience of making such profound decisions, both individually and as a group, cultivates democratic skills and an expectation of participatory processes in future governance. This phenomenon isn't found in movements that rely on violent tactics. (http://maryking.info/?p=920)

In a private email message Mary King told me:

In my mind the most important reason for the making of decisions by consensus in the SNCC context is that it simply would not work to use majority numerical voting to take a decision that could endanger the participants. How could someone who had doubts, or was not fully committed, be ordered into taking, say, direct action, if it might result in his or her being beaten, or worse? Only that individual could decide. In top-down armed struggle you could order someone to take an action, but not in nonviolent struggle.

PRIVATE EMAIL MESSAGE, 15 April 2014

The first target of SNCC was the segregated lunch counters in stores in the central business district of Nashville. Sit-in participants, who consisted mainly of black college students, were often verbally or physically attacked by white onlookers, abused, threatened, spat upon and had cigarettes stubbed out them. The students always remained polite and respectful despite the provocation. Despite their refusal to retaliate, over 150 students were eventually arrested for refusing to vacate store lunch counters when ordered to do so by police. On April 19, their lawyer's home was bombed and nearly 4,000 people marched to City Hall to confront the Mayor who stated that he agreed that the lunch counters in Nashville should be desegregated. After subsequent negotiations between the store owners and protest leaders, an agreement was reached and six downtown stores began serving black customers at their lunch counters for the first time. Whereas previous sit-ins had also been nonviolent, SNCC activists benefited from the intensive training that they had been given by Lawson, and whatever the source of the consensus mode of decision making, all agree that it came from the Nashville group trained by Lawson prior to the founding conference in April 1960.

In addition to sitting in at lunch counters, the groups also organized and carried out protests at segregated White public libraries, public parks, public swimming pools, and movie theatres. The response was often to close the facility, rather than integrate it.

In 1961, after a Ku Klux Klan mob attacked bus passengers defying segregation laws as part of the Freedom Rides organized by CORE, SNCC joined the campaign and put themselves at great personal risk by travelling in racially-integrated groups into Mississippi, but other bus rides followed, penetrating into the deep South. 440 people took part in the Freedom Rides during the spring and summer of 1961.

Following the success of these protest, SNCC moved to transform themselves from protest to community organizing, and the voter registration project became the centre of SNCC's activities from 1962 to 1966.

Registering Black voters was extremely difficult and dangerous. Blacks who attempted to register often lost their jobs and their homes, and sometimes their lives. SNCC workers lived with local families, whose homes were often firebombed as a result.

SNCC also played a significant role in the 1963 March on Washington for Jobs and Freedom. All of these projects entailed police harassment and arrests, KKK violence including shootings, bombings, and assassinations, and economic victimization of those blacks who dared to try to register.

The Freedom Summer campaign in Mississippi focused on voter registration and "Freedom Schools," bringing hundreds of Northern white students to the South where they volunteered as teachers and organizers. Three civil rights workers involved in the project, James Chaney, Andrew Goodman and Michael Schwerner, were lynched after having been released from police custody.

The Freedom Schools taught children to read and to to stand up for their rights, and the bolder attitudes of the children helped shake their parents out of the fear that had paralysed them for generations. The Freedom Summer project led to the formation of the Mississippi Freedom Democratic Party (MFDP), an integrated party, to win seats at the 1964 Democratic National Convention for a slate of delegates elected by disfranchised black Mississippians and white sympathizers. President Johnson offered the MFDP a 'compromise': two non-voting seats, while the all-white delegation sent by the official Democratic Party would take its seats. The MFDP rejected the compromise and walked out. From this time, SNCC leaders became more and more estranged from the mainstream civil rights movement.

The SNCC voting rights struggle in Selma, Alabama in 1963 had made little headway against the adamant resistance of Sheriff Jim Clark and the White Citizens' Council. Deep divisions began to grow in SNCC, and at a staff retreat in Waveland in November 1964 proposals for a more centralised structure were put but "practically no issue reached a consensus" (Pronley, 2008). In early 1965, SNCC activists in Selma asked the SCLC for help, and the two organizations formed an uneasy alliance. Following police attacks on protesters on 'Bloody Sunday', March 7 1965, SNCC activists became more and more disenchanted with nonviolent tactics and integration as a strategic goal, and cooperation with white liberals and the Federal government.

The group began to split into two factions – one favouring a continuation of nonviolence and integration within the existing political system, and the other moving towards Black Power and revolutionary theories. After the Watts riots in Los Angeles in 1965, more of SNCC's members argued that blacks needed to build power of their own rather than seek accommodation with the existing power structure. *Self-evidently, such fundamental differences could never be resolved by Consensus.*

Stokely Carmichael was elected Chair of SNCC in May 1966 and reoriented the organization towards Black Power and for black people to define their own goals and lead their own organizations. A vote was taken in December 1966 to exclude white people from SNCC, passed 19 to 18 with 24 abstentions. As a result, Mary King, Casey Hayden and others had to leave. It is fair to say that despite having *invented* Consensus, SNCC was no longer a vehicle for *transmitting* Consensus to the Civil Rights and Peace Movements after November 1964.

By early 1967, SNCC was approaching bankruptcy and close to disappearing. Stokely Carmichael began to generate resentment due to his celebrity status, and he was criticized for his habit of making policy announcements independently, before achieving internal agreement. In June 1967, Carmichael stepped down as chairman of SNCC and accepted the position of Honorary Prime Minister in the Black Panther Party, whilst remaining on the staff of SNCC, and attempted to forge a merger between the two organizations. The merger failed and Carmichael was expelled from SNCC. After leaving SNCC, Carmichael wrote his book, *Black Power*, and lectured, travelling throughout the world. Carmichael became more clearly identified with the Black Panther Party as its 'Honorary Prime Minister', but he was a public speaker, not an organizer.

The Rules of the Black Panther Party read like the regulations of an Army not that of a political party. There is no mention of collective decision making of any kind but there is repeated emphasis on obedience to commands and rules and obligations to report all activity, finance, expulsions and other matters to National Headquarters. The national leadership presumably arrived at decisions through discussion amongst themselves, but it is clear that the ethos was not Majority or Consensus, but at best that of Counsel.

The African and Slave Roots of the Black Baptist Churches

Myles Horton claimed that: "all the structures that white people hold so dear, parliamentary law, majority votes, what I call procedure sort of claptrap, ... Negroes have never mastered that way, their churches don't act that way. ... None of your poor people, Negroes or whites, fit these categories" (Horton, 2003, p. 180–1). Every people has *some* tradition of collective decision making. Horton disclaimed any credit for having *invented* Consensus, and James Lawson says he used it, despite the Majority practices of the Methodist Church, so we need to investigate the traditions of collective decision making in the southern black churches, specifically the Black Baptist churches and their roots in the slave plantations and ultimately in Africa.

African Decision Making

The specific deities and religious practices that Africans had known were lost in their removal to North America. In Brazil and the Caribbean, where there were larger concentrations of African slaves, they created religions that retained African deities and practices, combining them with Christian ritual and symbolism. In North America these African practices and deities were destroyed. However, an African worldview survived.

Even if we restrict consideration to West Africa, from where most of the slaves were taken, there was a wide variety of social formations – from centralized states to small, disparate village aggregations – and with that a variety of forms of collective decision making. However, there is a form of decision making which was a common denominator of African community life throughout the continent, known as Lekgotla, often translated as "African Consensus."

Descriptions of Lekgotla vary, but what seems to me to be the most authentic description is given by Wilhelm de Liefde:

> In African practice, the Lekgotla is a discussion in which the participants sit around an open fire in a semicircle. A central place is reserved for the chief, who occupies the highest position in the tribal structure and takes the final decision at the end of the deliberations. A council of wise people, also called elders, chooses the chief. The council represents all levels of society and the region. ...

[The chief] is an active listener, attentive observer and occasionally asks questions to elucidate an opinion. So he doesn't take part in the airing of different viewpoints, but listens and observes so that he can ultimately make a balanced judgment. ...

At the end of the Lekgotla, the chief takes a final decision that is accepted by the community. The opinions of every participant have been listened to with respect.

2003, pp. 58–68

Note that consensus is achieved at only *after* the chief has made the decision, which is binding upon all participants. All descriptions emphasize the virtues that are required, especially but not solely in the chief, if Lekgotla is to succeed. Also emphasized is that the voice of every participant is heard and attended to, just as St. Benedict emphasized that even the opinion of the youngest must be attended to. Again, the emphasis on the virtues of humility and respect for others is in agreement with St. Benedict, as is the familiarity with the myths and legends, written and oral, which underpin the ethics of the community, and function as precedents and exemplars for decision makers. So it seems clear: the traditional form of African collective decision making which the slaves would have brought with them to the New World, was Counsel, the same form of collective decision making which we also found in Anglo-Saxon England.

For slaves to reconstitute effective collective decision making it was therefore necessary to foster new leaders from amongst their own numbers, and to reform their spirituality on the basis of a new, shared mythology and theology. Since Africans in America did not share a single oral history, they appropriated the Biblical narratives for their own.

The Baptist Church under Slavery[1]

The Baptists arrived in New England in the seventeenth century and missionaries took the Word to the slaves in the late eighteenth century. The Baptists followed the congregationalist principle, thus offering greater opportunity for Blacks to practice their religion independently of white control than was the case with the Methodists. The early Baptists emphasized salvation through belief in Christ and anticipated a literal second coming, a belief which had obvious attractions for the slaves. In fact, belief in eventual liberation was the

---

1 My principal resource for this section is Cornelius, J.D. (1999). *Slave Missions and the Black Churches in the Antebellum South.* University of South Carolina Press.

central motif of slave Christianity. Early Baptists were also very demonstrative in their worship, believed in miracles and baptism meant full immersion, not just a sprinkle on the forehead. This kind of Christianity fitted well with African spirituality. In the late 1700s, in the early years of Baptist expansion in America, blacks were received as equal members of congregations along with whites, and were ordained to preach. Renowned charismatic black religious leaders preached to both whites and blacks and founded churches for both races. Under the loosely interpreted congregational principle, blacks formed their own congregations and chose their own preachers. Where slaveowners forbad worship, slaves built 'hush arbors' – makeshift chapels in the woods, where they met for prayer in secret during the night. The First African Church was established in Savannah in the late 1780s and by 1795, Baptists had 18,000 black members in the South.

Despite social and legal discouragement, white Baptists not only ordained and appointed black leaders, but encouraged their religious development, resulting in a generation of leaders converted, trained, and nurtured during slavery who took charge of an independent black church after the civil war. Typically, black watchmen and deacons conducted special services for black members of Baptist churches on Sunday afternoons, held prayer meetings during the week, and presided at discipline meetings where blacks voted to admit new members or release those having to move and reviewed each others' behaviour, recommending penalties for misdemeanours.

Nat Turner's 1831 slave revolt crystallized Southern white fears about the autonomy of the black churches, and they responded with a wave of legislation prohibiting blacks from preaching or assembling for worship and penalizing whites who taught blacks to read or gave them books. White Baptists then moved to incorporate black Baptist congregations within white ones or imposed white control, perhaps a white preacher and token white membership on black congregations, thereby abolishing the independence blacks had enjoyed in their own congregations.

At the same time, white Baptists began to seek the advantages other denominations seemed to receive from a trained ministry, a uniform theology and effective mission organization. More and more white Baptist churches abandoned the traditionally emotional worship style and congregational participation, whilst black congregations continued to prefer them and disliked their suppression during biracial services. Whilst formally remaining under white control, black Baptist congregations increasingly separated and practiced their own style of service, which in any case suited the desire of whites for physical segregation. Blacks had their own meetings and conferences, but whites made the decision on membership and on excommunication and other matters dealt with by the disciplinary committees. Usually these decisions were made by mutual agreement of black and white members, but blacks were not permitted to outvote white members of the committees. However, whenever whites actually exercised their control over black congregations, black members would desert that church and join another, in this way, gradually over time, re-establishing control over their own religious practice. De facto separation of Black and white Baptist churches was complete by the end of the 1840s, allowing blacks to continue the old-fashioned practices they preferred, and develop their own leaders.

In line with African practices exemplified in Lekgotla, the religious life of these black churches developed group solidarity based on strong moral leadership. The discipline exerted by leaders and accepted by the community had been an integral part of African life, and African American slaves endeavoured to replicate it through their churches. They took the language, ritual, and biblical traditions from the sermons, hymns, and catechism lessons given them by white missionaries and integrated and transformed them in their own worship. With the defeat of the Confederacy, the black churches quickly and decisively formalized their separation from the white church.

Similar processes affected the Methodists in the South. When the Union Army arrived and blacks were no longer forced to sit in separate galleries and be sermonised by White preachers, they left in droves. The Methodist Episcopal Church, South, suffered a decrease in black members from 210,000 in 1860 to 79,000 in 1866. Many of the former members of slave churches were recruited by black missionaries sent down from the North by AMEC and AMEC Zion; others turned to the new Black Baptist churches. Following the 1939 merger, the United Methodist Church had 300,000 African Americans as members but was still segregated in the South.

As black religious leaders began to build an institutional church that resembled a white religious structure, complete with buildings, associations, conferences, and colleges, they retained their root belief in liberation. Of all the privations of slavery, the most deeply felt were the separation of families by sale, and the denial of access to the printed word. Black leaders welcomed the help of northern missionaries in establishing churches but preferred to control their own education. In a single generation they tried to establish for blacks the associations, teacher training colleges, universities and church buildings it had taken the white denominations many generations to build.

The evidence suggests that the predominant form of collective decision making in the Black Baptist churches after the Civil War was Counsel. However, voting was not something foreign to the Baptist church. The most significant context in which voting took place was in the work of the disciplinary

committees which punished members of the congregation for moral trans-
gressions. However, it is hardly likely that the operation of these committees
would have endeared their practices to black members, as they were never
allowed to outvote the whites on these committees and despite the yawning
moral contradictions in the behaviour of the white slaveowners, it was invariably the votes of slaveowners who voted for the punishment of moral failures
of black members.

The Black Christian churches provided a vehicle for African Americans to
replicate the forms of leadership and collective decision making that had characterized the lives of their ancestors in Africa.

Conclusion

My conclusion as to how Consensus came to appear in SNCC is this. The difference between Consensus as practiced by SNCC, and Counsel as practiced in
Black Churches with a preacher like Lawson facilitating discussion rather than
the usual charismatic and often domineering preacher, is admittedly subtle.
I think it would have been unthinkable for a group of young black students
to engage in this practice without a more senior leader if it were not for Myles
Horton and James Lawson's training which gave them the self-confidence to
take charge of their own lives and the forbearance and solidarity to talk it
through. This style of Consensus, involving passionate debate stretching over
days on end, is a new invention. It is *not* how the Quakers did it. Such leaderless
egalitarian debate could *never* have existed in African communities. Mary King
and Casey Hayden both emphasized to me that SNCC decisions committed
people to life-endangering actions in which they could neither fight back nor
flee, and which were after all *voluntary*. People *had to be convinced* if they were
going to take part.

The SNCC students invented Consensus, drawing from what they had learnt
from Myles Horton, James Lawson and the Black churches, and developed it
as part of their non-violent, civil disobedience activism. However, the split in
SNCC, sealed by a vote, meant that SNCC was not the proximate source of Consensus in the wider Civil Rights and Peace movements in the later '60s.

Eleanor Garst and Women Strike for Peace[1]

The other individual to introduce Consensus Decision Making to social change activism in the u.s. was Eleanor Garst, who introduced it to Women Strike for Peace in Washington, in September 1961.

Eleanor Garst was born in Nebraska in 1915 into a conservative, small-town, Baptist family, destined for motherhood and homemaking. Her family moved to Spokane, Washington, where she grew up. Her father owned a pharmacy, and her mother was a housewife who did occasional work as a legal secretary but always considered herself a housewife, her main interest being the Baptist church – an old fashioned church that to this day advocates a literal reading of the book of Genesis. Eleanor was, however, a born rebel and at the age of ten she began to acquire radical notions from history books, began writing peace poems and after reading *The Origin of the Species* as a teenager she left the church.

Garst was a largely self-educated woman, although she did attend the University of Missouri for a short time. She dropped out to marry and spent several years as a housewife and mother. Although she loved her baby boy, she hated every minute of domestic life. She later worked in a bookstore in Spokane, run by a woman rumoured to be a Communist.

By 1940, Garst was divorced from her husband and had moved to Bethlehem, Pennsylvania, where she worked in a bookstore once again. When the war broke out in Europe, Garst was horrified, but incapable of taking any action because it seemed to her that the only alternative being offered to war was a reactionary brand of isolationism. She was very much opposed to the rise of fascism, but at the time she believed that Hitler could be stopped without u.s. military intervention. Shortly before the United States entered the War, Eleanor married Eugene Garst, a merchant seaman who shared her pacifist beliefs. Together they decided that he would refuse to be drafted. Without any contacts in the peace movement or support of any kind, Eleanor and Eugene spent their honeymoon writing an eighty-page brief opposing peacetime conscription, spending many days at the local public library, where they "learned the whole past history of conscription." Garst was fired from her job after her husband refused to be drafted. As they waited for him to be jailed, Quakers from the War Resister's League arrived to offer their support. This was her first

---

1 The principal source for this chapter is Swerdlow, A. (1993). *Women Strike for Peace: Traditional Motherhood and Radical Politics in the 1960s.* Amy Swerdlow was herself a participant in wsp from the beginning, and she is the only person to have documented wsp.

encounter with Quakers and she "loved them on sight" and "they changed her life" by inviting her to come to Philadelphia to live and work with them. From then on, Quaker teachings on peace and social justice were part of Garst's life.

During World War II Garst worked first as a publicist for WILPF (Women's International League for Peace and Freedom founded in 1915 by Jane Addams and others), which she had encountered for the first time when she moved to Philadelphia. She then became assistant director and lobbyist for the Women's Committee to Oppose Conscription, an ad hoc national committee of church and labour groups established to defeat a pending bill that would have conscripted women for wartime non-military service. She interviewed congressional representatives, sent news releases to supporting groups, and made a nationwide speaking tour on behalf of the campaign against female conscription.

At the war's end Eleanor and Eugene returned to Spokane, where she gave birth to a daughter, Jeannie, who was later to be an active participant in the peace movement. The Garsts were divorced a few years later, but Eleanor stayed on in Spokane where she became a professional organizer for social change, as the executive secretary of the International Centre, an umbrella group for the World Affairs Council, the Race Relations Council, and the local chapter of the National Conference of Christians and Jews. According to Garst, all interfaith, interracial, and international efforts in the Spokane area went through her.

In addition to her professional work for peace, Garst served as a volunteer secretary and program chairperson of the first regional branch of the American Association for the United Nations, which she had helped to organize. She was also regional vice president of the United World Federalists, and active in the Democratic Party.

In the late 1950s, while living in Los Angeles where she was working as assistant to the director of the Los Angeles County Conference on Community Relations, Garst became a founder of the Los Angeles chapter of SANE (National Committee for a Sane Nuclear Policy). She then moved back to Washington in 1958 to work as a community organizer for the Adams-Morgan Demonstration Project, a government initiative administered by the American University, aimed at keeping a Washington housing project racially integrated. During the late summer of 1961 Garst, along with millions of others, was experiencing 'nuclear anxiety' but felt alienated from the groups with which she had worked in the past. She began to correspond frantically with friends and contacts all over the country, communicating her fear of impending disaster and asking her contacts to report what they were doing in their own communities. Her friend, Carol Urner, who had started a women's peace group, sparked Garst's interest in the idea, as she had come to the view that women were more free than men to oppose entrenched national policies. In September 1961, her friend Margaret

Russell, invited her to an exploratory meeting with 5 other women, all of them housewives, at Dagmar Wilson's home. As a professional writer who had been published in the *Saturday Evening Post,* the *Reporter,* and the *Ladies' Home Journal,* Garst was the logical choice to draft the "Dear Friend" letter that became the call for the Women's Strike for Peace.

Garst taught the WSPers how to run a Quaker-style meeting in which there was no voting and frequent pauses or long, sometimes very long, periods of silence and quiet reflection and introspection, and under her leadership real consensus was usually found. According to Amy Swerdlow, it was Garst's simple, direct, moralistic, but non-ideological prose that played a crucial role in mobilizing and unifying WSP in its first five years. Garst's opposition to any form of bureaucratic structure, her faith in the grass-roots, and her conviction that consensus could always be achieved, struck a responsive chord in the key women across the country, most of whom had not previously encountered Quaker decision making.

WSPers invariably associated their consensus style of decision making with their inveterate mode of "unorganization" – remarkable considering that they had become extremely effective national organization which achieved high levels of policy consistency for a period of over 20 years. Eleanor Garst attributed the movement's success precisely to its lack of formal structure. "No-one must wait for orders from headquarters – there aren't any headquarters," she declared in an article in the FOR journal, *Fellowship.* "Any woman who has an idea can propose it through an informal memo system. If enough women think it's good, it's done. Sounds crazy? It is – but it utilizes the creativity of thousands of women who would never be heard from through ordinary channels."

In the words of the monthly bulletin of the Ann Arbor branch: "We are a do-it-yourself movement, depending on individual women who move freely in and out of our activities as their interest, concerns, energies, time, permit. ... We are unique in our non-structured, chosen, fiercely-guarded lack of organization – and yet we accomplish a great deal, learn even more, inspire each other." Notwithstanding the intervals of silence sometimes required for consensus, meetings were commonly noisy with more than one person talking at a time, babies crying while refreshments were being circulated.

Clearly, the successful implantation of Consensus in WSP entailed both Eleanor Garst, who had acquired it from the Quakers, and the readiness of the social stratum which made up Women Strike for Peace to embrace it and use it to good effect. To understand this readiness and how WSP transmitted the practice to the wider anti-war movement and the Women's Liberation Movement which followed, we must follow WSP through its early years.

It must be noted that none of the other organizations in which Eleanor Garst had hitherto participated were open to Consensus. SANE (of which all 6 founders of WSP had been members) was the first mass organization to oppose nuclear testing, but it was an *hierarchical* organization, anti-communist in its politics and focused on lobbying government rather than influencing public opinion. The Adams-Morgan community organizing project had plenty of opportunities to foster Consensus amongst the residents but it never did and it was run by means of a top-down management tree like any other quasi-governmental organization. WILPF was a chapter-based organization close to the labour movement which operated on the basis of Majority.

Both James Lawson and Eleanor Garst had been members of Fellowship Of Reconciliation (FOR). Jane Addams and US and British Quakers together with German Lutherans had founded FOR in 1914, but Addams never advocated Consensus. Gandhi had had contact with FOR, but again Gandhi was not an advocate of Consensus, and no-one remembers Consensus ever having been a feature of FOR.

All the evidence points to the meeting in Dagmar Wilson's livingroom on 21 September 1961, when Eleanor Garst attended the founding meeting of Women Strike for Peace, as being the moment at which the Quaker style of doing meetings took root in a social change movement beyond the Quakers themselves.

Women Strike for Peace

The six women who met in Dagmar Wilson's home in Georgetown, Washington were Dagmar Wilson, Eleanor Garst, Jeanne Bagby, Folly Fodor, Margaret Russell and one other woman, as well as two men who took no further part in WSP: Margaret Russell's husband and Quaker convert Lawrence Scott (all members of SANE). The meeting decided to call a one-day national peace strike of women for 1 November.

The call written by Eleanor Garst and issued on 22 September circulated rapidly through female networks, by word of mouth and chain letter from woman to woman, using personal phone books, Christmas card lists, contacts in PTAs, church and temple groups, women's clubs, and old-line peace organizations. The founders and those who joined them managed in only 5 weeks to organize 68 local actions across 60 cities that brought an estimated fifty-thousand white, middle-class women on to the streets or to protest rallies.

The call to strike contained no names, indeed none of the women were public figures. In response to demands, a second communication was entitled "Who are these women? – You ask." The organizers no longer referred to themselves merely as housewives, but as "teachers, writers, social workers, artists, secretaries, executives, saleswomen. ... Most of us are also wives and mothers, ...we are Quakers, Unitarians, Methodists, and Presbyterians, Jews and Catholics and many ethnic origins. First of all we are human beings." But the stereotype of housewives *stuck* to WSP forever after and was assiduously maintained. Celebrities such as Eleanor Roosevelt were invited to join the call, but no big names associated themselves with it. WILPF and SANE also kept their distance.

Dagmar Wilson was the spokesperson for the women and the press chose to identify her primarily as a mother, despite the fact that she had made it clear in the first press release that she was a "well-known children's book illustrator" which the press rendered as "woman who has three daughters and whose usual spare time occupation is illustrating children's books."

Dagmar Wilson was the only one of the founding group with whom the majority of the WSP women were able to identify and completely accept, and Wilson acted as an icon for the movement, rather than a leader. Educated in England she was an eloquent speaker and her diffidence, humility, gentle force, appealing, non-doctrinaire common sense and her thoughtful charisma communicated precisely the image of what an American woman of that time aspired to be and was expected to be. She claimed that she had no female role models and that her only inspiration for WSP was the civil rights movement, particularly the SNCC sit-ins. WSP made no feminist demands and its leaders generally knew nothing of earlier women's peace struggles and had barely heard of the suffragettes. WSP was decidedly feminine but not feminist.

It is noteworthy that demographically, politically and in terms of available means of communication, WSP was barely distinguishable from these earlier women's peace movements, but any thread of collaboration which might have linked them to their pre-War sisters had been severed, and in their form of collective decision making, they made a complete break.

Alongside the first strike call, WSP delivered identical letters to Jacqueline Kennedy and Nina Khrushchev, which served both to emphasize their non-partisanship, but also extended the interest of the participants and the press beyond one day. This would typify the canny use of the media which would continue to characterize WSP over the two decades to come. For example, a typical action would be a march on Congress, followed by delegations from all over the country going in to lobby their local Congressman, with weeks of interviews, letters to the Editor, etc., in localities before and after the march in the course of which the women would exercise themselves in political activity. WSP women made a special effort to dress and behave in a stereotypical fashion at demonstrations, vigils, and lobbies.

The women of WSP would transform themselves from "ordinary house-wives" and mothers into leaders, public speakers, writers, organizers, political tacticians, and analysts. Whatever their intentions, WSP created a female community in which reasoning ability, organizational skills, and rhetorical talents were valued above maternal competence. They also set an example of female courage, political responsibility, and leadership for their own children, male and female, who would make up the ranks of the social movements of the 1960s and '70s.

Most of the women who joined the strike and the movement that grew out of it, were in their mid-thirties to late forties, generally well educated with a pre-existing interest in public affairs and a commitment to political participation. They came from liberal to left political backgrounds, having been pacifists, Quakers, New Deal Democrats, socialists, anarchists, Communist sympathizers or CPUSA members in the years before and during World War II. By 1961, those who had been Communists had become disillusioned with both Soviet policies and the CPUSA, but most still believed that the US posed the greatest threat to world peace. They were the kind of women whose devotion to children extended far beyond their own. Most of them had withdrawn from the larger political arena into the PTA, League of Women Voters, church or temple social action groups, volunteer social services, local arts centres, or music societies. Where there was conflict with their husbands, it was not about politics but over division of childcare responsibilities and domestic labour.

The generation of which the WSP women were a part had their adolescence in the depression and young adulthood during World War II and raised their children in McCarthyite, Cold War America marked by a crushing conformism which silenced political debate and told women that their place was in the home. They were told from every angle to give up their jobs, careers and dreams of personal achievement to become full-time mothers. Although far more women quietly kept their foot in the workforce than was ever acknowledged, they on the whole consented to the image of domesticity which provided the shared language through which the WSP women could communicate with their base.

Most WSPers did not have to make a special effort to talk and act like 'ordinary mothers' – they had been talking and acting like that for years. They avoided 'ideological' language and continuously identified themselves with mainstream opinion, and rejected any tactic which they thought too radical to be understood by the 'average woman'. They found that their message could reach all kinds of women, political or apolitical, because they spoke to middle America in its own language. Nevertheless, they were always regarded by the political class as outsiders, a status which they wore as a badge of honour.

The maternal mask proved an exceptionally effective defence against red-baiting. The founders had learnt from SANE how *not* to defend themselves against McCarthyite witch-hunting. SANE was the first mass organization to mo-bilize against the nuclear arms race. Founded in November 1957, by June 1958, SANE had 130 branches. Under attack for being manipulated by Communists, SANE banned anyone with present or past Communist associations. A.J. Muste resigned and many individuals and whole chapters were either expelled or with-drew. The Washington D.C. chapter opposed the decision but did not withdraw. From the outset, WSP decided that they would have no formal requirements for membership or even keep membership lists. Their maternal persona deflected red-baiting attacks like water off a duck's back. Testifying before the House Unamerican Activities Committee, Dagmar Wilson said no-one could take over WSP because "we are the movement. We decide everything by group decision, nothing is dictated." Kay Hardman told the Committee: "No rigid authoritarian type personality could tolerate, for a single moment, the intuitive, agreement by consensus that is the *modus operandi* of women's peace groups." The perfor-mance of the WSP witnesses, who had actually *demanded* their right to testify before the Committee, and were applauded by the gallery and presented posies of flowers at the conclusion of their evidence, was probably the last nail in the coffin of the HUAC, which faded from history after making themselves a laugh-ing-stock in their cross-examination of the ladies from the PTA.

The "Structure" of WSP

After the strike, those who had participated wrote urging the founders to keep the women's peace strike idea going, but they also expressed a reluctance to es-tablish a formal organization. The antipathy to building yet another top-down bureaucratic peace organization was a shared view. By rejecting hierarchy and "boring meetings," the Washington organizers encouraged the strikers to speak out in their own voices and as they saw fit, and the loosely structured par-ticipatory approach which had successfully organized the strike set the tone for the national movement that followed. "Structurelessness" came to be the movement's hallmark and a legacy it bequeathed to feminist groups that fol-lowed. The WSP women insisted that every participant was equally qualified to speak for the movement. In the minds of those who participated in WSP, the structurelessness of the movement and the consensus style of decision making were inextricably linked together.

Without paid staff, designated organizers or spokespersons, WSP re-lied on the stereotypical maternal rhetoric which they all understood, and spontaneous direct action at the local level, for which there were clear models and limits implicit in the maternal ethos. This bypassed the need for policy documents, rules and regulations and processes of approval and oversight of the activity of the chapters.

Whenever WSP participated in wider actions, such as the draft resistance, they always operated from their separatist women's group, which decided on its own terms which issues, which groups, and which tactics it would or would not support.

Needless to say, WSP did not have a rulebook, but here is the structure they had.

Each local group was to observe a first-of-the-month strike day, but in any way it chose. The only requirement was that the groups call attention to the need to end the nuclear arms race. Each chapter exercised its autonomy and operated the same consensus-style of meetings with no appointed officers.

A *key woman* was someone who took part in local and national planning meetings and/or acted as a link in the telephone chain. The key women were appointed by their local groups, who were responsible for communicating information to and from the de facto national headquarters in Washington and regional, state and local contacts.

Like in the International Workingmen's Association, the 'leading section' (i.e., the Washington chapter), acted simultaneously as head office. The national office published the *MEMO*, which was sent to the key women, who were responsible for transmitting the news to their groups and supplying news and ideas for use in the *MEMO*.

In addition to the informal national office, *clearing houses*, or *task forces*, were also established for the dissemination of information and action proposals on specific issues. These were self-appointed women who took an initiative to organize some action. There *were* disputes over this structure, but they never developed into a faction fight.

On 9–10 June 1962, 105 self-selected delegates attended the first WSP conference in Ann Arbor. The conference ran for two and a half days and produced a unifying policy statement, a statement of goals and methods and consolidated the communications network. The policy statement which was agreed upon by consensus, proved to be so appropriate for WSP that it remained in use without revision throughout the 1970s and 1980s.

As was pointed out frequently during the conference, when there are no official delegates there can be no official decisions, nonetheless, the conference ended in unanimous agreement that national policy would be decided only at annual conferences and that local policy would remain the responsibility of each area.

Most of the key women believed that when there is no official hierarchy and no rewards for office, there can be no power struggle. However, an informal but entrenched leadership clique *did* develop in WSP, and the analysis that Jo Freeman put forward in 1970 in her speech, "The Tyranny of Structureless-ness," was irrefutable: the informal leadership was made up of women who knew the unspoken rules and possessed the resources and the networks to bid for decision making. Such resources included experience, recognized standing in other peace groups, personal friendships with the Washington founders or other national figures, professional standing or media recognition, powerful husbands, and most importantly, personal economic resources for travel and communication, including access to domestic help to free them from house-keeping and childcare responsibilities and freedom from the need to earn a wage – the kind of resources which are normally reserved for elected paid of-ficials. Decisions were made by those who happened to be present at a particu-lar moment and anyone who disapproved of a decision could simply ignore it. Later on, as WSPers became aware of the problem of being an all-white move-ment, they made special efforts to recruit women of colour and to pay their way to international meetings, etc.

The decision to not hire staff and for members to bear the cost of travel, telephone calls, and printing on a *personal* basis, freed them from the neces-sity to raise money, charge membership dues and all the paraphernalia of managing funds which has figured so largely in the organizational life of all other social movements. This was crucial in maintaining the creative, free-flowing spontaneity of the movement. However, there were costs for this freedom. It put the most active women under enormous pressure and simply excluded from leadership roles those who lacked the necessary resources. The lack of structure and the absence of paid office staff produced the great-est strains in Washington, where the local WSP chapter had to run a national office with no resources other than their own personal access to spare time and money. In 1968, Dagmar Wilson withdrew from her role in WSP, though still a committed activist, but just on a local scale, as a consequence of this kind of pressure.

When WSP succeeded in getting Bella Abzug elected to Congress as a Demo-crat, this tended to move the focus away from the movement and absorbed much of the energy of WSP into the Democratic Party, at the same time as delivering much-needed resources and even more effective access to Congress.

Some insight into how WSP's Consensus worked can be gained by reflecting on how it handled some of its most serious challenges.

The greatest difficulties arose over demands on WSP to take positions or participate in actions directed at other issues, such as racial segregation. Such demands required WSP to step outside the informal consensus on which unity of their structureless unorganization was based.

At its second national conference in June 1963, a group of women proposed from the floor that WSP condemn US intervention in Vietnam. It took almost 24 hours of constant debate, punctuated by pauses for contemplation and soul searching, to reach a consensus that in the coming year it would "alert the public to the dangers and horrors of the war in Vietnam and the specific ways in which human morality is being violated by the U.S. attack on...women and children." That is, the dispute was resolved by WSP making a public statement of principle.

The scope of WSP concerns did gradually broaden however. In October 1964, WSP issued a call to its participants to cooperate with Malcolm X in a campaign of writing letters to African heads of state and in March 1965, WSP participated in a march in San Francisco protesting *both* against the Vietnam war *and* racial injustice in Alabama.

In a radio broadcast in 1969, WSP declared: "We are profoundly a part of the total movement of the American people to change our society. ...but our major commitment and activities are still overwhelmingly dedicated to the single issue of peace."

WSP opposed mass draft card burning at one of the large antiwar mobilizations in April 1967 because civil disobedience had not been part of the original call. In a public statement presented to the head of the Draft Board, they justified their support for draft resistors:

> because we believe that these young men are courageous and morally justified in rejecting the war regardless of consequences, we can do no less.

Over time, as their base was radicalized by the burgeoning protest movements, the range of issues in which WSP participated continued to widen even including labour struggles. On the September 1967 March on the White House, confronted by a police cordon blocking their access to Congress, the women tore down the fence, trampled on it, pushed through or crawled under the line of baton-wielding policemen, to push their way on to the road directly in front of the White House gate, leaving a number of women battered and bloody on the ground.

WSP and Feminism

The great majority of WSPers had never been exposed to feminist discourse. Ironically, it was precisely because so many WSPers came out of the Left of the 1930s and 1940s that they had not been exposed to feminism. On the whole they had little awareness of their own contribution to sex-role stereotyping and female oppression, and embraced the culture of domesticity, even while belying it in their own activity. As was made transparent during the 1960s, the gendered division of labour and power was as dominant in the Left as it was in the general culture.

However, in the years of struggle, planning strategies, and making programmatic and tactical decisions, writing and speaking in public, challenging the political elite, WSPers began to feel their power, enjoy their victories, and savour their political acuity. They began to perceive the continuity between the strings that bound them to their homes and the forces that controlled public life.

When the WSP women found themselves under attack from their own daughters, they were generally already prepared to hear, understand, and embrace what their daughters were telling them about gender-stereotyping. Although the WSP women were far from being in the front ranks of feminist critique (a task that fell to their daughters), a decade spent demonstrating the capacity of women for political struggle and building the sense of female solidarity based on working in a separatist movement, justifies us in saying that WSP gave birth to and 'raised' the modern women's liberation movement.

Bit by bit, the WSP moms themselves became feminists. No women's history study groups or consciousness-raising groups were established within WSP, but many women were becoming aware that their own experiences had historical roots.

It was the Jeanette Rankin Brigade in 1968 which was the turning point in WSPers gaining a feminist consciousness. In 1967, a number of WSP activists joined forces with Jeanette Rankin (87-year-old Gandhian pacifist and the first woman elected to Congress) to organize a new broad-based women's coalition called the Jeanette Rankin Brigade to end the draft. Participants included Ella Baker, a key person in the founding of SNCC. The JRB consciously united war and poverty as twin issues, thus reaching across race and class lines. Jeanette Rankin had been a suffragist, and the JRB attracted a group of young women who decided to use the event to insert feminist consciousness and demands into the struggle for peace. It was this collaboration which won many key women in WSP to feminism and allowed them to see their own struggle in its full historical context as part of a history of women's struggle for peace and for their own emancipation.

Most of the women of WSP never returned to their domestic roles after the end of the Vietnam War. Things would never be the same again.

Mickey Flacks, who was a twenty-one-year-old member of Students for a Democratic Society (SDS), living in Ann Arbor in the early 1960s, recalls that she joined WSP because the women offered "a new vision of how to operate politically" and did not seem to be talking in old political terms. In 1980, Flacks told Amy Swerdlow that she still thought of WSP as "the most participatory organization of its time," and that WSP's "unorganizational" style, played a key role in shaping the later anti-war movement and the women's liberation movement. "It was never given enough credit for this," she stated in a 1980 interview.

Casey Hayden, who had been involved with WSP in Ann Arbor from the first strike, after having worked with James Lawson in SNCC, would go on to be one of the leading critics of SDS for the way in which it used women to do traditional female work and kept them from leadership. Hayden confirmed that WSP used the periods of silent contemplation to find consensus, and told me that:

> Mostly in SNCC, as I recall, everyone just talked a lot, but we didn't make decisions about actions until everyone was ok with the decision or had opted out and that was ok. I don't remember any silences like in WSP.
>
> private email message, 2 July 2014

Commenting on my quest to find the origins of consensus decision making, she said:

> I'd be interested to know if either of you ever come up with why we were committed to consensus decision making in SNCC. (I love it, myself, and have argued for it for decades in many settings. It was easier to achieve, of course, when we viewed love as our primary value, unity as a core issue, and our actions as nonviolent theatre, before we got into political theorizing which prefers/demands votes and splits.)
>
> private email message 23 June 2014

This difference – the presence/absence of silences – seems to have been the marker of consensus decision making having Quaker origins in the case of WSP, or African America in the case of SNCC. So far as my experience in social change activism has gone, the periods of quiet reflection have disappeared from Consensus decision making.

WSPers strongly associated their consensus style of decision making with the structureless of their "unorganization," which in turn was proudly held up in contrast to the "rigid authoritarianism" of traditional "male" organs of power and the failed peace organizations of the past. They also took it to be part of their maternal ethos.

For WSP, Consensus was also linked to the fact that participation in any action was *optional*. The fact that the organization nonetheless continued to exist and maintained consistency of policy, tactics and strategy over a period of twenty-years without any capacity to mandate or expel and was able to achieve consensus throughout can be put down to the commitment to the shared maternal ethos, the norms of which were well-known to everyone and met the expectations of the established society. Consensus and unity would always be put at risk if WSPers stepped beyond the boundaries of what was seen to be acceptable to "the average woman."

It is important to note that the adoption of Consensus for decision making has no necessary relation to WSP's "unorganization." The general workers unions of the early 1900s for example combined Majority decision making with branch autonomy within the Rules. Nor is Consensus necessarily tied to the absence of membership fees or clear criteria for membership. The connection between Majority decisions, membership fees and national discipline lies in the tradition from which these elements emerged, and traditions are powerful but not immutable.

I will reflect on the wider social and historical factors underlying the emergence of Consensus in the USA in 1960 at the conclusion to this part of the work. For now I must still review a couple of threads which turned out *not* to be decisive.

The Quakers and Movement for a New Society[1]

When I went in search of the origins of Consensus amongst social change activists in the US I found ex-Quakers and Quaker converts everywhere, and indeed, when I pushed back to find the earliest moment, it turned out that it was the Quaker convert, Eleanor Garst, who was responsible for introducing Consensus to WSP in 1961. I made note of Quaker converts wherever they appeared in the story of SNCC, but although they were there – A.J. Muste, Bayard Rustin – it appeared that they had no special role in introducing Consensus to SNCC. Despite Angeline Butler's impression, Highlander had nothing to do with Quakers and James Lawson is adamant that his use of Consensus owes nothing to the Quakers.

So this raises the question: where were the Quakers in all this?

During the first half of the 19th century, internal migration, the fragmenting effect of the autonomy of Quaker congregations and of the market, and the rise of evangelical Protestantism all combined to split the American Friends into numerous rival factions and splinter groups. At the same time, the Quaker doctrine forbidding individual participation in war faded. Quakers remained dedicated to the Abolitionist cause, as evidenced by their leadership in the Underground Railroad, and retained a consistent record of opposition to racial discrimination, but with the approach of the Civil War their pacifism came into conflict with their anti-slavery convictions. Many young Quaker men, the majority in some areas, served in the Civil War with the Union army, and suffered no reprove from their Quaker communities for it. During World War I, a majority of eligible Quakers served on active duty and numerous leading Quakers publicly supported the war effort and suffered no official admonishment. National Quaker assemblies invariably supported Conscientious Objectors, but no longer required that members uphold the position. Participation in war became a matter of individual conscience for Quakers and not a question for the Quaker faith as a whole. Recall that George Fox had preached pacifism in the context of lingering suspicions concerning the Quaker founders' radical position in the English Civil War, and the peace testimony was an affirmation of their acceptance of the Protectorate and the Restoration. Quakers were *good law-abiding citizens*. During World War II, 90% of eligible Quakers served on active duty in the U.S. Armed Forces, whilst the Quaker community concentrated on relief and refugee work, particularly after the end of the

---

1 My principal source for this section is Smith, A. (1996). The Renewal Movement: The Peace Testimony and Modern Quakerism, *Quaker History*, vol. 85 #2, Fall 1996.

War. Nonetheless, the Quakers did offer support to Conscientious Objectors, whether Quakers or not, and during World War II assisted the government in finding alternative employment for 12,000 men.

On November 12-13, 1960, to mark the 300th anniversary of George Fox's peace declaration, 1,000 Quakers held a Pentagon vigil officially sponsored by the Society of Friends thanks to successful lobbying by pacifists within a number of Quaker Yearly Meetings. The 1961 Easter Witness for Peace was an even greater success, bringing some 3,000 people to Washington while an additional 20,000 individuals participated in hundreds of local vigils around the nation winning active support for the Quaker initiative from the whole range of peace organizations. The action, however, brought out the simmering tensions within the Quaker community and investigations showed that only a small number of Quakers had participated in the Vigil, most of whom were opposed to the action. Although convened by Quakers, it was a largely non-Quaker event.

Nor were Quaker organizations quick to oppose the U.S. intervention in Vietnam. The 1964 New York Yearly Meeting statement on Vietnam, after "considerable discussion," called for neither negotiations nor withdrawal. This was hardly surprising given the anti-communist sentiment among leading Quaker proponents of peace. The Quaker peace lobby had refused to condemn the U.S. renewal of atmospheric nuclear testing in 1962, and in 1965, the most radical Quaker peace organization, the AFSC, called for a ceasefire, negotiations, withdrawal of all armed forces, including presumably Vietnam's own forces! and international peacekeeping force, which would presumably include US forces!

In short, throughout the century leading up to the events described above, the Quaker community was in fact on the side of those going to war, while at the same time offering support to Conscientious Objectors. And this is the irony: Quaker support for Conscientious Objectors provided a flow of active pacifists into the ranks of the Quaker community whenever there was a war. It was this inflow of 'convinced Friends' from non-Quaker Conscientious Objectors that provided the support for the very small minority of 'birthright Quakers' who upheld the Quaker peace doctrine which is responsible for the Quaker presence in the U.S. Peace Movement.

Beginning around the turn of the century there was a determined effort by pacifists within the Quaker community to recommit the Quakers to peace. The aim of the reformers was two-fold: both to renew the Quaker faith, and thereby to mobilize the Quaker community for a renewal of American democracy. The campaign took the form of efforts to draft a Peace Testimony which could be discussed and adopted across the various Yearly Meetings and tendencies within the Quaker community. These efforts continued up until the 1960s, but a consensus was never achieved! The only consensus among Quakers was to not rock the national boat.

The principal tactic used at first relied upon the continuing antipathy of Quakers to violence. Military service was excepted from this antipathy just as it is for any citizen. The reformers aimed to show, however, that a society geared up to make war was a society in which violence would characterize the life of its citizens and undermine the functioning of democracy. This tactic did not succeed, however, in achieving a pacifist consensus among Quakers.

So having failed to win a consensus for pacifism, reformers set out to mobilize those Quakers who were committed pacifists to take up the anti-war cause. In 1917, the reformers were based overwhelmingly in the Philadelphia Yearly Meeting (PYM) and the New York Yearly Meeting (NYAM). As noted in connection with the study of the PYM, and like the 'task forces' used by WSP, the reformers set up a committee based on the PYM which was open to membership of Quakers from any Yearly Meeting and non-Quakers: the American Friends' Service Committee (AFSC). This meant that the AFSC could effectively act as a law unto itself within the Quaker community. The move did not fail to generate resentment amongst Quakers who retained their 'law-abiding' convictions, but it did provide a vehicle for Quaker pacifist activity. During the 1930s, such peace leaders as Emily Greene Balch, Frederick Libby, A.J. Muste, and Mildred Scott Olmsted participated in AFSC activity. Newly 'convinced' Friends coming into the Quaker community as Conscientious Objectors turned the AFSC to continue their peace work. By the beginning of World War Two, 64 of the 850 Quaker meetings across the US were run by these 'convinced Friends', and the Wider Quaker Fellowship (WQF) had 2,000 members. At the peak of its activity, the AFSC employed 573 staff.

However, even within the AFSC, consensus could not be achieved about the nature of the nonviolent action which Quakers could support. While younger pacifists emphasized nonviolent action and civil disobedience, others, particularly older Quakers, could not condone methods which could stimulate a violent reaction from others. Further, as mentioned earlier, during the McCarthyite period, anti-communism reared its head even within the AFSC to the extent of condoning the resumption of U.S. atmospheric nuclear bomb tests in 1962. Even the most radical wing of Quaker pacifism proved incapable of effective action against war and racial segregation. With even the AFSC stymied, the reformers turned to ad hoc committees.

In 1966, Lawrence Scott (who had participated in the founding meeting of WSP in 1961) organized A Quaker Action Group (AQAG) to foment opposition to the war in Vietnam and "arouse the Society of Friends." AQAG tried to send relief supplies to North Vietnam and medical aid to the Red Cross Societies of

North Vietnam, South Vietnam, and the National Liberation Front, but were blocked by the US government. AQAG did manage to win support within the AFSC, and in the Fall of 1966, the AFSC called for the "complete U.S. military withdrawal from Vietnam, beginning now," and in 1968, AFSC sent medical supplies to the NLF for civilian use even after the U.S. government denied permission. This was the first time a Quaker group had directly disobeyed the government.

But it was clear: Quakerism had become a barrier to peace work. George Willoughby, a Quaker peace convert, declared that "working to renew the Society of Friends" was no longer important, and in 1971, George Willoughby, Lawrence Scott and Bill Moyer transformed AQAG into the *Movement for a New Society* (MNS).

While committed to personal change and social radicalism, and including numerous Quakers, AQAG abandoned all efforts to reform the Society of Friends. The MNS did however play a great role, not only in the Peace Movement, but in the second wave feminist movement and the emerging Environmental Movement. MNS promoted Consensus within this broad milieu of social change activists.

According to David Graeber (2010) and Andrew Cornell (2009), American anarchists owe to MSN the use of Consensus, the use of Affinity Groups for activist organization and the concept of 'prefigurative politics', that is, the principle that the kind of organization an activist uses prefigures the kind of society they are creating. As we have seen, Consensus was over a decade old amongst social change activists when MSN was founded.

The anarchist writer, Andrew Cornell, described the MSN thus:

> Though rarely remembered by name today, many of the new ways of doing radical politics that the Movement for a New Society (MNS) promoted have become central to contemporary anti-authoritarian social movements. MNS popularized consensus decision making, introduced the spokescouncil method of organization to activists in the United States, and was a leading advocate of a variety of practices – communal living, unlearning oppressive behaviour, creating co-operatively owned businesses – that are now often subsumed under the rubric of 'prefigurative politics'. MNS was significantly shaped by aspects of anarchist thought and practice developed both in the United States and abroad. Participants synthesized these elements with an array of other influences to develop an experimental revolutionary practice that attempted to combine multi-issue political analysis, organizing campaigns, and direct action with the creation of alternative institutions, community building, and

personal transformation. Although MNS never claimed more than 300 members, it bore an influence on 1970s radicalism disproportionate to its size, owing both to the strategy and skills training the group specialized in and to ways in which MNS vision overlapped with significant developments in the broader feminist and environmental movements.

CORNELL, 2009

But it was neither Quakers nor Anarchists who introduced Consensus to social change activism. It was the Methodist Theologian James M. Lawson, the hill-billy radical Myles Horton, the students of SNCC and the 'housewife' Eleanor Garst. After Stokely Carmichael's ascent to leadership in SNCC in 1965, SNCC was no longer a vehicle for transmitting Consensus to the wider movement, though a large number of activists had passed through their ranks in the meantime, and carried their experience with them. On the other hand, Women Strike for Peace were interacting with the Women's Liberation Movement and the Peace movement up to the 1980s. Even though SNCC may have been one of the inspirations for Eleanor Garst's organisational innovation as well as the Quakers, the housewives of WSP must be given a large share of the credit for giving the world Consensus Decision Making.

While Majority is an expression of the ethos of majoritarianism, Consensus is an expression of the ethos of *inclusion*. Majoritarianism does not rule out inclusion, in fact majoritarianism *protects* minorities, but only so long as minorities defer to the majority. Inclusiveness does endeavour to satisfy the wish of the majority, but will not sacrifice the minority to do so. So there is an inherent contradiction between the two ethics, even though they are not formally incompatible.

Courageous and politically astute young Blacks and middle-aged, middle-class housewives both demonstrated the power of the ethos of inclusion in mobilising the excluded.

Anarchism and Decision Making[1]

I began my search for the origins of Consensus with the book from which I first learnt about it in 1987, which led me back to the MSN in 1977. But as it happened, my attempts to implant this seed in my own activist milieu in Melbourne in 1992 failed because my socialist friends were affronted by the idea of Consensus, which they regarded as oppressive and unethical. Only the anarchists were interested, so Consensus was impossible.

The first occasion in which I actually participated in an activity organised by Consensus was in the S11 convergence at the World Economic Forum in Melbourne in September 2000, and this was initiated by young anarchist groups emulating the events in Seattle the previous year. So it seemed reasonable to explore the alternative route, which is in a sense more realistic than the route I have taken.

To explore this alternative route to the origins of Consensus I consulted my friend Jeremy Dixon, who had been a participant in the 1992 version of Socialist Alliance and is an anarchist. Jeremy first learnt about Consensus in 1977 from anarchists at Monash University. They were Communist-Anarchists, that is, anarchists of the Kropotkin type and they had imported the idea from their comrades in the U.S.

This would lead me back to the same origins via the Movement for a New Society, but as Jeremy pointed out, anarchists claim to have embraced Consensus long before the 1960s. So, I must investigate the history of anarchism, in particular communist-anarchism, as opposed to Bakunin's conspiratorial, collectivist anarchism and liberal individualist anarchism.

In this journey I was aided by the evidence of Murray Bookchin. Bookchin made his name in 1962 with the publication of *Our Synthetic Environment*, a landmark book for which Bookchin is recognised as a pioneer of the Environmental Movement. His next book, published in 1971, was *Post-scarcity Anarchism*. One of the informants who had assisted me via Jo Freeman's email list mentioned Murray Bookchin as having been a source of ideas for organization in the late-60s and this book may well be an example of his influence at this time. In *Post-scarcity Anarchism*, Bookchin has nothing to say about Consensus decision making. The book is concerned above all with the perils of *all* kinds of representative structure or hierarchy– which Bookchin reviews exhaustively – but it does not discuss Consensus. The book on which I will

---

1 In this section, I draw heavily on Bookchin, M. (1998). *The Spanish Anarchists: The Heroic Years 1868–1936*.

mainly rely in tracing the history of anarchism he first published in 1977: *The Spanish Anarchists: The Heroic Years 1868–1936.*

In the 1998 Preface to this book Bookchin says:

> In 1977, the year I originally published *The Spanish Anarchists*, surprisingly little was known about the movement. Although general surveys of Spanish anarchism and Syndicalism existed, they were sketchy... George Orwell's memorable *Homage to Catalonia*, ...appeared in 1938 but was virtually unknown to American radicals of my generation... Nor were my concerns merely historical. They were shaped by real-life issues that had arisen in the sixties left, with its often-professed anarchic beliefs. ...
>
> I began writing *The Spanish Anarchists* in the late sixties because I wanted to reclaim for a new generation this great revolutionary, indeed insurrectionary, upsurge.

So it is clear enough that what anarchists knew about the historical forms of organization used by the anarchist movement in times gone by were *not* transmitted by a continuously existing anarchist movement, but were *recovered* by Bookchin in his capacity as a historian, and introduced to contemporary anarchists around 1977. Nonetheless, this history has given today's anarchists their own resource from which to develop Consensus, so just as we had to trace Consensus back to the Quakers in 17th century England, we must also look back to the Anarchists in 19th century Spain. There is no national current of anarchism comparable in its richness and influence to that of the Spaniards.

Anarchism and communism have common roots. Anarchism is a social and political stance which arises spontaneously in any modern society as the rejection of political authority. Likewise, communism arises spontaneously from the rejection of economic inequality. Syndicalism, the doctrine which assigns a pre-eminent place to workers' unions, as against both the individual and the state, also arises spontaneously in those countries where trade unionism has taken root. All these spontaneous sentiments form part of the social-psychological ground from which (theoretical) Anarchism and Marxism grew. Communism and anarchism existed together as tendencies within the International Workingmen's Association of 1864.

The International Workingmen's Association 1864

When the First International was founded in 1864, as a mutual aid organisation to which tens of thousands of wage-workers and tradespeople belonged through their unions, cultural and political associations and trades councils. It included not only Marx and some of his associates, but also some followers of the Frenchman Pierre-Joseph Proudhon. Proudhon is regarded by some as the founder of modern anarchism; his social base was artisans and independent tradespeople and he envisioned a society in which independent tradespeople traded with each other without the need for a state or overall administrative bureaucracy. While the Proudhonists shared an interest in mutual aid, they were more interested in reading and discussion groups rather than organising trade unions or making revolution and their influence in the International waned.

In 1868, Mikhail Bakunin joined the International. A Russian aristocrat, Bakunin, was an inveterate revolutionary and a collectivist. Bakunin agreed with much of what Marx was doing and writing and made his own Russian translation of *Capital*. Bakunin's aims were the same as Marx's, but the two men came into sharp conflict. While Bakunin's ideals were socialist, his methods of political struggle were *conspiratorial* – consistent with his dualist conception of the social revolution as resulting from a putsch carried out by revolutionaries who would destroy the state while the organized workers took over management of the affairs of the society. The socialists' conception was of a seizure of state power *by* the organized working class, which would then proceed to dismantle the state as the conditions for a socialist society matured and the danger of counter-revolution receded. This difference in conception of how the revolution would arise was reflected in Bakunin's conspiratorial and factional work in the International. He saw the representational structure of the International as an incipient state formation and subverted it by the formation of a secret faction, the Alliance of Socialist Democracy. In the faction fight which ensued, no-one was covered in glory. Bakunin did however establish a firm base of support in Spain, where the working class was already acquainted with anarchism thanks to Proudhon.

In 1872, in the wake of the defeat of the Paris Commune (which, incidentally used Majority for its decision making), the International held its Congress in Geneva, and it was here that the final split between the anarchists and the socialists took place. Another Russian aristocrat, Prince Petr Kropotkin, was visiting Switzerland. It was the Swiss watchmakers, members of the Jura Federation of the International, founded in 1870, and their foremost theoretician, James Guillaume, who converted Kropotkin to anarchism and recruited him to the International, and for some this event marks the beginning of modern anarchism.

Soon after Bakunin's death, Paul Brousse advocated *propaganda by the deed* – "a way of grabbing these people's attention, of showing them what they cannot read, of teaching them socialism by means of actions and making them see, feel, touch." This approach, relying on spectacular acts of terrorism to stimulate the masses into action, was embraced by the anarchist movement after the 1880 Congress at Bern. Kropotkin, like many other anarchists, later distanced himself from this strategy, and in 1887 wrote in his journal, *Le Révolté*, that "a structure based on centuries of history cannot be destroyed with a few kilos of dynamite." The Spanish anarchists however remained wedded to this strategy in which spectacular acts of terrorism would demonstrate the fragility of the state, encourage the workers to struggle, and undermine the capacity of the capitalists to rule. Meanwhile the working class organizations, especially the trade unions, would prepare the working class to take charge of the economy and social life in general. Wage rises and improvements in working conditions were not important in themselves as they only dampened the workers' readiness to fight against capitalism.

The history of anarchism is very complex, but it was in Spain, where it found a genuine mass base in the working class and peasantry, that anarchism flourished. The history of Spanish anarchism, from 1868 up its definitive crushing by Franco in the Spanish Civil War, provides us with the only developed model of anarchist organization.

Before moving to this history, it is worth noting the identity of the visions of socialists and anarchists of this time. Kropotkin lived in London from 1881 to 1914 and while in London he became friendly with the foremost British Marxist of that time, William Morris. Morris expressed his vision of the social Utopia in his short novel *News from Nowhere* (1890), in which the narrator engages in an extended dialogue with an inhabitant of this socialist Utopia. In the following excerpt, the narrator is told about how collective decisions are made in Nowhere:

> "Well." said I, "I suppose there would be a difference according to circumstances in people's action about these matters."
>
> "I should think so, indeed," said he. "At all events, experience shows that it is so. Amongst us, our differences concern matters of business, and passing events as to them, and could not divide men permanently. As a rule, the immediate outcome shows which opinion on a given subject is the right one; it is a matter of fact, not of speculation. For instance, it is clearly not easy to knock up a political party on the question as to whether haymaking in such and such a countryside shall begin this week or next, when all men agree that it must at latest begin the week after next, and when any man can go down into the fields himself and see whether the seeds are ripe enough for the cutting."

Said I: "And you settle these differences, great and small, by the will of the majority, I suppose?"

"Certainly," said he; "how else could we settle them? You see in matters which are merely personal which do not affect the welfare of the community – how a man shall dress, what he shall eat and drink, what he shall write and read, and so forth – there can be no difference of opinion, and everybody does as he pleases. But when the matter is of common interest to the whole community, and the doing or not doing something affects everybody, the majority must have their way; unless the minority were to take up arms and show by force that they were the effective or real majority; which, however, in a society of men who are free and equal is little likely to happen; because in such a community the apparent majority *is* the real majority, and the others, as I have hinted before, know that too well to obstruct from mere pigheadedness; especially as they have had plenty of opportunity of putting forward their side of the question."

"How is that managed?" said I.

"Well," said he, "let us take one of our units of management, a commune, or a ward, or a parish (for we have all three names, indicating little real distinction between them now, though time was there was a good deal). In such a district, as you would call it, some neighbours think that something ought to be done or undone: a new town-hall built; a clearance of inconvenient houses; or say a stone bridge substituted for some ugly old iron one, – there you have undoing and doing in one. Well, at the next ordinary meeting of the neighbours, or Mote, as we call it, according to the ancient tongue of the times before bureaucracy, a neighbour proposes the change and of course, if everybody agrees, there is an end of discussion except about details. Equally, if no one backs the proposer – 'seconds him', it used to be called – the matter drops for the time being; a thing not likely to happen amongst reasonable men however, as the proposer is sure to have talked it over with others before the Mote. But supposing the affair proposed and seconded, if a few of the neighbours disagree to it, if they think that the beastly iron bridge will serve a little longer and they don't want to be bothered with building a new one just then, they don't count heads that time, but put off the formal discussion to the next Mote; and meantime arguments *pro* and *con* are flying about, and some get printed, so that everybody knows what is going on; and when the Mote comes together again there is a regular discussion and at last a vote by show of hands. If the division is a close one, the question is again put off for further discussion; if the division is a wide one, the minority are asked if they will yield to the more general opinion, which they often, nay, most commonly do. If they refuse, the question is debated a third time, when, if the minority has not perceptibly grown, they always give way; though I believe there is some half-forgotten rule by which they might still carry it on further; but I say, what always happens is that they are convinced not perhaps that their view is the wrong one, but they cannot persuade or force the community to adopt it."

"Very good," said I; "but what happens if the divisions are still narrow?"

Said he: "As a matter of principle and according to the rule of such cases, the question must then lapse, and the majority, if so narrow, has to submit to sitting down under the *status quo*. But I must tell you that in point of fact the minority very seldom enforces this rule, but generally yields in a friendly manner."

"But do you know," said I, "that there is something in all this very like democracy; and I thought that democracy was considered to be in a moribund condition many, many years ago."

The old boy's eyes twinkled. "I grant you that our methods have that drawback. But what is to be done? We can't get *any one* amongst us to complain of his not always having his own way in the teeth of the community, when it is clear that *everybody* cannot have that indulgence. What *is* to be done?"

"Well," said I, "I don't know."

Said he: "The only alternatives to our method that I can conceive of are these. First, that we should choose out, or breed, a class of superior persons capable of judging on all matters without consulting the neighbours; that, in short, we should get for ourselves what used to be called an aristocracy of intellect; or, secondly, that for the purpose of safe-guarding the freedom of the individual will we should revert to a system of private property again, and have slaves and slave-holders once more. What do you think of those two expedients?"

"Well," said I, "there is a third possibility – to wit, that every man should be quite independent of every other and that thus the tyranny of society should be abolished."

He looked hard at me for a second or two, and then burst out laughing very heartily; and I confess that I joined him. When he recovered himself he nodded at me, and said: "Yes, yes, I quite agree with you – and so we all do."

from Chapter XIV

Who could fault this vision of a rural Utopia? a vision in which all decisions of importance to the community would be made by Consensus or not at all.

But this pre-supposes a people who have already become accustomed living in an egalitarian society in which class divisions have been overcome. In short, Consensus is only meaningful insofar as the position from which discussion begins – the default should consensus fail to be achieved – already constitutes a consensus in itself. The *real* differences between anarchists and communists are about how to overcome *real* differences in the conditions of people's lives. There are no real differences about Utopia between socialists and anarchists.

The anarchist James Guillaume also expressed himself on the question of how differences would be resolved in the socialist Utopia:

> Furthermore, the producers' groups forming the federation will intervene in the acts of the bureau in a far more effective and direct manner than simply by voting. For it is they who will furnish all the information and supply the statistics, which the bureau only coordinates. The bureau is merely the passive intermediary through which the groups communicate and publicly ascertain the results of their own activities. The vote is a device for settling questions which cannot be resolved by means of scientific data, problems which must be left to the arbitrary decision of numbers. But in questions susceptible to a precise scientific solution there is no need to vote. The truth cannot be decided by vote; it verifies and imposes itself by the mighty power of its own evidence. (1874)

This idea that science and the development of an intellectual elite can bypass the need for any kind of collective decision making has a long history. It was promoted by the Diggers of Buckinghamshire in 1648, harking back to Anglo-Saxon times, and more recently was put forward by the social psychologists Moscovici and Doise (1994). But it is fatuous.

The Spanish Anarchists

In October 1868, Bakunin sent his Italian supporter, Giuseppe Fanelli, to Spain to establish a Spanish Section of the International. Departing Spain after only 4 months, Fanelli left behind him small groups of Internationalists in Madrid and Barcelona which would go on to build a powerful anarchist movement which dominated the political landscape of Spain for the following 70 years. Fanelli's recruits won over to the international the Federal Centre of Workers Societies in Barcelona, a federation of more than 60 workers' societies. The anarchists' aim was to promote socialist ideas "prudently" in the pages of the newspaper, strengthen their influence over the Federal Centre and gradually bring the Federal Centre into line with the principles and rules of the International.

At the Basel Congress of the International in 1869, the Belgian delegate, with the support of the delegates from the Swiss Jura, Spain and France first proposed a dual form of organization for the International: a federation of industry-wide "workers' associations" on the one hand, and a federation of local, regional, national and international "labour councils" on the other. This idea would later be taken up in Spain.

Barcelona's Federal Centre which entered the International in 1870, was an alliance rather than an act of organic unity, between a small group of Anarchist Internationalists and a large trade-union apparatus. This secret, elitist and highly centralized group of anarchist militants typified the modus operandi of Bakunin's "Alliance of Socialist Democracy."

The First Congress of the Spanish Section of the International was held in Barcelona in June 1870. Delegates from the affiliated associations sat in front row and had voting rights, though anyone could speak. But it was the *aliancistas* – the secret faction in Spain known to only a few initiates – that actually guided the proceedings.

The congress committed itself, as an organization, to an antistatist and abstentionist [i.e., nonparticipation in elections] policy, but left individual members free to act as they saw fit in the political arena.

The *aliancistas* were not happy with the Alliance not having any distinct identity beyond its secret existence within the Spanish section of the International and wanted to establish themselves as a separate body, whilst retaining their role within the International. However, the Congress established a Commission on organization which proposed a *dual structure* for the Spanish section of the International which reflected the way trade unions were organized in Britain at the time and was to become typical of the form of organization favoured by anarchists in Spain thereafter. On the one hand, there were to be local trade organizations grouping together all workers from a common vocation into a large occupational *Union* federation whose primary function was to struggle around economic grievances and working conditions; on the other hand, local *Sections* were grouped together, irrespective of vocation, into local federations whose function was avowedly revolutionary – the administration of social and economic life on a decentralized, libertarian basis. These local Sections would provide the ideal vehicle for anarchist activity, whilst the vital day-to-day business of trade union struggle over wages and conditions would be conducted by the Unions.

The members of the International elected the delegates to the annual congresses of the Spanish Regional Federation, which in turn elected the Federal Council.

The Third Congress of the Spanish Federation in 1872

The Anarchist delegates (mainly representing Switzerland and Spain) to the Hague congress of the International in September 1872, met at St. Imier in the Swiss Jura and formed an International of their own.

On 25 December 1872, 54 delegates representing 20,000 workers in 236 local federations and 516 unions, convened in Córdoba for the Third Congress of the Spanish Federation, but this was to be the last public gathering of the International in Spain for nine years. The abdication of the King and the proclamation of a Republic triggered a series of attempted insurrections, in which the anarchists of Barcelona were enthusiastic participants, and the repression which followed pushed the organization underground.

The Córdoba Congress created what is generally regarded as the typical form of Anarchist organization in Spain. The Federal Council was stripped of all authority over local organizations, responsible only for gathering statistics and conducting correspondence on behalf of the Federation. The trade sections and local federations were elevated to sovereign independent bodies, free to do as they pleased or renounce their affiliation to the national organization at any time if they so chose. There were no paid officials and the Alliance, in effect, continued to exist as a de facto leadership of the Spanish Federation.

The Workers' Federation of the Spanish Region 1880

The founding congress of the Workers' Federation of the Spanish Region was held in Barcelona on 24 September 1880. Organizationally, the Workers' Federation modelled itself on the decentralized structure of the old Spanish Federation, but there were modifications to the local unions which closely resembled the forms that were to be adopted later by the CNT. Over strong opposition from the anarchists, the Workers' Federation decided as a matter of policy to accumulate a strike fund. The anarchists were always opposed to the accumulation of strike funds (a practice which had defined the emergence of the organized working class in Britain), because they were opposed to the idea of withdrawing their labour, preventing scabs from coming in, and sitting it out until the bosses gave in; they were only interested in short, sharp struggles, involving sabotage, violent attacks and insurrection. As they saw it, strike funds only encouraged passivity. The 1880s were hard times for the Anarchist movement in Spain. By 1887, when the Federation held its fourth congress in Madrid, only 16 delegates showed up.

By the time of the last Anarchist International Congress in London in July 1881, Kropotkin had become the outstanding spokesman for 'Anarchist-Communism', and the 1890s was to see an explosion of support for "propaganda of the deed," an explosion which rumbled on for the next 40 years in the case of Spain.

The Anarchist Organization of the Spanish Region was founded at Valencia in September 1888 and consisted of several libertarian tendencies, mainly Anarchist-Communist in outlook. The base of this movement was organized around *tertulias*: small, traditionally Spanish groups of male intimates who gathered daily at a favourite café. Such groups formed spontaneously and the new Anarchist organization simply declared them its basic form of organization. It was this form of organization which took the Spanish anarchists into the new century. In October 1900, a conference in Madrid founded the Federation of Workers' Societies of the Spanish Region, adopting the same dual structure as its predecessors.

Meanwhile the Marxists had founded the Second International in 1881 and were building the Socialist and Labor parties that would represent workers in Parliaments and play a role in government throughout the twentieth century. A Socialist Party was established also in Spain, and created its own union federation, the UGT – *Union Generale de Trabajadores*.

The CNT (Confederación Nacional del Trabajo)

In October 1910, the Catalan Labor Confederation summoned delegates from local union confederations throughout Spain to Barcelona to found the CNT (*Confederación Nacional del Trabajo*), a new anarchist union federation to rival the UGT.

The CNT was built up organically around the Catalan Regional Confederation, bringing together seven other regional confederations, each established from local unions in one province. At the national level it was a loose collection of those regional confederations which in turn were loose collections of local and district confederations of individual unions. These individual unions were established on a trade basis and, according to the now well-established pattern, grouped into both local and trade federations. To coordinate this structure, the annual congresses of the CNT elected a National Committee whose primary functions were correspondence, the collection of statistics and coordinating aid to prisoners.

The general secretary of the National Committee and the secretaries of the Regional Committees were the only paid officials in the Confederation. No strike funds were established. Regular funds were established however for aid to prisoners and for secular schools run by reformers. The organization was committed to 'direct action'. Affiliated district and local federations were to be governed by the greatest possible autonomy, including complete freedom in all matters relating to the individual trades. Each member was expected to pay a small monthly subscription of 10 centimes, which was divided equally between the local organization, the Regional Confederation, the National Confederation, a prisoner aid fund and the CNT newspaper.

In exceptional situations, the committee consulted local bodies, either by referendum or written queries. In addition to the annual congress of the national movement, a regional congress was to be held every year at which the Regional Committee was elected; extraordinary congresses could be held at the request of the majority of local federations.

The delegations to the congress, who had voting power according to the number of members they represented, were elected by general assemblies of workers convened by the local and district federations. All the affairs of the local CNT were managed by committees staffed entirely by ordinary workers.

At annual congresses, many delegations arrived with mandatory instructions on how to vote on each major issue to be considered. If any action was decided upon, any delegation which disagreed was not obliged to abide by the decision. Participation was entirely voluntary. Nonetheless, *all decisions which the CNT made were made by Majority.*

A mere five days after its founding, the CNT announced without notice, a general strike, which rapidly spread across the country and exploded into a full-scale insurrection. Police rounded up 500 CNT militants, closed down their local offices and moved troops into all the major cities. The CNT commanded the loyalty of only a portion of the working class, and the strike was crushed and five anarchists put on trial for their life. The CNT went underground. Nonetheless, the CNT continued to grow and with the exhilaration affecting the masses in the wake of the Russian Revolution, by 1919 the CNT numbered close to a million members.

The CNT was a union, and cannot properly be regarded as an Anarchist organization, but the Spanish anarchists did what they could to win the mass membership of the CNT to anarchism.

The unions were completely restructured on an industrial basis, that is, all workers employed in the same enterprise would belong to a single 'united union', while maintaining craft based organization in trade sections within the united union. There was no strike fund – aid to strikers had to be made privately, outside of the union structure.

At the CNT's Second Congress in December 1919, despite their commitment to Anarchism, a proposal to fuse the CNT with the UGT was defeated by 325,000 to 170,000, and a proposal to adhere to the recently established Communist

International was passed, although never carried through. With far from total support for its anarchist politics within the CNT, the CNT was now competing with the Socialists and the growing influence of the Comintern for the loyalties of the Spanish working class, not to mention the fierce national rivalries within Spain. The years from 1916 to 1923 under the repressive Primo de Rivera dictatorship were however the bloodiest of a very violent history. A series of competitive assassinations were carried out by *pistoleros* on behalf of the government and employers' federations as well as by *pistoleros* from the anarchist *tertulias*.

Their more moderate political opponents had been able to retain a sense of unity by means of the politically limited work which conditions allowed within the trade union structures, an option which the anarchists were unable to utilize in this period. Their isolation from routine union work and the lack of real opportunities for insurrection, combined with the fact that the anarchist *tertulias* had no organization of their own meant that the Spanish anarchists had lived through these violent and dangerous times in isolation from one another. It had also bred a spirit of intolerance and inflexibility which was unsuited to the tasks facing the Spanish working class at this time.

Beginning in Andalusia in 1917, and then in Catalonia, the anarchist groups began to form themselves into federations and by the late 1920s, these had finally collected themselves together into a loosely organized national federation of anarchist groups the FAI – *Federación Anarquista Ibérica*.

The *FAI* (Federación Anarquista Ibérica)

The FAI's main purpose was to secure the adherence of the CNT to anarchist principles. They acquired a reputation as one of the most dreaded and admired organizations of revolutionaries to emerge in Spain. It based itself on the same nuclear groups, *tertulias* in effect, which Spanish anarchists had been using for 50 years. The FAI adopted the term *affinity group* to designate this basic unit of their organization. They were to be kept small to foster the sense of intimacy and mutual trust between members, and affinity groups rarely numbered more than a dozen people. Each member was drawn to others not only by common political principles but also by shared personal dispositions, or affinity, in effect an extended family with a strong sense of personal initiative and independence of spirit. The *faísta* (FAI-ist) affinity groups were secret and were not easily penetrated by police agents; membership lists were not maintained, and the FAI was highly selective in admitting affinity groups to membership.

The FAI was structured along federal lines: the affinity groups in a locality were linked together in a Local Federation and the Local Federations in

District and Regional Federations. A Local Federation was administered by an ongoing secretariat, usually of three persons, and a committee composed of one mandated delegate from each affinity group. The Local Federation convened assemblies of all members in its area, but we have no record of how these assemblies deliberated. All the local and District Federations were linked together by a Peninsula Committee whose tasks, at least theoretically, were administrative. The Peninsular Committee was responsible for handling correspondence, for dealing with practical organizational details, and for carrying through any decisions of the organization. Although the FAI did exhibit a degree of centralism, the affinity groups acted fairly independently and acted on their own in terrorist acts, even defying FAI policies at times.

Every member of the FAI was expected to join a CNT union, but the majority of *faístas* were young, highly volatile men and women whose preoccupation was not with the CNT business but with direct and usually violent action against the established order.

In the April 1931 elections, the UGT members voted for the socialist candidates, but an approximately equal number of Anarcho-syndicalists voted for the middle-class liberals – they preferred to vote for the middle-class republicans whose liberal views were more in harmony with their own than those of the Socialist candidates. This kind of intransigence was setting the anarchists on to a path to disaster. The Comintern was at the same time pursuing its own ultra-left policy which split the working class in Germany and opened the way for Hitler to come to power and was being applied in Spain. The UGT and CNT rarely cooperated with each other and all the working class parties contributed to the formation of a Republican government in which workers parties were divided amongst themselves and in a minority to boot.

In October 1931, the more moderate unions within the CNT formed a separate federation – *Las Sindicatos de Oposición* with a membership of only about 60,000 and later formed their own Party. This left the CNT under the complete control of the FAI. But the FAI was more a social stratum than an organization. It had no bureaucratic apparatus, no membership cards or dues, no headquarters with paid officials, secretaries, or clerks. They hatched their uprisings in the local café. And the FAI was not politically homogeneous. It had no official program and its demands upon the independence of the affinity groups were limited to periodic calls to action. There was no position within the FAI which had an overview of their own activity and was capable of formulating and executing any policy to position themselves for the approaching civil war.

The FAI decided to launch an insurrection on January 8 1933. The police knew all about their plans and the event was a total calamity. They went into the Civil War utterly incapable of defending themselves, far less of gaining political control of the country. The FAI-CNT fought bravely in the Civil War, and staring oblivion in the face, they participated in the Republican government and even allowed their fighting battalions to be absorbed into the regular army. But it was all too late.

Summary

The claim of anarchists to be the originators of Consensus is based on the idea that the *tertulias* of the FAI made their decisions by Consensus. Although I know of no evidence that they did, it is hardly conceivable that a group of a dozen or so intimate friends would decide on how they would carry out some terrorist bombing or whatever by voting! While it is common for groups of friends to collect around one charismatic individual (suggesting Counsel as the mode of decision making), it is more likely that there were egalitarian relations amongst the members of the *tertulias*. However, the very first moment a serious disagreement were to arise, such an affinity group would no longer *be* an affinity group and they would reallocate themselves accordingly. Collective decision making is quite simply not problematic for an affinity group, the problem arises *between* affinity groups when they don't agree with each other. The FAI had no answer for that. Everyone did as they wished. It was just as Blanqui had said in respect to the earliest uprisings in Paris in the 1830s:

> Neither direction nor general command, not even coordination between the combatants. Each barricade has its particular group, more or less numerous, but always isolated. Whether it numbers ten or one hundred men, it does not maintain any communication with the other positions. Often there is not even a leader to direct the defence, and if there is, his influence is next to nil. The fighters do whatever comes into their head. They stay, they leave, they return, according to their good pleasure. In the evening, they go to sleep.
>
> BLANQUI, 1866

There was no collective decision, only a social process which led by an imperious logic to its own destruction.

But the CNT, like the UGT and all labour movement organizations, made its decisions by Majority. But not only that, decisions were made by Majority at congresses of the Anarchist International such as that in London in July 1881, even though all the delegates to the Congress were avowed anarchists.

The dualism favoured by anarchists was a means of reconciling decision making amongst a group of co-thinkers in their affinity groups, with large organizations, the unity of which was an essential shared asset. That dualism could take the form of a Bakuninist conspiracy of a secret faction which aims to manipulate a mass organization. Or, it could take the form of affinity groups which act independently of one another within a larger body, possibly with privileged access to communications. Or it could take the form of 'caucusing' – where a leadership group hammers out its differences, with or without voting, behind closed doors, and then maintains 'caucus solidarity' in order to control the larger body of non-initiates. Or it could take the form described by Jo Freeman and other critics of Women Strike for Peace of an informal group of activists who simply work themselves into the job of making decisions on behalf of the larger organization.

Consensus implies something more than affinity groups. Consensus is real only when on-going unity in action is achieved by surmounting genuine differences. This was exhibited in WSP and the SNCC. Affinity groups were and remain an important and valuable innovation, but they are Consensus bodies only in a trivial sense. Making decisions without voting does not equal Consensus. Consensus between a small group of intimates within an affinity group means nothing. It does not solve the problem of making collective decisions across a large number of such affinity groups.

In any case, the Spanish Anarchists did not transmit Consensus to 1960s USA. The anarchists of that time learnt Consensus from Movement for a New Society.

PART 3

The Post World War Settlement

∵

Consensus appeared in the US in 1960/61 in the Civil Rights and the Peace Movements. Quaker meeting practice turned out to be more or less incidental to the introduction of Consensus to social change activism. It was an historically original departure. What was it about this historical conjuncture which gave rise to such a novel innovation?

The new alignment of geopolitical forces after World War Two and the postwar settlement which secured the new arrangements had a profound impact on social and political life in every country.

At the end of the war, the Red Army was left in occupation of half of Europe, and would soon be nuclear armed. The old European colonial powers had been mortally wounded. The US, on the other hand, had overwhelming military, industrial and financial power, but the prospect of the troops coming home posed real problems as Western Europe itself teetered on the brink of social revolution. The Soviet Union had been devastated however and was in no mood to lead a world revolution. Both sides were anxious for a deal. Roosevelt and Stalin divided up the world between them at Yalta and Marshall Aid money and the Bretton Woods monetary arrangements were used to underwrite Keynesian policies of public enterprise, low unemployment and a comprehensive state Welfare in Western Europe and North America. The Communist Parties – who were in leadership of the poorest sections of the working class in the West – were enlisted in the cause of peace. Working class mutualism was destroyed by mediating welfare through the state, institutionalising the Social Democratic parties as part of the system and satisfying the most pressing demands of the organised working class in Europe and North America. McCarthyite witch-hunting and Cold War brutality beat down any who failed to fall in line. The workers movement in its most powerful centres was demobilised, enjoying full employment, with austerity giving way to relative prosperity, universal welfare services and peace.

This was an *historic compromise.* But what took place next was *the revolt of those excluded* from this compromise: the people of the former colonies, African Americans and women.

Martin Luther King said it all in his 1955 letter from Birmingham jail:

> We have waited for more than 340 years for our constitutional and God given rights. The nations of Asia and Africa are moving with jetlike speed toward gaining political independence, but we still creep at horse and buggy pace toward gaining a cup of coffee at a lunch counter. ...The yearning for freedom eventually manifests itself and that is what has happened to the American Negro. Something within has reminded him of his birthright and freedom, and something without has reminded him that

it can be gained. Consciously or unconsciously, he has been caught up by
the Zeitgeist, and with his black brothers of Africa and his brown and yellow brothers of the Asia, South America and Caribbean, the United States
Negro is moving with a sense of great urgency toward the promised land
of racial justice.

KING, 1963

The American Negroes identified themselves as an *interior colony* of the United
States. Although feeling themselves a part of the vast anti-colonial movement
gathering pace across the world expressing the right of the majority to free
themselves from the rule of a tiny minority, the Negroes differed from their
"black...brown and yellow brothers" in that the Negroes were a *minority*. This
not only obligated a critique of majoritarianism, it also ruled out the armed
strategy of the Comintern-led National Liberation Fronts. (The Black Power
movement was the exception to prove the rule in this case.) Their strategy had
to be civil disobedience against laws which unjustly excluded them, for which
the model was the Indian Independence movement, which had after all been
the first to achieve national liberation after the war, in 1947.

WSP appealed to housewives and mothers, who, though freed from economic pressures, were *excluded* from public life, their opinions deemed worthless.
Even in the Peace Movement they had been excluded from activity which had
focused on lobbying government. The majoritarian ethos made no sense here;
the ethos was *inclusion*.

The Nuclear Disarmament Movement and the Civil Rights Movement were
overtaken by the escalation of the Vietnam War and the Anti-War movement
which grew mainly in response to the conscription of hundreds of thousands
of young men to kill Communists in Vietnam and brought millions on to the
streets across the globe. This movement included the Labor Movement which
had organic connections with the National Liberation Fronts. This movement
electrified an entire generation, and out of this upsurge rose the social movement which was to transform the world more than any other before or since:
the Women's Liberation Movement. The changes in the labour processes
which had been accelerated by the War now placed women in an anomalous
and patently unjust position.

The daughters of the WSPers soon put two and two together. The Negroes
characterized their exclusion as *racism*, and by analogy, it was *sexism* which
excluded women:

The study of racism has convinced us that a truly political state of
affairs operates between the races to perpetuate a series of oppressive

circumstances. The subordinated group has inadequate redress through existing political institutions, and is deterred thereby from organizing into conventional political struggle and opposition.

Quite in the same manner, a disinterested examination of our system of sexual relationship must point out that the situation between the sexes now, and throughout history, is a case of that phenomenon.... Through this system a most ingenious form of 'interior colonization' has been achieved.

MILLETT, 1969

The Women's movement emerged in situation where both the ethos of majoritarianism and the ethos of inclusion were in play. The Women's Liberation Movement arose almost exclusively among women who had already been mobilized by the Anti-Vietnam War Movement which was predominantly majoritarian, including women who either belonged to the Communist Party or were active in the New Left. The sexism in these Anti-War groups was a significant trigger. Women who came into the Women's Liberation Movement from Left political groups brought their majoritarian principles with them, but many who had *not* been educated in the Labor Movement were receptive to the inclusive ethos introduced from WSP and SNCC. Some women's groups (e.g. New York Radical Women) used Majority, others (e.g. League of Women Voters) used Consensus. My informants all agreed that whether Majority or Consensus was used, when differences arose, there was always protracted discussion and only rarely did a matter have to be *decided* by a vote. It was however very often these votes, when consensus could not be achieved, which proved to be fateful for a group.

By the time the Women's Liberation Movement reached Australia in the late 1960s, Consensus was the dominant method of decision making and inclusion the dominant ethic. Magazine, books and media reports from the Women's Liberation Movement in the US, including Murray Bookchin's writings, were influential as the women worked through the problems of organization, trying to understand what Consensus meant, and these discussions often involved a lot of anguish.

Lyn McKenzie, who was active in Women's Liberation from the beginning in Melbourne says she only remembers one vote, that was the vote to ban the Spartacists (who opposed women's liberation) from the Women's Liberation Centre.

The Women's Liberation Movement never attempted to construct a Front, let alone a Party – it was an archetypal *social movement*, containing many different tendencies, working in small groups on issues and projects making common cause. Large events, such as an International Women's Day march, would be organized by an ad hoc group of women who participated as individuals, not as delegates. So it was always possible for a group of women to find a consensus but there was neither need nor opportunity to find a consensus among a large number of women.

The way Consensus worked was this: a group of women would come together around some project, and policies would be worked out through exhaustive discussion which would arrive at agreed principles by Consensus. These policies would accumulate over time and framed what the group stood for, and women joined on the basis that they agreed with that orientation. These groups could be relatively large, larger than the dozen or so in a Spanish *tertulia*. In working out the tactics and strategy for pursuing those policies, inevitably disagreements would arise which could not be resolved, but it was understood that if you didn't agree with a particular action or tactic, you simply didn't take part in that action. This was how internal differences were managed.

This is the nature of a social movement: it is not a front or a party, nor an institution or a government-in-waiting, though all of these may be subject to it. But a social movement is essentially a process with a finite life span; either by its success or by exhaustion, it must pass over into something else.

The Negation of Social Movements

A new conjuncture emerged in the early 1970s, from which time all the social movements began to be demobilised.

The public sector and the universities had absorbed many of the activists, before the boom turned into 'stagflation' and unemployment began to grow. The Vietnam War ended with the defeat of the US, while many of the demands of the Women's movement were institutionalised.

Later, the policies of Reagan and Thatcher put millions out of work, demoralised whole communities and destroyed all bases of mutual aid to clear away resistance to their neoliberal agenda. Neoliberal government policies reflected the changes taking place in the labour process: microeconomic reform replaced the failed efforts at macroeconomic control of the economy; privatisation, outsourcing, multitasking and a kind of 'Taylorism in reverse' had workers doing the work of management and put an end to key elements of the Fordist compromise. Corporate restructuring, franchising, one-line budgeting and export of capital went along with niche marketing. Naomi Klein later reflected on how the Women's Liberation Movement had undergone a parallel process of transformation:

> We knew the fast food chains were setting up their stalls in the library and that profs in the applied sciences were getting awfully cosy with pharmaceutical companies, but finding out exactly what was going on in the boardrooms and labs would have required a lot of legwork, and, frankly, we were busy. We were fighting about whether Jews would be allowed in the racial equality caucus at the campus women's centre, and why the meeting to discuss it was scheduled at the same time as the lesbian and gay caucus – were the organizers implying that there were no Jewish lesbians? No black bisexuals? ... When it came to the vast new industry of corporate branding, we were feeding it. ...
>
> The need for greater diversity – the rallying cry of my university years – is now not only accepted by the culture industries, it is the mantra of global capital. And identity politics, as they were practiced in the nineties, weren't a threat, they were a gold mine.
>
> KLEIN, 2001

How did this come about?

Just as socialism had been taken as a claim of a *better deal* for wage workers, rather than as a social movement for the *abolition* of wage labour, the Women's

Liberation Movement was taken as claim for a better deal for women rather than for the abolition of female gender roles. The Women's Liberation Movement was launched largely by educated, white, middle-class women, and their universal claims were widely taken to reflect the experiences and grievances of a unique social position, and consequently to be oppressive in relation to women who were not heterosexual, who were poor, disabled or Black or immigrant or working class. Given that the ideas, the literature and the aspirations of the Women's Liberation Movement were authored by women generally from this privileged social position, this relatively narrow social position was indeed reflected in their representations. This kind of misunderstanding is in the nature of a social movement; in order to recruit proletarians to the cause of Socialism – something which is essential to the realisation of Socialism – it is necessary to enhance the capacity of workers' organisations to win material benefits for workers. Likewise, women inspired by a revolutionary vision of a world in which patriarchy and sexism would be abolished recruited women to the cause by working for a better deal for women here and now, rather than waiting for the Socialist utopia. But that was not really the point!

When a new universal conception of 'woman' was put forward at a certain historical juncture, it had to be recognised in terms of the dominant attributes attached to 'woman' at that juncture. As such, the image of the white middle class woman moving into work is linked to the Black woman who replaces her domestic labour, the problem of female access to management positions ignores the lousy pay available to females on the production line, and so on.

A new concept arising from a new social movement identifies a newly-exposed social problem; that concept becomes deeper and more concrete through successive efforts at resolving the given problem as contradictions arise. On the other hand, the recognition of the new concept in terms of *contingent features* can obscure the true concept at the heart of the new social movement, and render it in terms of a claim for a 'better deal' for some section of society. The fate of a new, revolutionary concept is not predetermined, but in the context of the various pressures bearing down on the Women's Liberation movement at the time and particularly the fragmenting impact of neoliberal politics and corporate restructure, this objectification had a deadly effect.

The Women's Movement was rendered as a claim for recognition by a particular social group and was followed by an unending series of like claims (all of them justified) and any critique of late capitalism was rendered likewise as a particular claim for recognition. The trade unions and socialist parties were rendered as claims for a better deal for white, blue-collar workers; even the Environmental movement was rendered as a claim for better living conditions for the urban middle class. The resulting demobilisation was not the outcome of the Women's Liberation movement, but of neoliberal politics and corresponding changes in the labour process.

I doubt that any form of organisation could have maintained the social movements in the face of the neoliberal demobilisation of the time; what was *needed* was to hold the movement together and through discussion achieve a successively more concrete concept of emancipation in the process of fighting through the diverse struggles posed by the neoliberal turn. What happened instead was the break-up of the original universal concept into rival particular concepts.

A particularist claim is above all for a claim for *recognition*, which in political terms means self-determination. So it is unlikely that *any* form of decision making could have held back the process of disintegration which resulted from the successive competitive claims for recognition. The Women's Liberation movement never aspired to any kind of integral wide-scale organisation – their shared Identity as women was sufficient to constitute them as a movement. The ethic of *inclusion* which underpinned Consensus gave way to *Liberalism*, shared *Identity* gave way to *recognition of Difference*.

The powerful moral force attached to being part of the majority had been inverted. It was taken for granted that the status quo expressed the concrete will of the majority; majoritarianism was ipso facto then an oppressive and reactionary ethic. The archetype of the minority was no longer Mr. Moneybags, but the marginalised and excluded. The archetype of the claimant for justice was no longer the exploited majority, but the neglected minority. All this was presaged on the historic compromise of the Post-war Settlement which had emancipated millions from the worst privations of capitalist exploitation.

The Negation of Negation – The Rise of Alliance Politics

By the end of the 1990s, the combination of Identity Politics and Neoliberal economic reform had so fragmented social and political life that a social movement mobilising around a broad world-changing progressive idea was impossible. (See Klein, 2001 and Maeckelbergh 2009). The environmental movement could still stage media events and identity groups could still expose isolated elements of discrimination and make gains for themselves; opposition to the First Gulf War had brought hundreds of thousands on to the street, for a few hours, but governments had learnt to simply ignore such occasional mobilisations.

Protests at a meeting of the WTO in Seattle in 1999 marked the opening of a new period. The 9/11 attack provided the opportunity for the second Bush administration to launch a new war fever which undoubtedly set back progress towards a new wave of resistance, but the success of the Occupy Wall Street protests September-November 2011 demonstrated that the depressive effects of the War on Terror had exhausted itself. These events marked the most spectacular instances of a new kind of politics however, most remarkable because they succeeded in putting the political-economic *oppressed majority* back in the spotlight.

The new landscape which had been bequeathed by Identity Politics was Alliance Politics. Alliance Politics is the character of the present times, but I will limit myself to the following brief observations.

© KONINKLIJKE BRILL NV, LEIDEN, 2016 | DOI 10.1163/9789004319639_023

Alliance Politics

The first premise of Alliance Politics is that no-one, no single party or group, has sufficient political weight to alone make any significant impact on the major centres of power. Each has a specific grievance or objective which it pursues, but everyone knows that they are just tinkering around the edges of vast social processes which confront them almost as forces of nature.

The second premise is that the capacity of any party or group to mount activity outside of their own focus is extremely limited; petitions can be signed, occasional rallies can be attended or a donation made, that is all.

The third premise is that parties and groups can collaborate on some project only if the objectives are *strictly limited both in time and space* as well as in political and intellectual depth. Occupy Wall Street was such an event; it lasted for 8 weeks in one location in New York and made one point: that political-economic inequality had gone too far. There were ripples across the world and then the protests faded away. But it did have a huge impact on the way we all see the world; inequality is back on the political agenda, but doing something about it remains firmly in the hands of the same institutions which brought it about.

In short, protests are protests, that is all.

The organisers of these protests have generally been anarchists and the centrepiece of the protests has been the general meetings which strive to be models of Consensus. Ingenious techniques have been invented to scale-up Consensus as far as possible, but it has never extended far beyond shouting range of the podium. Discussions are generally limited to the practical goals of the protest: who will be where when, or for providing relevant information. Selection of demands and slogans is based on the principle of the most extreme demand possible, and mutually irreconcilable demands are embraced on the principle that no responsibility will ever be taken to garner support for them in the wider population, far less implement them. The events are generally triumphs of organisation, but only until something happens which requires a change of plans, at which point things quickly descend into chaos and/or deadlock. Discipline is inconceivable – people do as they wish. Resources, such as printing and broadcasting, are usually provided by NGOs or labour movement organisations who for all their faults have accumulated assets over the years. The only asset of the alliance itself is each other.

The point is that the garment worker who joins a protest against the WTO aspires to different vision than the student who is in favour of globalisation, albeit 'from below'. The *only* thing which needs to be agreed upon is the

© KONINKLIJKE BRILL NV, LEIDEN, 2016 | DOI 10.1163/9789004319639_024

practical action to be taken. No vision, no program of action is required. And that is the *great strength* of alliance politics – a new concept was put in the centre of public consciousness – inequality – without any program to address it, or even an analysis of why it exists or exactly what it is. But such an abstract concept cannot function as an ideal for an ongoing political project. The ideals which do motivate people can bring them along to an alliance protest but that is all.

The ethic of Alliance Politics is this:

> What we do together, we decide together.
> But apart from that we go our own way.

Consensus Now and Then

For a period of 4 or 5 years the SNCC practiced Consensus in small groups in connection with specific actions. WSP was able to practice Consensus on a nationwide scale on the foundation of historically exceptional cultural homogeneity and by strenuously confining themselves to protesting a single issue. No Consensus process has successfully transcended these limits. In both cases, intense schooling in Consensus was required to embed it in the movement, and the planning meetings in today's alliance politics also function as 'movement schools'.

Large scale alliances by a limited number of parties, from the mediaeval Hanseatic League to NATO, give consent to an action by some form of Consensus, but here it is delegates not individuals who make their alliance by Consensus, with laissez faire relations between sovereign parties outside the scope of what is to be done together. Such national and international alliances presuppose substantial corporate actors as components of the alliance and such actors have *never* been constructed by Consensus.

Consensus between actors in an Alliance presupposes the narrow scope of agreed action complemented by laissez faire beyond that. Participation in a Consensus is invariably *voluntary*. The scope of action which can be pursued through Consensus depends on the strength of the tacit consensus across the social stratum to be mobilised. The social movements constituted by the Spanish Anarchists, Women Strike for Peace and even Women's Liberation rarely achieved consensus between the participating groups beyond the abstract ideals that constituted the movement.

When Majority is extended beyond a small group who share some asset, to a wider group sharing a larger scale asset, various complicated arrangements are deployed but the underlying ethic of majoritarianism remains unchanged. In a sense, Majority is at home on the scale of the entire community. When

Consensus is extended beyond a small group participating in some action to a larger group participating in a large scale activity, the ethic of inclusion gives way to laissez faire – toleration without solidarity. Consensus is at home in a meeting of intimates, but does not scale up beyond a certain limit.

A new order could never be instituted by Consensus, because *participation in a new order is not voluntary*. The minority should offer its solidarity to the majority in that instance, and on their side, enjoy the tolerance and protection of the majority.

Conclusion

I set out to discover the roots of the deep antipathy between two paradigms of collective decision making – Majority and Consensus – by tracing the historical roots of each paradigm. In the course of this I discovered that there was a third paradigm, Counsel – the most ancient form of collective decision making, practiced in traditional communities in which a Chief consults his advisers and then makes the decision. This is still the dominant mode of collective decision making in many boardrooms and in families.

Further, collective decision making among a group of individuals in the same project has to be distinguished from bargaining between delegates representing distinct projects such as labour and management negotiating a new contract. Just because there is no voting does not mean that there is Consensus. In Negotiation, there are always essentially two sides, so majority is meaningless in this context. Sometimes meetings which have the appearance of Consensus, with a large number of individuals engaged in the debate, are in reality nothing more than negotiations between a number of parties entering into a temporary alliance.

Majority originated over 1,000 years ago in voluntary associations of merchants and artisans who had no place and no rights in a feudal system based on the land. Their guilds were the first organisations to be based on voluntary relations of equality and they made decisions by Majority. In the absence of social support they depended for survival on the solidarity of their fellows; laissez faire was not an option. Throughout, Majority has been linked to equality and solidarity.

These guilds evolved over time, giving birth to Parliament, companies such as the East India Company, universities and trade unions. For centuries these organisations were inward looking and marked by particularism, and their democratic life gradually degenerated. The French Revolution injected a new democratic spirit into working class communities and, drawing on forms of organisation introduced by the Methodist Church, new forms of democratic organisation were developed. With the emergence of the modern working class in the Chartist movement, Majority became a universal moral principle standing in opposition to the rule of a privileged minority in the nobility and the bourgeoisie.

Consensus first emerged with the Quakers in the wake of the English Revolution, and was transmitted to Quakers in twentieth century America more or less unchanged. The Quaker way of doing meetings was one of the inspirations for Consensus decision making which arose in 1960–61 in the Civil Rights and

© KONINKLIJKE BRILL NV, LEIDEN, 2016 | DOI 10.1163/9789004319639_025

Peace movements, but it was not the principal source. The Nashville branch of the Student Nonviolent Coordinating Committee were the first to develop Consensus in its modern form. Although the traditional style of decision making of the Southern Black Churches was their starting point, the young activists of SNCC developed Consensus with the help of the Methodist Minister James Lawson and the labour educator Myles Horton. A different style of Consensus was developed independently by Women Strike for Peace, an anti-war movement made up of middle-class, middle-aged women. Thanks to SNCC and WSP, Consensus took root in the burgeoning social movements of the post-war period.

As a result of the post-war settlement, the growing stratification of the working class, and the bureaucratisation of the trade unions, the labour movement was no longer seen as the emancipatory force it had once been. Increasingly seen as part of the establishment, its majoritarian ethos was under challenge. The Women's, Civil Rights and other movements representing the 'excluded' eschewed Majority in favour of Consensus, with its ethic of inclusion and respect for difference.

Having their roots in antipathetic historical traditions, Majority and Consensus appear to each other as morally reprehensible. In point of fact, neither Majority nor Consensus can be ethically justified without reference to tradition. They are each part of a tradition.

Insofar as participants in a meeting fail to coordinate their actions for the purpose of achieving a shared object, then no collective decision making is entailed and there is no subject-formation – each party is simply an object to the other. "Coordinating actions" does not mean "doing the same thing," but agreement to not coordinate actions is just life in the world of neo-liberal capitalism. Difference is not indifference.

The only decision principle which can be ethically justified is: "We decide together what we do together." So the decision procedure must be agreed at the outset. This is usually settled by a project being initiated within one tradition, and inviting others to join, which entails acceptance of the decision procedure. However, decision procedures only engender commitment if they are seen to be ethically valid by the whole community which is affected by the decision. The Left has to talk these issues through on the basis of mutual respect.

The problem that the Left has with collective decision making is not whether Majority or Consensus is the right way for a group of people to decide what they're going to do together – both procedures facilitate fair and rational decisions where the will exists. The problem is that all the decisions which really matter are excluded from collective decision by the application of the laws of private property in the public domain. The food industry poisons us, the media spreads lies and misinformation, and so on, because these activities are deemed to be 'private property'.

The ethical principles expressed in Majority and Consensus can be respected in a well conducted meeting under either procedure. Which is the most appropriate procedure depends on the circumstances. In some circumstances even Counsel is appropriate. If there is to be a dispute about how to conduct a meeting, then we need to recognise the roots of the different approaches in tradition. Neither Majority, Consensus nor Counsel is inherently unethical. If we stick to the concrete questions which arise in collaborating with one another, and the purpose for which we have joined together, then differences can be overcome.

The really tough questions are who gets to participate in which decisions.

The evidence is well and truly in that bureaucracy and hierarchy are problems which affect *all* organisations which survive longer than the social movement on which they rest. This is true whether decisions are made by Consensus or by Majority. The SNCC split when it could no longer reach consensus; WSP was run by a clique of women with privileged access to resources. The Soviet Union degenerated because of a lack of voting not from too much voting. On the other hand, labour movement organisations need to learn the merits of diversity in action as well as unity.

But so long as the social movement itself is in flow, then the problems of representation and bureaucratism are immaterial; when the movement ebbs, no decision making procedure can save it. Attention must be paid to achieving reforms which are by their nature very difficult to undo, as far as possible institutionalising participation in the regulation of social life. An educated and empowered citizenry which routinely participates in decision making is the best guarantee against bureaucratism.

With or without the aid of voting, there is no chance whatsoever of the Left making any headway against inequality, or any progress in building a rational social and economic order without some form of delegation and representation. Local autonomy is not incompatible with national and international co-ordination. But before we can solve the problems which arise from extending decision processes beyond those who are present in the room, we must first solve the ethical problems which already arise in making a decision here and now. Different decision procedures can be used in different circumstances. If we can overcome the ethical problems of decision making itself, then I am sure we can go on to resolve the problems arising across the *whole* of the decision making process from beginning to end. The kind of creative energy that has been mobilised to develop Consensus to its current form needs to be directed to developing forms of collective decision making and collaboration which can be extended in time and space as well as imagination.

These are not new problems. Radicals have been wrestling with them for centuries. I hope that this brief record of the efforts of previous generations will provide a resource for meeting the challenges our times.

References

Addams, J. (1902). *Democracy and Social Ethics*, Macmillan.

Alinsky, S. (1971/1989). Rules for Radicals. A pragmatic primer for realistic radicals. New York: Vintage Books.

Anonymous Digger Pamphlet (1648). *Light Shining in Buckinghamshire.* http://www.marxists.org/history/england/english-revolution/light-shining.htm.

Baker, P. (2007). Ed. *The Levellers. The Putney Debates*. London: Verso.

Black Panther Party, Rules, http://www.marxists.org/history/usa/workers/black-panthers/unknown-date/party-rules.htm.

Blanqui, L.-A. (1866). *Manual for an Armed Insurrection.* http://www.marxists.org/reference/archive/blanqui/1866/instructions1.htm.

Bookchin, M. (1962). *Our Synthetic Environment.* AK Press.

Bookchin, M. (1971). *Post-scarcity Anarchism.* AK Press.

Bookchin, M. (1998). *The Spanish Anarchists: The Heroic Years 1868–1936.* AK Press.

Bureau des "Temps Nouveau", Paris (1896) *Les révolutionnaires au congrès de Londres : conférences anarchists, de londres.* http://gallica.bnf.fr/ark:/12148/bpt6k817808/f6.image.r=congres.

Burrough, E. (1834). Letters, In *The Yorkshireman, a religious and literary journal, by a Friend*, ed. Howard, L., London: Longman &Co.

Chartist Ancestors website http://www.chartists.net/.

Chase, M. (2000). *Early Trade Unionism: Fraternity, Skill and the Politics of Labour*, Farnham, UK: Ashgate Publishing.

Chase, M. (2007). *Chartism. A New History.* Manchester University Press.

Citrine, Sir W. (1939). *The ABC of Chairmanship, All about Meetings and Conferences*, Co-operative Printing Society Ltd.

Communards: The Story of the Paris Commune of 1871, As Told by Those Who Fought for It. Texts selected, edited, and translated by Mitchell Abidor, MIA Publications, 2009.

Coover, V., Deacon, E., Esser, C. & Moore, C. (1977), *Resource Manual for a Living Revolution. A handbook of skills & tools for social change activists.* Philadelphia, PA: Movement for a New Society.

Cornelius, J.D. (1999). Slave Missions and the Black Churches in the Antebellum South. University of South Carolina Press.

Cornell, A. (2009). Anarchism and the Movement for a New Society: Direct Action and Prefigurative Community in the 1970s and 80s, *Perspectives*, http://archive.is/MYEmo#selection-345.0-979.71.

Daniels, B.C. (2012). *New England Nation. The Country the Puritans Built.* Palgrave Macmillan.

de Liefde, W.H.J. (2003). *Lekgotla. The art of leadership through dialogue.* Houghton South Africa; Jacan Media.

Dickerson, D.C. (2014). "James M. Lawson, Jr: Methodism, Nonviolence and the Civil Rights Movement," *Methodist History*, 52:3 (April 2014).

Dimitrov, G. (1935). Unity of the Working Class against Fascism, *Selected Works*, vol. 2, Sofia Press 1972, pp. 86–119.

District of Columbia. Office of Urban Renewal (1964). *Adams-Morgan – democratic action to save a neighborhood : a demonstration of neighborhood conservation in the District of Columbia*, Report prepared by the Office of Urban Renewal District of Columbia, in cooperation with Stein and Marcou Associates and the American University.

East India Company (1621/1903). *The Lawes or Standing Orders*. University of London.

Epstein, J. & Thompson, D. (1982) eds. *The Chartist Experience. Studies in Working-Class Radicalism and Culture, 1830–1860*. London, UK: Macmillan.

First International (1964). *Documents of the First International. The General Council of the First International, 1864–1866. The London Conference 1865. Minutes.* Moscow, Foreign Languages Publishing House.

Freeman, J. (1970). *The Tyranny of Structurelessness.* http://www.jofreeman.com/joreen/tyranny.htm.

Fry, T. (1980). *The Rule of St. Benedict.* Collegeville: The Liturgical Press, 1980.

Gadamer, H.-G. (2005 [1960]). *Truth and Method*, London, UK: Continuum.

Gandhi, M. (1929/2010). *An Autobiography: The Story of My Experiments with Truth*, Routledge & Chapman Hall.

Gastil, J. & Levine, P. (2005). Eds., *The Deliberative Democracy Handbook*, San Francisco, CA: John Wiley.

Glen, John M. (1988). Highlander. *No Ordinary School, 1932–1962.* University Press of Kentucky.

Graeber, D. (2008). There Never was a West: Or, Democracy Emerges from the Spaces in Between, in *Possibilities: Essays on Hierarchy, Rebellion and Desire.* Oakland, CA: AK Press.

Graeber, D. (2010). The Rebirth of anarchism in North America, 1957–2007. *Historia Actual Online*, Núm. 21 (Invierno, 2010), 123–131. http://www.historia-actual.org/Publicaciones/index.php/haol/article/view/419/337.

Graeber, D. (2013). *The Democracy Project: A History, a Crisis, a Movement*, Random House.

Gramsci, A. (1926). "Some Aspects of the Southern Question," *Selections from Political Writings (1921–1926) with additional texts by other Italian Communist leaders*, 1978.

Guillaume, J. (1874/1971). Ideas on Social Organization. In *Bakunin on Anarchy*, edited by Sam Dolgoff, 1971.

Hardy, T. (1842). *Memoir of Thomas Hardy, Founder of and Secretary to the London Corresponding Society.* London: James Ridgway.

Hayden, T. (2012). *Inspiring Participatory Democracy: Student Movements from Port Huron to Today*, Paradigm Publishers.

Herbert, W. (1836). *The History of the Twelve Great Livery Companies of London.* Published by the author, London.

Hill, C. (1975). *The World Turned Upside Down: Radical Ideas during the English Revolution*, London: Pelican Books.

Hogan, W. (2007). *Many Minds, One Heart: SNCC's Dream for a New America.* Chapel Hill, NC: University of North Carolina Press.

Holsaert, F.S., Richardson, J. & Noonan, M.P.N. (Eds.) (2012). *Hands on the Freedom Plow. Personal Accounts by Women in SNCC.* University of Illinois Press.

Horton, M. (1990). *The Long Haul. An Autobiography.* Doubleday.

Horton, M. (2003). *The Myles Horton Reader. Education for Social Change.* Ed. Dale Jacobs. Knoxville, TE: University of Tennessee Press.

Isaac, L.W., Cornfield, D.B., Dickerson, D.C., Lawson, J.M., Jr. & Coley, J.S. (2012). "'Movement Schools' and dialogical diffusion of nonviolent praxis: Nashville workshops in the Southern Civil Rights Movement." *Research in Social Movements, Conflict and Change*, vol. 34, 155–184.

James, B. (2001). *Craft, Trade or Mystery: Part One – Britain from Gothic Cathedrals to the Tolpuddle Conspirators*, Takver Initiatives.

Journeymen Stockingmakers of Dublin (1749). *Reply to Committee into the causes of disputes between masters and journeymen.*

Kautsky, K. (1892). *The Class Struggle.*

Kautsky, K. (1909). *Road to Power.*

Kilham, A. (1796/2010). *The Progress of Liberty, Amongst the People Called Methodists. To Which is Added, the Out-Lines of a Constitution.* Gale Ecco Print Editions.

King, M. (1999). *Mahatma Gandhi and Martin Luther King Jr. The power of nonviolent action.* Paris, France: UNESCO.

King, M., Private email messages.

King, M.L. (1963). *Letter from Birmingham Jail.*

Klein, N. (2001). *NO LOGO*, Flamingo.

Lawson, M. (1996). *The International People's College 1921–1996. A Celebration of 75 Years of Working for Peace and International Friendship.* IPC Denmark.

Lenin, V.I. (1905). "Two Tactics of Social Democracy in the Democratic Revolution." *Collected Works*, vol. 9, pp. 77ff.

Lenin, V.I. (1917a). April Theses, *Collected Works*, vol. 24, p. 19.

Lenin, V.I. (1917b). Alliance Between the Workers and Exploited Peasants. *Collected Works*, vol. 26, p. 333.

Lenin, V.I. (1921). Speech to Tenth All-Russian Conference of the R.C.P, 26 May 1921, *Collected Works* vol. 32, p. 399.

Liebermann, F. (1913). *The national assembly in the Anglo-Saxon period.* Halle.

Loyn, H.R. (1984). *The Governance of Anglo-Saxon England, 500–1087*, Chicago, IL: Stanford University Press.

Luxemburg, R. (1906). "The Mass Strike," *The Mass Strike, the Political Party and the Trade Unions*.

Maeckelbergh, M. (2009). *The Will and the Many. How the alterglobalisation movement is changing the face of democracy*. London, UK: Pluto Press.

Maeckelbergh, Marianne. (2011). "The Road to Democracy: The Political Legacy of "1968"." *International Review of Social History* 56: 301–332.

Mann, T. (1923). *Memoir*. London, UK: The Labour Publishing Company.

Manniche, P. (1952). *Living Democracy in Denmark*, with an introduction by H.J. Fleure, The Ryerson Press.

Martin, J. (2010) *Popular political oratory and itinerant lecturing in Yorkshire and the North East in the age of Chartism*, 1837–60, PhD Thesis for University of York, Department of History.

Marx, K. (1843). "Introduction to the Critique of Hegel's Philosophy of Right," *MECW* vol. 3.

Marx, K. (1845). "The German Ideology," *MECW* vol. 5.

May, T.E. (1843). *A treatise upon the law, privileges, proceedings and usage of Parliament*. http://www.marxists.org/history/england/1844/parliamentary-procedures.pdf.

Millett, K. (1969). *Sexual Politics*.

Minute Book of the Goggleshall Combers Purse (c. 1685). Courtesy of Malcolm Chase.

Minute book of the London Working Men's Association from 18 October 1836, British Library, http://www.bl.uk/learning/timeline/item106691.html.

Minutes (1864–6). *The General Council of the First International 1864–1866. The London Conference 1865*. Foreign Languages Publishing House, Moscow [n.d.].

Minutes of the Paris Commune (1871) *Journal officiel de la République française*, Paris. http://gallica.bnf.fr/ark:/12148/cb328020920/date.r=journal+officiel+de+la+commune+de+paris.langEN.

Morley, B. (1993). *Beyond Consensus. Salvaging Sense of the Meeting*, Wallingford, PA: Pendle Hill.

Morris, W. (1892). *News from Nowhere*. http://www.marxists.org/archive/morris/works/1890/nowhere/nowhere.htm.

Moscovici, S. & Doise, W. (1994). *Conflict and Consensus: a General Theory of Collective Decisions*. Sage.

panarchy.org *Resolutions of Congress of the Anti-authoritarian International*, Saint-Imier (15–16 September 1872), http://www.panarchy.org/jura/saintimier.html.

Parliament of Great Britain (1803). *Cobbett's Parliamentary Debates*.

Pronley, M. (2008). *Waveland, Mississippi, November 1964: Death of SNCC, Birth of Radicalism*, PhD Thesis for University of Wisconsin.

Ricœur, P. (1984). *Time and Narrative. Vol. I*. Chicago: University of Chicago Press.

Robert, H.M.R. (1915/1876). Robert's Rules of Order. Revised for Deliberative Assemblies. Chicago, IL: Scott, Foresman.

Select Committee on the Combination Laws (1825). *Report.*

Sheeran, N.J. (1996). *Beyond Majority Rule: Voteless Decisions in the Religious Society of Friends*, Philadelphia , PA: Philadelphia Yearly Meeting of the Religious Society of Friends.

Smith, A. (1996). The Renewal Movement: The Peace Testimony and Modern Quakerism, *Quaker History*, 85(2), Friends Historical Association, Haverford College Library, Haverford, PA. http://www.quaker.org/renewal.html.

Society for the propagation of the faith in foreign parts (1706). *Standing Orders.*

Starhawk (n.d.). Star Hawk's Guide to Consensus Decision Making, http://www .marxists.org/glossary/terms/c/consensus-decision-making.htm.

Swerdlow, A. (1993). *Women Strike for Peace: Traditional Motherhood and Radical Politics in the 1960s*, University of Chicago Press.

Tarrow, S. (2005). *The New Transnational Activism*. Cambridge, UK: Cambridge University Press.

Taylor, F. (1911). The Principles of Scientific Management, *Scientific Management.*

Thale, M. (1983). *Selections from the Papers of the London Corresponding Society, 1792–1799*, Cambridge University Press.

Thompson, D. (2013). *The Chartists: Popular Politics in the Industrial Revolution*. Breviary Stuff Publications.

Thompson, E.P. (1963). *The Making of the English Working Class*, Penguin Books.

Tillett, B. (1910). *A Brief History of the Dockers' Union*. Dock, Wharf, Riverside and General Workers' Union of Great Britain and Northern Ireland.

Townsend, W.J. (1909). *A New History of Methodism*. London: Hodder & Stoughton.

Trotsky, L. (1932). For a Workers' United Front Against Fascism, December 8, 1931, *Bulletin of the Opposition*, No. 27, March 1932.

Trotsky, L. (1938). "The Lessons of Spain," January 1938, *Socialist Appeal.*

Winstanley, G. (1941). *Works*, with an introduction. Ed. G. Sabine. Cornell U.P.

Yeo, E. (1982). "Some Practices and Problems in Chartist Democracy," in *The Chartist Experience: Studies in Working-Class Radicalism and Culture, 1830–1860*, ed. James Epstein & Dorothy Thompson, London: Macmillan, pp. 360–362.

Index